THE
POWYS
JOURNAL

Volume V

THE POWYS SOCIETY

President Glen Cavaliero

Chairman Morine Krissdóttir
Vice-Chairman Paul Roberts
Hon. Treasurer Stephen Powys Marks
Hon. Secretary John Batten

The Powys Society is a registered charity, No. 801332

The Powys Society was founded in 1967 to 'establish the true literary status of the Powys family through promotion of the reading and discussion of their works', in particular those of John Cowper Powys (1872–1963), Theodore Francis Powys (1875–1953), and Llewelyn Powys (1884–1939).

The Society publishes a journal and three newsletters a year, and has embarked on a publication programme. In addition it organises an annual weekend conference, occasional meetings, exhibitions, and walks in areas associated with the Powys family.

The Society is an international one, attracting scholars and non-academics from around the world, and welcomes everyone interested in learning more about this remarkable family.

Correspondence and membership enquiries should be addressed to:

John Batten, Hon. Secretary
Keeper's Cottage, Montacute, Somerset, TA15 6XN
(tel. 01935 824077)

THE POWYS JOURNAL

Volume V

1995

Editors
Louise de Bruin   Peter J. Foss

Contributing Editor
Charles Lock

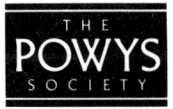

The Powys Journal is a publication of The Powys Society, appearing annually each summer. Its aim is to publish original material by the Powys family — in particular, John Cowper Powys, Theodore Francis Powys and Llewelyn Powys — and scholarly articles and other material relating to them and their circle. It also carries reviews of books by and about the Powys family and their circle.

The Powys Journal is grateful to the copyright holders of the individual estates: Mr Francis Powys and Laurence Pollinger Ltd for their permission to quote from the writings of John Cowper Powys and Theodore Francis Powys, and Mrs Sally Connely and Laurence Pollinger Ltd for their permission to quote from the writings of Llewelyn Powys.

MSS for publication, correspondence about the contents of the *Journal*, and books for review should be addressed to Dr Peter Foss, *The Powys Journal*, 82 Linden Road, Gloucester, GL1 5HD. *The Powys Journal* has a refereeing policy, whereby material is submitted for independent reports, in which the anonymity of the author and the referee is preserved. MSS should, therefore, be submitted in duplicate, or on disk preferably in ASCII or text-only format with one paper copy, with the name and address of the author on a separate sheet. MSS will be acknowledged but cannot be returned unless accompanied by a stamped, self-addressed envelope. Authors of printed articles will receive two copies of the *Journal*.

Orders for copies of the *Journal* should be addressed to the Society's Publications Manager, Stephen Powys Marks, Hamilton's, Kilmersdon, near Bath, Somerset, BA3 5TE (tel. 01761–435134).

© 1995. Copyright is retained by the authors and, for other material, by the Editors or as otherwise stated.

Cover and title-page design: Bev Craven

Typeset in Garamond
in PageMaker 5 on a Macintosh computer
by Stephen Powys Marks

Printed by Future Trading (Bath) Ltd

ISSN 0962–7057
ISBN 1 874559 12 0

CONTENTS

Janina Nordius
Life at One Remove:
Solitude in *Maiden Castle*   7

Diana Petre
Living with Louis   23

Ben Jones
Surprised by Frances:
Travel and Recognition
in *The Mystic Leeway*   35

John Cowper Powys
The Influence of Personality:
Who wants his Inmost Self
Meddled with and Invaded?   54

T. F. Powys
The New Broom   62

Llewelyn Powys
Hedgecock   67

Katie Powys
Brothers and Sisters: A Selection
from the Diaries 1927–41   72

Robin Wood
Owen Glendower:
Powys's Faustian Prince   92

Llewelyn Powys
'In his Great Old Age'   108

Charles Francis Powys
A Sermon for Montacute
Club Day, May 1894   113

The Sons to the Father:
Six Letters written on the
Occasion of the Sixtieth Birthday
of Charles Francis Powys   117

A. R. Powys
The Crippled Child   122

Mary Casey
Family Portraits: A Selection
from the Journals 1951–53   129

T. F. Powys
Letters to Valentine Ackland   148

John Cowper Powys
Letters to Gerard Casey,
1937–40   153

Phyllis Playter
'On the Departure of Powys
for England'   176

REVIEW-ARTICLE

Charles Lock
Not the Lost Generation: John
Cowper Powys and American
Literature, a review of *Elusive
America: The Uncollected
Essays of John Cowper Powys*,
Volume One,
edited by PAUL ROBERTS   178

REVIEWS

John Gray
*Petrushka and the Dancer: The
Diaries of John Cowper Powys
1929-1939*, selected and edited
by MORINE KRISSDÓTTIR   198

Glen Cavaliero
Sylvia and David: The Townsend Warner/Garnett Letters, selected and edited by RICHARD GARNETT
The Diaries of Sylvia Townsend Warner, edited by CLAIRE HARMAN   203

Anthony Head
Jack and Frances: The Love Letters of John Cowper Powys to Frances Gregg, Volume One, edited by OLIVER WILKINSON, assisted by CHRISTOPHER WILKINSON
Powys to Glyn Hughes: The Letters of John Cowper Powys to Glyn Hughes, edited by FRANK WARREN   206

Jeremy Hooker
A Net in Water: A Selection from the Journals of Mary Casey, edited by JUDITH M. LANG and LOUISE DE BRUIN   209

Ben Jones
Paint It Today
H.D. (HILDA DOOLITTLE), edited by CASSANDRA LAITY   212

Margaret McCullough
The Mystic Leeway
FRANCES GREGG, edited by BEN JONES   216

Robert Mighall
The Supernatural and English Fiction: From The Castle of Otranto *to* Hawksmoor
GLEN CAVALIERO   219

John Williams
Mock's Curse
T. F. POWYS, edited by E. & M. B. MENCHER   224

Notes on Contributors   231

Wood-engraving by G. M. Powys,
illustrating 'A Moon Circus', in Llewelyn Powys's
Earth Memories *(1934)*

6

JANINA NORDIUS

Life at One Remove: Solitude in *Maiden Castle* *

Among John Cowper Powys's novels, *Maiden Castle* holds a central position, most significantly because it involves a crucial critique of the author's whole philosophy of solitude. The full implications of this critique have been obscured by the many cuts made in previous editions. In the 1990 restored edition, however, the idea of making solitude the basis for a personal philosophy appears not only as far more controversial than in earlier novels but also, due to an increased complexity in the notion of solitude itself, as potentially more rewarding.[1] It is Powys's achievement in *Maiden Castle* to show how in a situation where solitude seems to have well-nigh exhausted itself as a modus vivendi, a 'philosophy of solitude' may nevertheless — against all odds — provide a new opening.

Critics have often pointed to the 'self-parody' or even self-castigation they find in *Maiden Castle*.[2] Such comments obviously draw on the affinities between the author and his protagonist, Dud No-man. Like Powys, No-man is a writer of romances, and like Powys he returns to Dorchester after a long absence. More important than these external parallels, however, is the fact that both No-man's personality and his attitude to life are clearly modelled on the persona that meets us in Powys's other writings, most explicitly in his essays and the *Autobiography*. Narratologically, this self-duplication means a doubling of authority in the novel, since Powys's presence may be felt not only in the character of No-man but also in the voice of the impersonal narrator. It is in the impersonal narrator's attitude to No-man that we can sense the self-parody which is undeniably there; but at the same time it is clear that the narrator's attitude to No-man is not consistently critical or derisive. On the contrary, as often as not it seems to be

* *A revised version of a paper read at the Powys Society Conference, Dorchester, 1993*

one of complete agreement. This vacillation on the narrator's part is particularly noticeable in the novel's treatment of solitude.

It is in his attitude to solitude that No-man's closeness to the Powys-persona shows particularly clearly. He is a solitary person whose 'happiest moments' occur when he is safely cut off from human company—alone in his attic study or in his long solitary walks. Yet the chief appeal of 'these interludes of solitary self-indulgence' (191) is that they allow him to enjoy a state of inner solitude which belongs, as it were, to another level of reality—a state that I shall discuss here as 'transcendental solitude'.

Most of all, it is in his private philosophy of solitude that we can sense No-man's dependence on his author.[3] No-man's philosophy is, in all essentials, an elaboration of the philosophy Powys presented in *In Defence of Sensuality* and *A Philosophy of Solitude*. That is to say, it is both a 'life-illusion' and a system of thought-control. It is the expression of a belief, not only that every 'human being is alone in the core of the mind', but that it is in this state of existential solitude that 'our unique and singular happiness' is to be found;[4] moreover, it is also a carefully thought-out strategy to attain this goal of happiness. That we may regard No-man's philosophy of solitude as more or less identical with that of Powys does not mean, however, that it is never questioned in the novel. On the contrary, Powys's constantly renewed examination of his own philosophy is an ongoing project in all his novels, and it is as part of this project that we should see his treatment of No-man's philosophy in *Maiden Castle*.

A central idea in No-man's philosophy is that by deliberately forgetting such aspects of life which he regards as 'alien, hostile, [or] uncongenial' (184), he can acquire 'the power to enjoy life on the barest, the most stripped, most winnowed terms' (185). This power manifests itself basically in two different but complementary ways. One concentrates on a sense of 'the present', and the other draws on 'a sense of the continuity of the centuries' (185).

What No-man thinks of as the 'intense awareness of the present' may perhaps better be understood as some kind of 'extra-present': it is the sensation of something out of the ordinary, something much more intense, than what we ordinarily think of as 'the present'. The *ordinary* 'present' is something from which to escape, as No-man escapes in his 'solitary excursions' from 'the pressure of the immediate' (228). In doing so, he is 'lifted ... for a passing second to the edge of another dimension' (228), and it is there, on the edge of this other dimension, that the extra-present belongs. Psychologically, No-man's experience of the extra-present is understood as a heightened sensuality. The cult of his sensations is what gives meaning to his life. 'What I really live for', he claims as he is carried away by the sight of some road-side flowers, 'are sensations like this!' (183). But the ontological implications are never obscured: the chief importance of No-man's sensations is that they allow him to get a glimpse of another, extra-ordinary, reality — 'a reality just beyond our reality, a reality that I've been longing for all my days' (187).

On the other hand, No-man also needs the 'sense of the pathos and significance of the past before he could enjoy to the full this present he made so much of' (185). To No-man, the sense of the past reveals 'a less personal element in his subjective life' (185), an element which manifests itself as 'the feeling of being a *medium* through which the overtones of human life upon earth, purged of its grossness, flowed through the present into the future' (103-4). What we have here is obviously not just a mental substitution of the past for the present; rather, No-man's feeling of being a medium implies the simultaneous access to *all* times, an intense awareness of the *continuity* of human life on earth. This sense of solitary communion with the human past does not get much attention in *In Defence of Sensuality* or *A Philosophy of Solitude*. It depends to a great extent on the psychic atmosphere of certain places, and hence it is perhaps significant that it is mainly developed in the novels where we have a definite geographical setting. Thus, in *Maiden Castle* the town of Dorchester 'with its layers upon layers of human memories, semi-historic and prehistoric' has 'a magical power over Dud's imagination' (91). But here too, in this historical, and 'less personal' side of No-man's mental withdrawal from the pressure of the immediate, the main appeal for him is the anticipation of another level of reality than the ordinary: 'History to him was life *at one remove*, life purged and winnowed of its grosser impact! It was a second reality, so to speak, ...' (185).

The sense of the past and that of extra-present sensuality thus represent different aspects of No-man's transcendental solitude. To be sure, the boundary between them is not absolute. The two sides constantly mix and intertwine in his solitary trances, one side often being triggered by the other, as when the sight of some cuckoo-flowers growing in a ditch calls forth a vision of 'generations of burgesses and artisans, their lads and their maids, their baby-boys and baby-girls', pausing 'transported with delight in the presence of these lavender-tinted tremulous entities' (186). Nevertheless, a distinction is clearly being made in the account of No-man's philosophy: the sense of being a medium to the 'overtones of the centuries' (185) represents a step even further away from the ordinary world of human relations than does his escape into extra-present sensuality. It is a double escape, or a double stripping away, because in order to respond fully to this second and 'winnowed reality of his', No-man's soul has to free itself not only from the pressure of daily reality, but also 'from the burden of subjective sensuality' (185). When this happens, his solitude becomes depersonalised, bordering on the mystical.

In the novel's account of the ideological content of No-man's philosophy of solitude there is, then, no sense of irony or parody; on the contrary, we can sense a sincere commitment here on the narrator's part. Yet the narrator is not always equally affirmative when he describes the practical implications of No-man's solitude. It is, in fact, in the clashes between No-man's idiosyncratic solitude and the reality of other people that Powys's self-sarcasm can be felt particularly strongly. The effect on the narrative of this self-sarcasm is, however, rather odd, and may need some comment before we embark on a closer examination of No-man's encounters with outside reality.

The narrator's division in respect to No-man and his solitude — now committed, now critical — need not in itself present a problem in these post-modern days. Even if we tend to look for a 'final stance' in the novel's attitude to solitude, we may accept that this 'final' stance is not finalised — that it is one of 'both/and' rather than exclusively 'either/or'. What may be felt as puzzling, however, is No-man's reaction — or rather, lack of reaction — to the criticism that is launched against him. He never seems to take it to heart or question his own philosophy, remaining in all essentials confirmed in his initial position. Although he reflects, at the end of the novel, that the outcome of events 'had changed everything for him' (476), he himself is not shown to have changed in any substantial way. On the other hand, though, No-man's confirmation of his initial philosophy is remarkably weary and subdued. Not being the result of a serious reconsideration, it lacks the enthusiasm and fervour that would effectively refute all criticism once and for all. There is nothing in No-man's final stance like Wolf Solent's flash of revelation in the field of golden buttercups, or of Sam Dekker's sense of sudden release after emerging from his inner struggle with asceticism. As a result, the reader is left at a loss at the end of *Maiden Castle*: even though we may be prepared to accept the narrator's divided attitude of both criticism and commitment to No-man's solitude, we feel that both these positive options are undermined by No-man's own negativity. His 'revolt ... against being placed' in any given context within the fictional world (191) seems to extend also to the narratological level; he consistently turns down the role of Bildungsroman-hero assigned to him by the narrative, neither heeding the reproach he meets with, nor displaying any affirmative zest when confirming his own initial stance.

Still, puzzling as No-man's attitude may seem, it will perhaps be easier to understand if we take a closer look at the philosophy of solitude he shares with his author. The discrepancy between our expectations of a resolution that would, as it were, release a hidden store of insights and truths in the protagonist, and the absence of such a dénouement may be put down to an opposition, or quasi-opposition, that inheres in his philosophy. This is the tension between freedom and self-control which is generated in the field between the philosophy's two basic components — the goal of solitary happiness, and the strategy to achieve this goal. When No-man is ascending the hill fortress of Maiden Castle, feeling 'as if he had been lifted up' into 'some kind of aerial keep ... within the ramparts of which he was floating free, free of all the worries of his life', free of all emotional demands implicit in his ties with other human beings (231), he is enjoying the sense of liberation which is the ultimate aim of Powys's philosophy. Such trances are often unpremeditated, but not always;

and it is in order to be able to attain this state of solitary freedom by an act of will that No-man imposes on himself his 'rigorous system of thought-control' (184). Although this system of control *aims* at liberation, it is obviously in itself far from free. Self-control thus becomes an equivocal force — being at once opposed to and promoting the force of liberation. Normally, the tension between liberation and self-control does not cause any problems in Powys's novels; in *Maiden Castle*, however, it becomes central to our understanding of No-man's stationary attitude, and thus, implicitly, to our understanding of what is being said about solitude in the novel. As I shall argue, No-man's self-control is to a large extent rendered in terms of 'deliberation': in matters that concern his solitude, his dealings with outside reality and with himself are characterised by thorough and careful forethought.

The event that instigates the plot is No-man's 'blind plunge into reality' (250), a 'plunge into that terrible real life which from his childhood he had dodged' (126). This is how he represents to himself his falling in love with Wizzie, a young circus girl. In practice, however, No-man's confrontation with reality turns out to be more like the dip of a toe than a bold 'plunge'; it is only half-hearted, since in spite of his involvement with the real world through Wizzie and their circle of friends, he is not prepared to compromise with his life of solitude.

Ambivalent though it may be, it is, nevertheless, through this plunge into reality that No-man's philosophy and his attitude to solitude are put to the test. One of the major questions that arise here concerns the moral justifications of his philosophy: do we really have the 'right' to be 'selfish' and seek our happiness in solitude when there are others who suffer?[5] This question is raised on a general level when the novel's communist, Claudius, attacks No-man's cult of solitude as being an upper-class privilege belonging to the past, something both anti-egalitarian and parasitic. While the working-classes live in poverty and degradation, 'without privacy or solitude' (402), the 'simple life' led by No-man and his likes is 'the luxury of the comfortable' (402). But if, as Glen Cavaliero has argued,[6] Claudius can be seen as merely a 'mouthpiece', the same could be said here about No-man who, replying to Claudius's attack, seems simply to recycle an often rehearsed speech. Pledging his solidarity with the oppressed and declaring himself willing to 'share the world's drudgery', he all the same argues for his right 'to snatch every moment' he can 'for being alone' (402). Despite its unmistakable sincerity, No-man's declaration has nothing of the emotional 'liberation' that we saw in Wolf and Sam when they finally arrived at a similar insight. Rather, the fluency with which No-man delivers his well-balanced speech gives it away as being the result of long and careful deliberation.

Still, if No-man refutes Claudius's rather impersonal accusations swiftly enough, his relationship with Wizzie presents a more serious test to his philosophy of solitude.

Shifting from No-man's to Wizzie's point of view roughly at mid-novel, the narrator becomes at times quite vicious in his criticism of No-man and his cult of solitude. It is not only No-man's 'obsession with the town's past' that 'constantly excludes Wizzie';[7] the same goes for his immersion in his own sensations. That nothing 'as it really was' had the least interest for him', is a constant source of irritation to Wizzie. The thought of having 'to live in a damned second-hand mirror, if she lived with him at all' (413) makes her both furious and frustrated. Most serious in this respect is his love-making, which 'always left her cold because it wasn't her as she was in herself that he caressed' (363); rejecting Wizzie-in-herself for one of his mirror images, No-man insists on turning her 'into what he called his Bronze Age girl before he could get his pleasure' (312). Thus, by privileging his 'own selfish sensations' (260) before the reality Wizzie wants him to share with her, No-man exiles Wizzie from their supposed love relation. Her alienation becomes a tacit accusation against No-man's 'selfishness' and hence implicitly works towards an undermining of his philosophy of solitude, bringing to a head the question whether we really have 'the right' to concentrate on our own 'solitary awareness of existence',[8] when this occurs at the expense of someone else's happiness.

If we look to No-man for an answer to this question, it is clear that he is aware of the criticism implicit in the narrator's portrayal of Wizzie's alienation, but also that he is not prepared to be shaken by it. No-man is aware of Wizzie's objections to his solitary self-indulgence, not because he suddenly wakes up to reality and fills with empathy for *her* individual case, but because his philosophy has already long ago anticipated these objections. No-man knows already, it seems, what Powys points to in *The Art of Happiness*, namely that there are indeed different *kinds* of selfishness. There is 'egoism' (a positive term) and 'egotism' (its negative counterpart): 'What is popularly known as "Egoism"', Powys writes, is 'a mental attitude, not only lawful, but inescapable and inevitable, ... whereas what is popularly known as "egotism" ... is simply the abuse of egoism'.[9] It is this insight that makes it possible for No-man to justify his behaviour towards Wizzie. Although he knows that 'his way of separating himself from life, of picking and choosing from life, for the mere pleasure of his personal sensations' is 'a bitter grievance' to her, he claims that for him not to do so would be impossible (473). This deterministic attitude is based on the conviction 'that, living together as they were, they really lived in two separate worlds' (473); the basic axiom of his philosophy posits absolute loneliness as the ultimate condition of existence for every human being, and the logical consequence is, it seems, that we are all egoists. 'I'm alone', No-man thinks, 'as we all are. I'm alone, *and I'm mad in my egoism*, as she is in hers. Her crazy selfishness takes a different form from mine, that's all' (94). It is because he deduces the defence of his own egoism from this general premise of his philosophy that we feel it is so heavily charged with deliberation. Thus, as far as No-man at all acknowledges the moral dilemma that the narrator points to here, he is neither shattered by remorse, nor shown to reach a liberating anagnorisis; he just remains coolly the same as always.

It is not only the ethical aspect of No-man's philosophy of solitude that is questioned through his relationship with Wizzie, however. If, instead of focusing on Wizzie's experience of Noman's solitariness, we turn to No-man's experience of Wizzie, and particularly to his loss of Wizzie at the end of the novel, we approach another problematic topic. This is the issue which Powys has called life's 'most difficult task', that is, the solitary individual's 'adjustment' of solitude to love.[10] The question that arises here is to what extent failure to achieve such adjustment will affect the individual's possibility to find happiness in solitude, and thus, ultimately, the effectiveness of a philosophy that claims to hold *the* key to happiness. It is my contention that in No-man's case, although the loss of Wizzie affects his *experience* of solitude, his basic *attitude* to solitude nevertheless remains essentially unshaken. This is to say, he deliberately clings to his philosophy, even when his experience of solitude seems to be directly contrary to happiness, and accordingly would seem to undermine the claims of his philosophy.

As has already been intimated, No-man's love for Wizzie takes place in the realm of his own solitude rather than in a reality Wizzie can share. It is a typical, although extreme, instance of the kind of one-sided relation that we always find at the centre of Powysian love. In *A Philosophy of Solitude*, Powys describes how the 'rarified "eidola"' of our loved ones only grow nearer to us when we are alone: we 'carry them with us in our mental flight from the noises and confusions of the world.'[11] Bearing this idea in mind, then, it might perhaps seem as if no adjustment of solitude to love would be needed, since love is already solitary. Such a solipsistic view is, however, emphatically rejected by the impersonal narrator of *Maiden Castle*; although No-man's is a solitary love, it is nevertheless dependent on the real Wizzie. The extent to which Wizzie's actual presence in his daily life informs No-man's experience of love emerges clearly if we compare two scenes where Dud's whole attention is absorbed by the absent Wizzie. His sense of liberation on Maiden Castle shows us just such a 'mental flight', propelled by love, as *A Philosophy of Solitude* describes:

> [H]ere, with his real girl — No-man's girl — ensconced in his soul like a flint in a cairn, here, with no link with the world ... he was free to float on a wave of pure sensation, upon which — for what he felt, *she* felt — Wizzie might drift with him for ever and ever! (231)

But when Wizzie has left him, No-man's deflated realisation that an eidolon is not enough is communicated in a passage that moves closely to the ground:

> [T]his diffusion of her desirability through the earth he walked on, through the grass and the rocks and the stones and

the trees he passed, became, now that he had lost her, a perpetual reminder of her, and an increasing craving for her presence. (475)

What No-man realises here is the importance of *contrast* — 'the crucial role played in his life of sensation by contrast with something else!' (475) It must be noted at once, however, that this insight does not imply a reversal of views; No-man is by no means prepared to downgrade solitude in favour of reality. On the contrary, the whole point of 'contrast' is to heighten the experience of solitude; and when contrast is lacking, it is very clearly solitude that suffers. Although No-man misses Wizzie 'in every possible way', what troubles him most is perhaps that he misses her 'as the general background of his life' (474). Deprived of its background, 'his grand cult of sensations ... lost in some subtle way much of its finer edge' (475). The loss here, then, seems primarily to involve his sensations of the extra-present: his walks give him 'nothing approaching his former delight', because 'half the pleasure he got from them' had been the anticipation of telling Wizzie of his 'adventures' when he got back (471). But the other and 'less personal' (185) side of No-man's transcendental solitude, the sense of solitary communion with the past, also suffers when contrast falls away. This is the state of mind where he finds the inspiration for his writing: normally this state is triggered by the 'aura' of Dorchester, which has 'a magical power' over his imagination (91).

> [S]ince he had snatched Wizzie from the circus, he had displayed an almost savage resolution in his concentration on his writing. Morning after morning ... he left the girl in bed at Mrs Dearth's and came over to his attic ... The moment he sat down at that table in front of those old roofs, the spirit of the past seemed to obsess him. Sometimes he actually wrote so fast ... that it was as if he became a medium, writing he scarce knew what under some unknown control. (91)

But without Wizzie, and without 'the contrast that lay at the bottom of all' (476), the magic of his attic is gone too:

> Less than a month ago his escapes into this attic had been

moments of stolen bliss, whereas now it was hard for him to realise what on earth there was in the place that had pleased him so much. ... How heavenly had been that passing backwards and forwards between Wizzie and his attic! (476)

Failure in love, or failure to adjust solitude and love to each other, thus strikes at solitude. When Wizzie leaves him, solitude withers for No-man, becomes insipid and fatigued. Like Wolf Solent at the depth of his crisis, he even for a brief moment thinks of suicide (474). Yet in this situation, when solitude has lost so much of its attraction, and when the goal of solitary happiness set up by his philosophy seems merely a mockery, No-man again reverts to deliberation. The strength of his philosophy is that it is a philosophy of 'in spite'; it has a built-in preparedness to cope with such setbacks that one would otherwise expect to wreck it. As we know, its strategy is to *deliberately* enjoy the existential loneliness that we cannot escape anyway; and the first step towards this goal, the deliberate *forgetting* of those aspects of life which are 'alien, hostile, uncongenial' (184), also includes the forgetting of such aspects of *solitude* that are contrary to the goal. Thus, No-man fights his depression by deliberately clinging to the philosophy he has embraced all the time. After 'gathering up his forces' (474) and deliberating with himself for several pages, his assertion that he will neither give up his life in a physical sense, nor his life of solitude by letting 'objective' reality swamp it, does not come as a great surprise. '"I'm not going to give up", he said to himself, "because Wizz got bored with me. And I'm not going to become objective either, for all old Claudius's eloquence"' (480). The novel ends on a note of dogged determination. No-man is resolved to stick to 'his own way' of life: 'Well! He must go on as best he could in his own way. ... He must be faithful, after his fashion, to Wizzie. He must hold fiercely to all those sensations of his!' (483).

Thus, in all the attacks that the narrator has reality launch against No-man's solitude (questioning its ethics, turning it into desolation when love fails), No-man responds with extreme deliberation. It is this never-failing self-control that makes him appear static: although the near-automatism with which he is able to resist attacks on his life-illusion shows the strength of his philosophy, in terms of narrative development his preconceived answers to every new objection produce a standstill. No-man's initial stance as regards his philosophy is confirmed again and again, while never really shaken: the 'conclusion' he reaches or the 'resolution' he arrives at at the end of the novel is no different from what he started out with, nor from the stance he has upheld during the whole course of the action.

This standstill should not, however, be regarded as just a narrational accident; on the contrary, the non-progression that marks the novel's whole discussion of solitude is only a way of emphasising, on the level of narration, the chief 'message' advanced by *Maiden Castle*. This message may be summed up by No-man's statement at the end of the novel, that 'all this progress that old Claudius praises is only a return, a return with a difference but still a return to the centre from which we spring!' (474). Although this Nietzschean-sounding phrase could obviously be read as an allusion to the circular plot or to No-man's abortive plunge into reality, my interest here is primarily in the way it epitomises the novel's critique of No-man's philosophy of solitude. More precisely, I am interested in the 'difference' produced by No-man's non-progressive returns. As I will show, his deliberate strategy *does* produce the desired effect: in the midst of the compact self-control at the end of the novel there is an indication of a new liberation, and it is here the 'difference' is to be found — not in the actual passing from self-control to liberation, but in the *quality* of this 'new liberation'.

No-man's strategy to exorcise the pain of loneliness is, then, not to alleviate it by looking outward, for 'company', but to accept and intensify our inescapable existential solitude in order to transform it into happiness. This means that the way 'out' of depression does not lead out at all, but further in.[12] The model for such a break-through has been established early on in the novel; No-man is said always 'to analyse his moods to the very bottom — and often beyond the bottom, for his imagination was like an irresistible plummet sinking into the centre of the earth and liable to *come out on the other side*' (102; emphasis mine).

Not surprisingly, then, it is when No-man increases his self-discipline in order to resist the fatal tide that threatens to sweep him away, when he deliberately applies his 'rigorous system of thought-control' (184) to penetrate to the bottom of his philosophy and his self, that the first suggestion of a break-through comes to him. Holding on to his identity 'in the midst of the flowing away' (474), he returns to what 'is *in* us' (474), to his 'individual soul' (474), and in doing so he forces a passage to something *beyond* personal identity and his own subjective self. What meets No-man at the bottom of self is 'the great cloud of witnesses that emanated from the very foundations of this old Durnovaria' (474), and these are the ones who, he finds, 'could bear him up' and carry him through — 'clouds and vapours though they were' (474). This meeting with all the other 'personal souls that had held to their identity in the midst of the flowing away' holds, then, the seed to a new liberation: at the same time as it confirms No-man's belief in the solitary identity of the personal soul as the basis of existence, it is also, in its suggestion of a collective store of human memories, a going beyond this belief.

However, this suggested break-through does not constitute a climax or final resolution of the novel, for two reasons. Firstly, even though No-man may have penetrated to the bottom of his self, he has not yet, as the following pages show, reached the bottom of his depression; it is only on the penultimate page that we find him facing, 'without flinching but with an immense weariness the long ascending path up' (483). Although his break-through *is* the beginning of an ascent, it is the result of a sustained and deliberate effort rather than of a triumphant victory over self-doubt. And so, instead of the golden revelation of a Wolf Solent, we have a corroboration of his philosophy of solitude, marked by 'apathy', 'numbness' and 'a strange quiescence' (483).

Secondly, and more importantly, No-man's 'new liberation' is not really new at all, because his sense of communion with the past was already part of his life of sensations. We have already seen how subjectivity is transgressed in No-man's sense of becoming a medium, when his soul frees itself not only from the pressure of objective reality, but also 'from the burden of subjective sensuality' (185). But what is *different* in No-man's break-through at the end of *Maiden Castle* is that this less subjective side emerges as the dominant and most viable aspect of his transcendental solitude. While his subjective sensuality still torments him, evoking the image of Wizzie in every detail of the material world around him (475), it is emphatically his sense of communion with a collective past that promises to 'bear him up' (474) and let him feel again 'the magic of the generations' (480). There has been a shift of emphasis *within* No-man's solitude, and it is in this refocusing of his imaginative vision that the significant difference is to be found.

This new focus is also what gives *Maiden Castle* its central position among Powys's novels. It is not only in No-man's philosophy that we have a shift of emphasis, but in that of his author too; and the result of this shift is immediately noticeable in the novels to follow. Wilson Knight's opinion that '*Maiden Castle* is a transition work' has become a commonplace among the novel's critics.[13] However, while these words are mostly taken to refer to a shift in themes and settings — from contemporary domestic Wessex to historical and mythological Wales — I would argue that the important 'transition' takes place primarily on the level of imaginative vision. That is to say, the interest in historical Wales which Powys displays in novels like *Owen Glendower* and *Porius* is only secondary to the shift of emphasis that occurs in *Maiden Castle*, where the less subjective side, the sense of being a medium for the continuity of human life on earth, emerges as the dominant aspect in the writer's vision of solitude.

In the earlier novels from *Wolf Solent* on, the problematisation of subjective solitude was an important driving force. The solitary individual was perpetually questioning, dissecting, defending, motivating, affirming, his own solitude. In the novels following *Maiden Castle* this theme is virtually dropped. This is not to say that subjective solitude or subjective sensuality is gone from Powys's novels — on the contrary! But while it is certainly there, it is no longer questioned or haunted by guilt or fear, and since it is no longer problematised it is no longer at the centre of dramatic interest. Powys seems to be finished with these particular questions, just as No-man is already finished with them in *Maiden Castle*.

This leaves Powys free to develop his sense of the past. Yet even though his historical writings are less anxious in their attitude to the subjective, they are still visions of solitude. Their main aim is not to convey an air of historical realism, in the scientific sense of the word, but to capture the 'over-tones and under-tones' of human existence.[14] In fact, No-man's views on history may well be taken as a 'genre manifesto' for Powys's own historical writing: 'He was no historian, in a scientific sense ... History to him was life *at one remove*, life purged and winnowed of its grosser impact! It was a second reality, so to speak, a reality passed through the sieve of one man's peculiar imagination ... ' (185).

NOTES

[1] J. C. Powys, *Maiden Castle* [1936] (Cardiff: University of Wales Press, 1990). The first edition of the novel, published by Simon & Schuster in New York in 1936, from which all subsequent editions up to the 1990 one were derived, was heavily cut by the publisher's editor. My references will be to the 1990 restored edition and will be given parenthetically in the text.

[2] See G. B. Blake, *Autobiography and Romance: The English Novels of John Cowper Powys* (Ann Arbor: UMI, 1973), 95. Glen Cavaliero, in *John Cowper Powys: Novelist* (Oxford: Clarendon Press, 1973), 100, connects the portrayal of No-man with 'the same impulse which led Powys to castigate himself in the *Autobiography*'.

[3] See especially 184 ff. This account, which in my view is absolutely essential to an understanding of what happens in the novel, and consequently to an understanding of *Maiden Castle*'s central importance in Powys's authorship, was cut from earlier editions of the novel (as were a number of other passages relevant to my reading here).

[4] J. C. Powys, *A Philosophy of Solitude* [1933] (London: Village Press, 1974) 43.

[5] In his Foreword to *In Defence of Sensuality* (London: Gollancz, 1930), Powys asks: 'How far has the individual the right to be what is called "selfish"? How far has he the right to concentrate on his own solitary awareness of existence and make this alone his life-purpose?' This problem is also addressed in *Wolf Solent* and *A Glastonbury Romance*, as well as in *The Art of Happiness* (London: John Lane, 1935), 74, where Powys discusses what he calls 'the ultimate question': 'How have any of us a right to be happy at all, still less to make an art of happiness when so many fellow-organisms, both human and animal, are enduring unthinkable anguish?'

[6] Cavaliero, *John Cowper Powys: Novelist*, 100.

[7] *Ibid.*, 96.

[8] Powys, *In Defence of Sensuality* [Foreword].

[9] Powys, *The Art of Happiness*, 21–2.

[10] Powys, *In Defence of Sensuality*, 10.

[11] Powys, *A Philosophy of Solitude*, 177.

[12] What No-man envisages is a 'breaking through' of the kind his father Urien seeks.

Urien hopes to achieve his break-through by storing up a highly charged potential of unreleased emotion, and as we have seen, the strategy of No-man's philosophy of 'in spite' resembles that of Urien in its stress on intensification rather than relief.

13 G. Wilson Knight, *The Saturnian Quest* (London: Methuen, 1964), 49.
14 See my 'Prince and Outlaw: Visible and Invisible Solitudes in *Owen Glendower*', *The Powys Journal* III (1993), 69–87.

Gertrude and John Cowper Powys in Corwen, 1936

DIANA PETRE

Living with Louis *

At ten o'clock on a Monday morning in King's Road, Chelsea, I hurried along to meet the man who, the day before, after six hours of persuasion, had finally got me into his bed. The rendezvous was at the top of Oakley Street.

I saw him before he saw me. He looked quite unlike all the other people in the street. They were going about their business, on their way to the shops or the bank or a bus, while he looked like someone who had suddenly materialised for the first time in a city street and was trying out, not entirely successfully, the unique experience of walking on pavement. He looked totally out of place. I ran across Oakley Street and reached his side.

'Hello.'

He looked up from his scrutiny of the ground. 'Ah,' he said, surprised and pleased, 'so you got here. Well ... er ... well.' He looked into my face and blinked several times. 'I've got some addresses here, if I can find them. Ah, here ...'

He brought out a crumpled fragment of paper, quite small. He was a crumpled sort of man. His clothes had a secondhand look, not dirty, but not clean either; his hair was crumpled, and so was his intellectual face. He was fifty, but to me, at nineteen, he might have been eighty. Only his voice made up for the shabby appearance: it was a beautiful voice, deep and masculine and full, like cello music.

I said: 'Addresses? Whose addresses?'

He looked at me in surprise. His low untidy eyebrows cut across his vision here and there, as with some dogs, but nothing could mask the vitality that bore through the hairy veil. He gave a low chuckle.

---

* *First published in the* London Magazine, *October/November 1976, reprinted here with the permission of the author.*

'Well, we've got to live somewhere,' he said. 'I've only got the flat in Bloomsbury for a few more days. It isn't mine, you know, I borrowed it from a woman friend. I've jotted down the addresses of one or two furnished rooms. There's one quite near here in Sydney Street. I thought we might start with that.' He lifted his glasses and peered myopically beneath them, holding the scrap of paper up to his nose. 'Yes, here it is. It's not, I'm afraid, the Sidney Street to which Churchill called out the troops. That's in the East End. You know the story, of course.' And he gave me a vivid account of the siege of Sidney Street.

I said: 'You mean we're going to *live* together?'

He was even more astonished than I was. His hand with the paper in it fell to his side, and his bright little eyes blinked as he stared at me. He was almost bouncing with pleasure.

'Well, of course we are,' he said, 'what did you think? Did you imagine that after yesterday we'd go on living separately? What would be the point? When you're absolutely sure of something — seize it. It isn't often in a lifetime that one is sure of something like this, but when it comes along the great thing is to trust one's judgement. Of course we're going to live together. Anything less would be madness.'

We had been standing quite still on the pavement during this conversation, the rest of the world passing us by on either side, and we went on standing there as though alone in a room.

'You'd better, you know,' he went on. 'Of course it can't last, that's in the nature of things, but if you go on living as you are now, sooner or later you'll get into trouble. As one gets older one comes to see that certain things are inevitable, and this is one of them — that a girl like you can't fail to get into trouble if you go on as you are now, whereas if you come with me you won't. What you need is an anchor, even a temporary anchor, and I can be that for you. I thought we might ...'

After the word 'we' I stopped listening. My sole ambition was to be a half of 'we'; until that should come about I was incapable of further planning. Ever since I had left home over two years ago I had been scratching a living as best I could. Every morning on waking I had been aware that today might well be *the* day, the day that must eventually arrive, and produce, within its span of twenty-four hours, my first romantic partner. I can only say that as Louis explained his plan to me that morning I experienced a strange compulsive feeling as though my destiny had crept up behind me to give a great shove onward. Without more ado I thrust my hand through his arm, brushing against the dingy mackintosh of this old man to whom, it seemed, I now belonged, and set off with him down the street, matching my stride to his professorial shuffle.

The room in Sydney Street turned out to be the ground floor back. It had a double bed, a small ancient armchair, an upright chair, a wardrobe and a chest of drawers. It was very shabby. There was barely space for both of us to stand in the room unless close in each other's arms, but that, after all, was the principal purpose of being there. Undaunted, he looked around in a blinkered sort of way.

'What do you think?'

I was unshaken by the awfulness of the room; I despised riches. I knew that simply by my own presence and that of this shaggy man who was almost old enough to be my grandfather, but was, instead, incredibly, my lover, the grime and the deadness would soon quite cease to be. Of that I had no doubt at all. This sordid room would quickly become a haven of love and learning.

'It's fine,' I said.

'Very well then. I don't think there's anything to be gained by looking further. We'll move in this afternoon. I expect you'd like me to pay you in advance,' he said to the landlady who was standing in the doorway. Then he searched for his money in the way that he had fumbled about for the paper with the addresses, and when finally he extracted a pound note and a ten shilling note from a sort of pouch, he did so with the grave concentration of someone dealing in foreign currency. 'I think you said thirty shillings a week. We'll take it for a week and see how we go.'

This is how I came to live with Louis Wilkinson in the spring of 1931. I had not wanted to be seduced by him. I had met him briefly twice before that fateful Sunday and not liked him. Both times he had been with his second wife, Nan, who had now been dead for about three months. I thought I had not liked Louis; nevertheless, when he asked for my telephone number I gave it to him, and when he invited me to lunch, Trilby-like, I went. I had arrived soon after midday and he had tried to make love to me almost at once, before lunch. It was nearly six o'clock in the evening before he finally wore me down and I gave in. I could have left at any time; I stayed because he was a practised seducer, a capital companion, and because I was lonely. He read poetry to me. He kept getting up and taking a book from the bookshelves and reading aloud from it. He told witty anecdotes. I was nearly but not quite a virgin at this time. He made me tell him about the couple of hours I had spent in a hotel bedroom with a middle-aged man I knew who had promised never to ask me again if I would go with him once. 'I think I'll go mad if you don't,' he had said. I had thought him already

Louis Wilkinson
(by courtesy of Mrs Diana Petre)

mad and was so sorry for him that finally I had gone. It had been rather alarming — I had believed that the navel played an important part in the sexual act, and I had never before seen a naked man — and also something of a let-down. Was that all?

I enjoyed telling Louis about it; I enjoyed telling him all sorts of other things as well. He listened. He made me feel that everything I had to say was interesting, and this was something quite new to me. Also he had a particular quality which seemed to me admirable: except in matters of artistic judgement he was totally free from prejudice. I had never before met tolerance on this scale and I was deeply impressed. But his attitude towards writing was something else: he had a passion for literature, and when he believed some work to be less than artistically true he would come down on the author with withering contempt, calling him second-rate or *faux-bon* or someone who had had his withers wrung. A writer himself, he also lectured on Eng. Lit. He wrote a novel every two years and published under the name of Louis Marlow.

He was a marvellous lecturer. On a platform his stooped height — he would have been well over six feet standing straight — and his intellectual head, dark eyes piercing from behind spectacles, gave him a presence, and his actor's voice, of which he was rather vain, and total absence of nerves did the rest. Perhaps, too, he had learnt something about delivery from his father, now long dead, who had been a parson. But in my opinion — so carefully nurtured by Louis himself — he was not a good writer. No doubt I expected too much from someone of such inflexibly high standards.

The first time he gave me one of his novels to read I told him I thought it had 'not quite come off'. I was afraid of hurting his feelings, but I need not have worried about this; he had areas of insensitivity. While I was with him he sent a manuscript of his latest novel to his old friend Somerset Maugham asking for his opinion of it. Mr Maugham returned it with a short letter asking to be excused from comment; he never gave his opinion of a friend's work, he said. But Louis was not to be put off. 'He's too sensitive,' he said, 'I shall send it back and explain that I don't mind *what* he says. I just want his opinion.' I argued with him until I ran out of words; nothing could make him see that he was forcing his old friend into an intolerable position. 'He doesn't like it,' I cried, 'can't you see? It's not *you* he's trying to save, it's *himself*.' Louis sent the manuscript. It came back in an otherwise empty envelope and for a moment or two Louis was disappointed in his friend. 'I thought better of him,' he said. 'Perhaps if I write again explaining more fully ...'

There had been no men in my childhood and youth so that I had no yardstick for male behaviour other than Hollywood style in the movies, and Louis's behaviour towards women was certainly not like that. In the three years that I lived with him he never gave me a present, not even a bunch of violets, and when eventually we got married he used his mother's old ring, and later, when I left him, asked for it back. I was not bothered by this unsentimental attitude; I saw myself as one of H. G. Wells's New Women, and talked energetically about equality of the sexes. Besides, Louis was not entirely without sentiment. I once woke to find a love poem stabbed by a safety pin to my pillow. He had written it in the night while I slept. I despised the sort of woman who allowed herself to be kept by a man and insisted on giving Louis a pound out of my wages of three-pounds-a-week-and-no-tips earned as a waitress in a Greek restaurant in Chelsea.

I never considered the male ego. I talked to Louis exactly as I had always talked to my two elder sisters, that is to say, into the air, since they were both outdoor types and not interested in talk. But Louis listened and answered, whereas my sisters, not unnaturally, had done neither. Louis was my teacher and my confidante; I thought I should never tire of the daily miracle of someone so clever to talk with. He read aloud to me; he suggested that I try to write a novel about my own experiences; he said the flotsam aspect of my life, the way in which I belonged absolutely nowhere, was in itself an interesting theme. I talked my head off and he never told me to stop. When we were at home he mostly sat upright on the bed with his feet up, and I, the better to see him when talking, sat on a cushion on the floor. We used the one armchair for putting things on.

When Louis fondly pronounced me a good student my cup was full. He also told me he had never known anyone to be, as I was, completely devoid of sexual tact. It was refreshing, he said, but an ex-mistress of his expressed a different view: 'Diane is pure poison,' she said.

We lived in the drab bed-sitting room for nearly six months and were very happy there. After a while I consented to give up working in the restaurant. I already knew that Louis was friends with, or had at least met, most of the writers of the day. Now that I was free I went with him to the Café Royal, to parties, and to long alcoholic dinners in Soho. I often saw double and my pulse jiggered about with idolatry when I shook a famous hand. And there were disappointments. And surprises. Sometimes I was prudish about behaviour when, for instance, Louis's heterosexual friends — so old and so eminent — turned out to be bottom pinchers. Louis always laughed when I told him. He said I had a streak of the puritan in me and if I wanted to be a writer I should get rid of it.

We left the room when I had my appendix out and for some unexplained reason stayed in the hospital for over a month. During this time — which included our first proposed marriage date — Louis lived with friends in a house in Chiswick Avenue. He had never wanted a place of his own or belongings of any sort; he used libraries and borrowed books, and his clothes were of the one-on-and-one-off variety, all, except for a dinner jacket which was permanently housed in a friend's cupboard, easily contained in a cheap fibre suitcase. He was blind to surroundings, even to beautiful surroundings; deep dust, chipped cups and glasses, stained tablecloths, meant nothing to him. So long as he could settle himself somewhere at the right angle to negotiate a small three-tier typewriter which he accurately tapped with two fingers, and had the books he wanted, he was happy anywhere.

He was the happiest man I have ever known. His deep absorption and devotion to himself were a teasing joke among his friends. He looked after his own health with a cherishing affection that left little room for other priorities. It would be inadequate to call him selfish although few people could manage to be more so; with Louis it was more a question of ivory tower impenetrability; totally wrapped up in himself he was unaware of the wants of other people — all other people — and if this was pointed out to him he seemed unable to grasp what was being said. In other ways, too, it sometimes seemed as though a part of his brain simply failed to function. In a friends' house he would ask the way to the lavatory on twenty or thirty occasions and the next time set off yet again in the wrong direction, and when putting on his mackintosh he would stab with his hand at the *outside* of the shoulder for minutes on end in the belief that it was the inside opening of the armhole. He wore glasses, but with them on he was neither blind nor loopy; simply, he was an odd man, living in a world of his own, who must have been old fashioned even as a boy. And he was mischievous. Once, lunching in Soho, he leant across the table and spoke to me urgently. 'Darling, would you mind changing places with me? I'm in a terrible draught ...' Even for Louis this was a bit steep. I laughed and he asked me why I was laughing. When I explained he said, doubtfully, 'I see ...' Then he got up and went to fetch his mackintosh from the hat-stand where he had hooked it up. He put it on, ostentatiously turning up the collar, and ate his lunch, huddled down. When we left he murmured, 'To be on the safe side I think I'll have a hot toddy when we get home.'

His egocentricity flourished in restaurants. Like a tall, short-sighted Mr Magoo, napkin flapping from the hand, he would follow a waiter through the swing doors into the kitchen, getting in everybody's way and never knowing it, to add a word or two about his order.

When I came out of the hospital we got married at Hampstead Registry Office and made plans for a three-month honeymoon. Louis was an old hand at travelling. On coming down from university — he was up at both Oxford and Cambridge — he did the lecture circuit in America for three months of the year and for the remaining nine spent his dollars and his own small income exploring Italy, Spain and France. I don't think he was ever interested in more distant travel. For some time now he had given up the American lecturing and was a University Extension Lecturer in England, earning far less money and spending quite a lot of time in third class railway carriages which he loved, claiming them to be the best possible environment for getting work done.

Louis wrote to friends abroad to say that we were coming and worked out an itinerary. He also gave me ten pounds to buy clothes.

This had never happened to me before and I was ecstatic. For travelling in boats, trains and buses I assembled an outfit of unrelieved white surmounted by a wonderful white Garbo hat from Scott's. My feet — in white shoes — barely touched the ground as we set off one morning, an incongruous looking couple, Louis with his dotty-professor manner and ancient mackintosh, and me, now twenty, got up like a fashion plate. As it turned out no one ever believed that our passports told the truth, that we were man and wife, and twice in Spain I was taken to a room by women officials and stripped naked to prove my sex. I had had my hair cut very short, almost to an Eton crop, and was thin with a flat chest like a boy. At the sight of me naked the women officials doubled up laughing and prodded each other and me in great gusts of merriment.

It was an unforgettable trip. Mostly we stayed with Louis's friends, including Mr Maugham. In cities like Venice and Florence Louis was a perfect guide, knowledgeable, ardent, experienced, happy in the role of teacher. Unwilling to tire himself he planned excursions with minutest care, and never, as might have been expected, mislaid passports or tickets and money. He had planned our movement to give the maximum variety: a spell of city life with its galleries and churches and café sitting would be followed by a visit to the country, talking, reading, walking, and then perhaps a longish journey to the next destination.

My moods were very unstable in those days; I seemed incapable of feeling less than intensely and was consequently always in a state of emotional excess. I had started writing a novel. Louis said I showed promise but that no amount of promise would work for me until I learnt to manage myself. He held the view that whether I would eventually be able to do this or not still lay in the balance. Himself he was like a rock: day after day the same, imperturbable, amused and amusing. It was impossible to imagine him unhappy. In the same way that he lacked prejudice to an almost impossible degree he also appeared to be impossible to hurt. Really hurt. He had feelings, of course, strong feelings, but perhaps not on the scale that might have been expected of him, or perhaps, simply, he protected himself from hurt more successfully than most. He liked to be seen as a bit of a dog with women and was amused when I told him that in my opinion he had no idea what women were really like; he used them, I pointed out, as most of his friends did, merely for his convenience. He encouraged me to talk like this, to say exactly what was in my mind, and looking back I am glad I recognised even at the time how kind and long suffering he was with my moods and my opinionated ignorance. Sometimes, unthinkingly, I must have bruised his pride, but I don't think I hurt him gravely, although once, certainly, I gave him a fright.

We were in a train on our way to Pisa. I was still rather weak from the month in hospital and the black/gold stripes and whit-whit-whit of the telegraph poles and avenues of trees that we tore through were ripping at my nerves. As usual Louis was unruffled and sympathetic; he prescribed a glass of ice-cold beer in the restaurant car. It was delicious. He also invented a game to distract us: with a time limit of one minute by his watch we were to write simultaneously a word picture of another passenger seated at one of the tables in the long restaurant car. Louis's pockets were always stuffed with scraps of paper and pencils. We set to. It was a lovely game and we went on playing it until we had 'done' almost everyone in sight. Each time we congratulated each other and I proclaimed myself the winner and Louis a cheat since he used quotations while I, unable to do this, wrote an original portrait. It was thirsty work and we drank glass after glass of beer. Arrived at Pisa in the best of spirits we found a restaurant for lunch within no distance at all of the leaning tower, indeed we seemed to be sitting just underneath it. Luck was still with us: Louis proclaimed the wine that we drank with our lunch quite exceptional. We drank several carafes. Dawdling over coffee and Strega he said did I have the energy to climb the tower to the top. 'Of course,' I answered, 'what's more I'll run up it.' I had no idea I was drunk.

I did run up it. Nothing was beyond me that afternoon; even my horror of heights had left me. Once, in Austria with my mother, I had had to walk a few steps across a short iron bridge from a funicular to a landing cabin; at the sides of the bridge there were only railings and under foot a pattern of holes through which eternity was visible stretched out below. Terror, and shame at my terror, had battled inside me. Shame had won, and I had somehow got across without betraying myself.

Today I was fearless. The spiral staircase was deserted and so was the platform at the top. Arrived there I made for the side that leant over. In those days there was just a simple railing, like the Austrian railing, around the edge. The view was superb. I rested my elbows on the railing and looked about me, and then, for greater comfort, I sat down on the floor, holding on to nothing, with my legs draped over the side.

I had never felt more in command of myself and my situation. I sat there for some time, ecstatically happy, on top of the world, and then I heard Louis making gruntings as he reached the last few steps of the staircase. I turned to welcome him to my citadel. I waved my arms above my head and cried out:

'Come and give me a push and all your troubles will be over!'

Then I saw his face.

I had not meant to be cruel. It was not until I was down on the ground again and looking up at my pinnacle that my legs gave way and I sat on the grass and begged him to forgive me.

Our marriage came to an end as he had said it would, but his influence on my life had gone very deep. I have often wondered what would have happened to me had he not persisted on that first Sunday. Many years later I tried to thank him for his endless patience with me in those early days and he was astonished that I had found it remarkable. I had not made the mistake of supposing myself to be in love with Louis but while I was with him I made another mistake: I thought I was grown-up. Perhaps neither of us properly understood that my immaturity was essential to our relationship. And so, uncomfortably, it continued to be. Whenever we met in later years I felt the insidious tug of childish behaviour, if only of showing off, and all too often succumbed to it. Once, just after the war, when I knew he was staying in a borrowed flat in London I rang up at noon. 'Shall I come round?' I said.

When I arrived I dropped into a chair. 'Guess what I've been up to all night — well, nearly all night.'

He was standing in front of me, not quite as tall as he used to be, over seventy now, in his unvarying state of shabbiness, looking down at me. He smiled.

'I don't have to guess,' he said, his beautiful voice unmarked by the years. 'I know that look. Yes, I remember that look on your face. It was always a wonderful thing to see it the next morning and know that it was I who had been the cause of it.' He blinked several times, his bright little eyes kindling behind the thick spectacles. 'I wish I had been the cause of it now ...'

'Well,' I told him, 'you may like to know that in the course of the night's activities my companion said to me, "At some time in your life you've had a very good lover".' Elated, I jumped up from the chair and gave Louis a hug. 'Can't think who he meant,' I said.

BEN JONES

Surprised by Frances:
Travel and Recognition in *The Mystic Leeway* *

> But Zarathustra was a friend of all who travel far and do not like to live without danger.
> ... To you, the bold searchers, researchers, and whoever embarks with cunning sails on terrible seas — to you, drunk with riddles, glad of the twilight, because you do not want to grope along a thread with cowardly hand ... to you alone I tell the riddle that I *saw*, the vision of the loneliest.
> — *Nietzsche*

> As to Frances, who can predict anything or assert anything or deny anything? Would you be where you are if you could? Would either of us? It is this very devilishness which makes her irresistible. These diabolic surprises that made her — Frances.
> — *John to Llewelyn*

In this paper I shall offer four encounters, each of which is marked, for me, by surprise, by strangeness, by what Freud called *das Unheimliche*, the uncanny, and by what Jack called 'devilishness'. The word 'surprise' means, from *surprendre*, overtaken, and it is in this sense of being 'taken', taken over, that I use the word. In tracking these surprises, I hope to tell you something about how others saw Frances Gregg, and how she saw herself.

The most arresting look of surprise was Frances's own as she encountered herself in writing *The Mystic Leeway*,[1] although this was certainly not the first time that she turned inwardly to explore herself. Hers must have been a life of self-examination, but mixed, at times, with action and with looking outward. Frances's own surprise will be my main concern.

The second is Jack's surprise at encountering Frances, carrying with it the mythology of the somewhat wild colonial boy, of the 'boy's own' occupation of virgin land, believing himself to be on some frontier

* *An abbreviated version of a talk given at the Powys Society Conference, Cirencester, 1994*

(the mythology that drives *Autobiography*). If there were at times frivolity, some excess, and some villainy (as Jack himself says[2]), it was an encounter that continued to the end, an encounter that leaves its written trace in *The Mystic Leeway* that Jack urged Frances to write.

I shall also refer to passages from Hilda Doolittle's *Paint It Today*. Frances is the Josepha of the text (the cover is transparent since Frances's middle name was Josepha, and Julia, Frances's mother, appears under her own name). The encounter here — the 'shock of

Frances Gregg with her son Oliver, reproduced from The Mystic Leeway

recognition' — between these two women is one of a profound and, as yet, unwritten intimacy.

There is another surprise, a fourth encounter — that between Oliver Wilkinson and his mother — of which I will not say very much because he himself could say it much better.

I shall discuss these surprises, these 'over-takings', in reverse order, starting with the one I will say least about. Oliver, I think, was always surprised by his mother; by her toughness, by her tenderness, by her restlessness, by her excitement, by her resourcefulness in times of trouble — *The Mystic Leeway* recounts many troubles; and by the people she met. He was surprised by her incessant work, by her accessibility to danger, by her courting of it, and, like every son, he would have been surprised by her anger. The temptation here to become anecdotal is very great: she tells good stories, and so does he. What did Oliver think when Frances and her mother, the redoubtable Julia Vanness Gregg, decided to take up vegetable gardening for a profit? How did he share the disappointment when it was discovered that nothing would grow? And what of the many, many times when a barren place, a hillside, or an empty room were turned by special powers into a home? I know, from Oliver's account of his mother in *The Mystic Leeway*, about his surprise when a strange and secret room was transformed by Frances's magic:

> Our journeys as a family were beset by lack of money, were often dangerous, as we rode on the rim of existence, but most of them were, in fact, happy, extraordinarily happy. When, for instance, I was ten and my sister was eight, in 1925, we were in Oaken Hill Hall — that Elizabethan mansion with no running water or electricity, but with secret rooms and passages. Frances and her mother, Julia, prepared a Christmas room for us. They had been making — out of the wood of packing-cases, mostly — furniture, vast furniture that could hardly be moved, but which, when padded, were comfortable thrones. Now they prepared this room which could only be reached by a steep ladder. Betty and I saw them going up and down this ladder. We knew they spent a great deal of time there. We had no idea what they were doing, except that they were making a

Christmas room as a present to us. On Christmas morning, Betty and I were allowed up there for the first time, through the trap-door. The room was glowing with decorations, tinsel and Christmas stars, with an oil-stove burning brightly. The floor was spread with pictured rugs. A punching-bag was stretched from floor to ceiling. A doll's house, with lighted windows, stood near the window, every room filled with furniture. There was a big horse, that Frances had made from a plank covered with cloth, and stuffed with rags, with a mane and tail of coloured strips, and a head smiling with painted teeth, the whole of it hanging by ropes and hooks from the ceiling, and strong enough to swing endlessly on. It was a magic Christmas: but then all our Christmases were magical, and so were many other days.[3]

What Oliver knew, and learned over and over, was that there was an aura of magic around Frances. She could transform the unfamiliar into the familiar. She was herself uncanny. Others knew it, too. Not all the time, of course. Anxiety, sickness, struggles for power, distress, even malice: these were there. At times the familiar became the unfamiliar.

But life was to be affirmed. Frances travelled. She was a nomad, someone Zarathustra would pause to look at, to be surprised by, to speak to: 'Come along, Frances. You know all about "the vision of the loneliest".' She was one of those for whom *Zarathustra* was written — Zarathustra, a 'friend of all who travel far and do not like to live without danger'. Friends of 'bold searchers, researchers, and whoever embarks with cunning sails on terrible seas', those who are 'drunk with riddles, glad of the twilight', who 'do not want to grope along a thread with cowardly hand'.[4] Frances had the vision of the loneliest.

I know that Oliver Wilkinson was surprised, was sustained by surprise, and that he would not forget to exchange gifts with Frances, to return her writing to her.

Surprised by Frances. Frances Gregg's name has been connected to Hilda Doolittle's since their first meeting in Philadelphia in 1910. They enjoyed something of instant fame within their little realm, attributed likely to their close friend Ezra Pound who was always making something famous, or infamous. The realm did not remain little for long. Europe opened its doors. Or did they open Europe's doors? There are no doubts about the intimacy between Frances and Hilda. And there are no doubts about Hilda's surprise. Some will know Frances's portrayal as Fayne Rabb in *HERmione* which recounts a triangular love relationship between Hilda, Frances and Ezra Pound.[5] The text I would like to mark here is *Paint It Today*. Composed in 1921,[6] and spanning the years 1912 to about 1919, it has until recently only been available in portions. It is of interest to Powys studies, mainly for the role that Frances Gregg plays in it (as Josepha), but also for Louis Wilkinson's role as Josepha's husband, named Seaford (51), and for its references to Josepha's 'true lover', an unnamed Irish dramatist (identified by Cassandra Laity as Llewelyn, but it was John Cowper). The relationship with Frances began with a look. Frances had just come through the door:

> It was not that the girl, Josepha, was beautiful, judged by the ordinary standards. She came into the room, stood stiff against the oak doors that closed heavily behind her.
> The other [Josepha] sat down. She had on a raincoat that fitted closely and a stiff straw hat wound with a stiff gray veil. This gave her an old fashioned appearance, a distinction in this room filled with the daughters of lawyers, doctors, professors, and oversuccessful wholesale merchants. (8)

She was without class distinction, insofar as lawyers, doctors, professors, and oversuccessful wholesale merchants offer such distinction. The heavy closing of the oak doors takes us immediately into the Gothic scene, the site of the uncanny, enclosed. In the text Hilda is known as Midget, a name — along with 'Wee Witches' — that Hilda and Frances exchanged affectionately. Hilda's gaze is precise, moved by both physical and mythological perceptions:

> It was her eyes, set in the unwholesome face; it was the shoulders, a marble splendor, unspoiled by the severe draping of straight cut rainproof; it was her hand, small, unbending, stiff with archaic grandeur; it was her eyes, an unholy splendor. ... Her eyes were the blue eyes it is said one sees in heaven; eyes, Angelo would have garnered in a group of holy boys, copied

for one face and recreated for another; eyes a Messalina might have wrought (to stab a Caesar) into bright steel; eyes the color of wet hyacinths before the spikes have broken into flowers. (9)

Others looked at them. The 'fiancé [Ezra Pound] twitched his very young mustaches and thrust out his slightly underdeveloped chin and said: "You and the girl, a hundred years ago, would have been burned at Salem, for witches"' (9). The text is formed from these repeated encounters: Hilda and Frances are separated from everyone else, separated even from the separated (the artists around them in a so-called Bohemian London). They touch only each other, and they speak a secret language:

> When she and Josepha, after the inevitable preliminary rambling together in the present, the present that was dead, found themselves for the first time face to face, the present which was dead melted away and they were together in the past and in the future. They spoke a few words, at least it was Midget who spoke the words. Midget knew that she was speaking simple words and understandable words. She understood them herself and Josepha understood them, but she felt somehow that she was speaking the wrong language. She was speaking English. (12)

This intimacy fused with the thoughts that were to move and to haunt H.D. throughout her life: not living in a present, but in an uncanny mix of past and future, speaking a mysterious language that only special people could understand. Josepha/Frances was one of those who understood.

Awareness of speaking the 'wrong language' takes us into H.D.'s profound sense of language and her desire to find a new language, to create a new poetics, and it connects Frances/Josepha to this process. Frances and Hilda speak to each other, but the English words, the 'wrong' words, are mere markers for a communication that cannot be spoken. This is the uncanny, the unfamiliar, the possessed. This was not just 'Imagism'. It could only be approached by relentless experimentation with other languages, with ancient, primordial languages and rituals, certainly with the language of dreams and psychoanalysis, and it would likely never be found. English, as she heard herself speak it, was wrong, but all the languages of the social order were wrong. The intimacy between Hilda and Frances took a variety of forms, and one of them was that they understood each other's language.[7] Such understanding set them apart: after such knowledge there was no forgiveness. And, although they went different ways, they were unforgiven.

The 'hounds of Hecate' dogged Josepha's footprints (9). They had earlier agreed upon their vocation as witches. But even among witches there are surprises. And there was the great surprise when Josepha wrote: "'I am going to marry — I will be married when you get this — a passable person. He gives University Extension lectures. We may get across to Berlin in the spring'" (32). She gives no details, no explanation.

Josepha was not allowed to forget: 'Josepha, I have not forgotten you. I pretend that I have forgotten you because I pretend that I have forgotten everything. I have a new game. I am a shell. There is nothing in the shell' (52). Midget's (Hilda's) words are both benedictory and maledictory: 'See, oh Josepha, great in your pride. I have made a bitter prayer at last. To spite you and to spite myself and to spite your glorious baby. Sleep, Josepha. Are you dead? What is this birth you speak of? I would cry if I had any tears. Sleep, Josepha. Are you dead? If you are dead, I will make a song for you' (57).

Hilda's connection to Frances did not end with their separation to join their lovers. In the 1930s, Hilda met Freud, was close to him as a friend, and was his patient. She records in *Tribute to Freud* a session with Freud in which Frances figures: 'She [Frances] came in my dream and said, "Do you remember ... so-and-so ... and so-and-so ...?" — as if to hurt or humiliate me'.[8] She discusses Frances with Freud: 'When I told the Professor that I had been infatuated with Frances Josepha and might have been so happy with her, he said, "No, — biologically, no." For some reason, though I had been so happy with the Professor (Freud/Freude), my head hurt and I felt unnerved. Perhaps it was because at the end I tried to tell him of one special air-raid when the windows of our room in Mecklenburgh Square were shattered' (152).

It is an extraordinary passage, and I have tried to think it through. The date of the session was 11 March 1933. *Tribute to Freud* was begun in 1944, not published until 1956. Given the date of the session, the air-raid would have to have been in the First World War. This is a possibility.[9] Hilda tells Freud about a dream she had in which Frances returns and asks her to remember 'so-and-so', to hurt her, Hilda thinks. We do not know what or who 'so-and-so' is. She tells Freud that she thought she could have been happy with Frances. Freud says no, 'biologically no'. Freud has 'killed' Frances. Hilda is happy with Freud — she connects him with *Freude* (= joy), yet she becomes sick (head-ache, unnerved). The dream-telling ends, and she tries to tell Freud about one 'special' air-raid when windows 'in our room in Mecklenburgh Square' were shattered. 'Our' was probably Hilda and Richard Aldington's. The session seems broken. But why the air-raid, why the shattered window? Windows are like doors. Was this something outside, wanting to get in, something uncanny? Freud should know about this: he wrote the book on the uncanny. Is this something about Frances? Frances, already killed by Freud, will be killed in an air- raid in 1941. Much shattered glass. Surprised by Frances? Yes.

I turn now to John Cowper and the surprise he encountered in the face of Frances. Frances had admirers, but, as we shall see, she says in strong words that no man had ever allowed her to be Woman. She was constantly being made into something Other, into some being out of someone else's text: she is Messalina, or Faustine, or, in a bit of theatre concocted by Jack, a Lucrezia Borgia. Someone with whom Jack could play dress-up. There must have been an extraordinary sense of play in her makeup. She didn't mind crossing over. Jack was astonished, ecstatic about the 'boy-girl' scene in Italy. Jack writes to Llewelyn on 4 January 1914 that she is 'in a curious way dreaming over something behind a mask. Some new departure — some mental change — is evidently occurring in her', and that she was a 'little wild treacherous thing!' '[She] is looking round for something new — some unknown new person who will not turn up!'[10] In all the photographs that I've seen of Frances she displays a serious face, melancholic. Perhaps she was always 'dreaming over something behind a mask'. But I think she must have been lots of fun, too.

SURPRISED BY FRANCES

Jack wrote a poem to Frances, shortly after their first meeting, at one of his lectures in Philadelphia, in 1912. The Swinburnian speaker addresses the 'spoken to' as Sadista. The poem is 112 lines long, and carries out a Swinburnian project. Reading Swinburne together must have been a kind of courting ritual at that time. We know that Hilda and Frances read Swinburne together — that's where Hilda got the name Faustine.[11] Here is an extract:

> Shall I not be really cruel to you?
> Just a little really cruel to you, Sadista?
> Shall I not make you tremble, O victim, prepared for me —
> Prepared for me from the foundation of the world —
> Tremble and pitifully cling, with imploring wrists,
> With imploring wrists and suppliant child-like fingers?
>
> ...
> Is it not strange?
> That a shy white body like yours, Sadista,
> Should only grow more and more delicious,
> The more it is made to quiver under the lash —
> The more it is bruised by the Panther's tongue?
> O little gasping cries!
> O little arms that vainly struggle!

And the ending:

> Hush! What is that?
> That sword-flash, that laughs like a merry child at the ruin
>   of worlds,
> That is my spirit, Sadista —
> That sword-flash is my spirit —
> Mocking, mocking, mocking, mocking forever
> At earth and air and sky and shore and sea—
> That is my spirit, Sadista — mad — mad — mad — mad —
>   mad!
> But the one thing in a thousand universes
> At which it doth not mock —
> Is the breast towards which this blade is pointed

Pointed, pointed forever —
Thy breast, Sadista![12]

Jack surprisingly found in Frances someone to whom he could confess his sadistic bent, albeit somewhat obliquely, that is, in the Swinburnian mode. Here is a mixture of the ludic (and the ludicrous), the embarrassing and the sinister. Whatever kind of violence Jack discloses here, with his blade pointed forever at her breast, he is saying 'Look at me.' Surprisingly, perhaps, Frances did just that. I hope they laughed together about Sadista: it would have been a sign of health. But it has its dark side, too.

In a letter probably written just before 'Sadista', Frances is assigned the role of priestess cleaning up Jack's shores: 'Even as I write this your being and essence flow over me, like a flood, and I am clean of all — The salt-cold Frances at her priest-like task of pure ablution round Jack's human shores ....'[13] The allusion to Keats' "Bright Star" is conspicuous: courtship by literature again.

The Sadista poem is not likely to gain much recognition except as an item of psycho-sexual curiosity. But we are here talking about a profound relation, Frances and Jack, a relation based on drives towards recognition, and a relation that culminates with Frances's writing of *The Mystic Leeway*.

John Cowper's fetishism is well-known. It forms a line of narrative in a number of his fictions, and in its sadistic mode it is central to his confessions in *Autobiography*. In the poem, Frances is marked as fetish, as the desired object that can be subdued. This fetish-making does not change over the course of his writing. Certainly the central problem in *Wolf Solent* is Wolf's realisation that his perception of the world, particularly his perception of Gerda and Christie (Christie is, to a degree, Frances Gregg), has been devastated by his obsession for fetish-making. Such revelations, and even the addiction to the woman as fetish, inform us of a particular kind of desire fulfilling itself in narratives that position the woman as an object in another person's eye, the position that Frances occupied in Jack's gaze (and Hilda's, and Ezra's, and Llewelyn's, and Louis's). This, we know, is the usual position of the woman in modernist texts. We think of epiphanies: Bloom's and Stephen's, and the schoolgirls on Brighton Beach.

Frances in her Mirror. What did Frances see in herself? We have recorded so far some views of Frances from the outside. She knows that, after so many encounters, she had yet to be recognised:

> So far, in all my life I have met no single Man — though I have done my best to make one of Oliver Marlow — nor has any man encouraged me, or indeed been willing for me, to be a Woman. Mumbo-jumbo, superstitions, muddled mythologies, have been my fate among these artists and prelates and magicians, these escapists from life — from Life![14]

Now, as she writes, she seeks out a leeway. The leeway itself is a space, a space away from the wind, from turmoil, violence, from otherness, from the gaze of the Other. It is a space in which one may recover: perhaps a private space, but also a space to re-affirm, re-assert, re-form, a connection to the world. Gregg's project here is to use her own life-writing to discover, re-discover, and recognise herself, to re-establish her speaking voice. She sums up this enunciation of herself in these words: 'To me all that I am is most necessary' (170). This was the answer to those artists, prelates, magicians, and the others, who had used her. But a 'leeway' is not just a space. It is a 'way'. More exactly, it is a deviation from a set course, a drift. Both of these meanings — shelter and drift — are in the text. Early on she says: 'This tale was begun as a record of those people who, in the hurly-burly, the wash and silt of life, seemed to me keen and reputable, not beggars in the mart of their shiningness wrapped all about with the rags and gauds and trappings of other people's thoughts and other people's laws and other people's conventions' (133). But the writing takes a turn:

> These were the people [Pound, H.D., John Cowper Powys] about whom I set out to write, the people whom I knew best, but more and more it is becoming a tale of the one whom I knew least, the baffled, hag-ridden, bewildered I, about whom I shall never come to say she was this, or that, for, by turns I am a grand and wise superhuman being moving with sure and stately tread where truth is, and a scrambling ape tearing their silken woven scarves into idiot tatters, making a mock of their

human gestures, chattering ribaldries with my high ape gods. And for the actual living of life I have but one law — I serve. Oh, if I can but find you, strange companion who is I, then I shall know the secrets of life and death, but I shall not find you, neither I nor anyone. (133)

Her comment here, with its uncertainties of movement between assertion and malice, its confessional and bitter 'I serve', and its awareness that she will not be recognised, sets out a course.

The Mystic Leeway begins with a surprising visit by gypsies to Frances's caravan. She is afraid, but they ask only for water, and she makes her own identification with them. She, too, is a gypsy. They have treated her 'on terms of dignified equality' (55). 'I am a caravanner', she says. 'I want to claim no country for my own,' and she continues: 'I do not know why I do it, nor what I seek, nor towards what bourn I am eternally pressing. I don't know. Nor do I know who it is who weeps darkly within me, longing for its "home"' (55).

Travelling and 'home' are the motifs — indeed the motives — that control the text. But they are always at odds. As Jack discerned: there seemed always to be a 'new occurrence' in the offing. Certainly the most important journey she took, perhaps the most important event in her life, was the trip she took to Europe with her mother and Hilda Doolittle in 1911. There are some contraries in her recording of the trip: the ocean voyage itself she recalls as the 'happiest and most exciting adventure of my life', and she wonders why all the other passengers, as she learned at the end of the voyage, were waiting 'patiently', with some anticipation, for her to throw herself overboard (108). But she knows why her countenance was so sad, and she tells us. She had abandoned hope: 'I can still feel that awful emptiness, loneliness, grief, of those hours of struggle. It had to be and I had to face it. I remember the feelings of my sharp chin pressed down upon my cold salt hands that clasped the rail, just that frail barrier of flesh between me and nothingness. This left me with an awful tenderness for the flesh, the pitiful poor thing' (115). This was the context of the voyage into exile, taken with her mother and her lover.

Frances did look into mirrors. She recalls a special moment of revelation in the presence of Hilda. The two of them are travelling by train at night in France, looking out the window, seeing themselves reflected in the glass, against the darkness. It was a moment of 'mystic communication of beauty'. She stares at Hilda's head and sees, like a 'second medallion', her own:

> To that was added the mysterious excitement of being borne on and on through space while the eyes of those phantom girls met, out there, where no thing was. I remember ... the tragic, unstressed melancholy of their gaze upon each other. We were beautiful, and we were doomed, — as indeed, in a sense, we both were, for life was to deal harshly with each one of us in many ways. Dauntless and untried, as we were then, I think that we knew, for those few peerless moments, all that we were ever to know of the meaning of life. Afterwards we elaborated upon the theme, and tried it out upon the lovers of our choice who, with marked unanimity, and painful regularity, deserted us. (57–8)

One of those lovers who 'deserted' them was that 'bright-haired poet who first kissed the lips of Frances', Ezra Pound. Pound was no passing fancy, and Frances, in the following passage, tries to even the score:

> Mr. Pound, explain yourself. I have raged enough. For your sake I have torn my lovers from dithering limb to limb. You had something — in those first kisses you scattered so widely like stars upon a cerulean field of flowering maidens, you had something of which your poetry has been no more than a dim and vapid echo. Believe me, we have been faithful to you, lover Micawber, though, in very truth I forgot you years ago. So much I know, that a woman has but one lover, one only, one whom she is destined never to know, never to find and to whom she is to be forever faithful. (92)

There is no sense in this text of her recovery either from love of woman or love of man, nor is there any sense that she should have tried to recover. But there is a strong sense that she remained Other to all lovers. Perhaps writing *The Mystic Leeway* for Jack was her exception:

perhaps she found herself in this text. But, as she has told us already, no man ever allowed her to be a woman, nor did any woman, except, perhaps, Amy Hoyt: flat body, angular hips, little sculptured hands. Amy is entitled to one short paragraph that ends: 'I have known no other woman who was good' (100). We have little choice but to accept sexual strangeness in Frances's text. In matters of the uncanny, she was not a dilettante. That's what made her different.

We do not need to read confusion into her recitation of her sexuality. Confusion is already there — she admits her own bewilderment: 'Male and femaleness in sexual matters is remarkably inconclusive and fluid; male and female characteristics weave and intertwine, and run the gamut of a dual expressiveness bewildering to the protagonists ...' (94). Jack would, I think, have liked that — Jack who had invented Persephone Spear and the 'automatic young lady from the Farmer's Rest'.

Within a year of her return from the trip to Europe with Hilda, she found (was found by?) three male lovers (the already married Jack, Llewelyn, and Louis), she married (Louis), and she committed herself to motherhood. Remembrance of Hilda remained. And as late as 1934 she writes to Hilda: 'I wanted the original woman who poked her head through the womb of time. You are it, and I am your still born twin'.[15] Surely this is Frances's search for recognition: the origin, uncanny, doubled, yet homeless. Ezra, Jack, Hilda, Llewelyn, Louis: none had found for her a home.

But her mother was at hand — that strangest of mirrors. Julia was, likely, always at the door: 'In the first place the Mother is an awful burden.'[16] The figure of the Mother is constantly before us as a counter-Persephone myth: instead of Ceres searching out the lost daughter, we have the lost daughter unable to escape from the perennial Mother, indeed, lost because of the Mother. The myth pattern is told with resentment, with an unsparing bitterness.

The trip to Europe, which, of course, was made possible by Julia, was one long argument. Frances remembers it as a struggle between her deep devotion to Hilda and her necessary obedience to Julia. 'Needless to say,' Frances records, 'my mother wept, wailed, and gnashed her teeth across two continents, accusing Hilda of robbing the widow of her orphan, destroying its morals, besmirching its innocence, leading it to betray the sainted duties of daughterhood' (109). Several pages later, after recording her mother's accusations that Frances's conversation 'is abominable and filthy' learned from her friends, Frances moves immediately into one of the most lyric descriptions of Hilda's beauty in the text: 'her heavy-lidded eyes, her chiselled lips, that something glaucous and yet flowerlike that was her very essence, and the mystic light that glowed within her like a flame globed in alabaster' (123). Yet, one of the most devastating comments on her mother is her two-page treatment of her mother's own lovers, Rowena, Harriet and Katy. 'Once I came upon her and my mother locked in passionate embrace' (97). She adds: 'Had I hissed "Lesbian" at her, she would have yelled the house down' (99). Each is given a repulsive end. Rowena 'trundled towards her tomb, ranting in jangled imbecility.' Harriet dead by starvation. An aged Katy the object of the mother's scornful laughter because of her pathetic love gestures. There is no evidence to validate Frances's reporting, but Frances's malice is obvious enough. Immediately after this scene, she invokes Amy the Good: 'My own friend, Amy, was not like any of these' (99).

In one of the final statements about Julia, she does not mince words:

> By one of the freakish elements in my mother's character I had grown up to these years of over twenty in complete ignorance of the phallic in life. I had grown up, too, in a morbid isolation that she had imposed upon me. I was the solitary stamping ground for that centaur-lady of the blue and fiery eye, the limpid moist eye, the lascivious languishing eye. Upon me she poured out all the phials of her perversity, of her thwarted sex, of the hot flight of her blood. ... What it [sex] was all about came as, first, a ludicrous anticlimax, and then as a menace, a terror in life, a thing by which everything had to be re-stated and revalued, but worst and most fatal of all it robbed man of his dignity, and [robbed] life of free will and real personality. (156)

The three lovers (Ezra, Hilda, herself) had had no chance: Hilda 'came out of the nothingness with a message that none could read'; Ezra and

Hilda together remained 'just out of the range of my comprehension' (156). 'I, too, was attracted to them, each, the sex made no matter' (156). Sex 'made no matter'.

Frances connects her own sexual strangeness directly to her mother. Although she has written about other women, and about women as other, there is no sign so powerful as the sign of the Mother, the sign of Julia Vanness Gregg. This writing was done well before the theorising of the Maternal — of such significance in current literary debate — had been formed. We can learn something from such theorising. I want to comment on Kelly Oliver's remarks on Julia Kristeva:

> Kristeva identifies two relations a woman can have with her mother. One possibility is that she doesn't ever 'get rid' of her mother. Rather, she carries with her this 'living corpse', the mother's body that no longer nourishes. Kristeva claims that usually women close their eyes to this corpse. They forget about it. And they certainly don't eroticize it. As a defense, some women devote themselves to the Symbolic order. Kristeva identifies feminism as one such defense. Presumably, politics, art, and science are others. Kristeva warns that if a woman enter this 'combat' with her mother without any such defense, it can lead to 'fairly serious forms of psychosis'.[17]

The Mystic Leeway, whatever claims it makes to calm space, is 'combat'. It is a combat against artists, prelates, magicians, lovers, and against The Mother, those who have betrayed the child, failed to recognise the child, man or woman, and impaired that child's entry into the world, either as child or adult. *The Mystic Leeway* was, for all its anecdotes, defence — defence against the unseen hand, against what Jack came to call the malicious First Cause, the Great Eye that stared at the helpless figure on the Waterloo steps and haunted Wolf Solent. Frances had carried the living corpse of the Mother long enough. But Julia was, nevertheless, the kind grandmother who transformed an empty attic into a child's delight.

Frances, who lived with the first choice — with what she must have known to be the 'living corpse' — for too long, took, in the writing of

The Mystic Leeway, Kristeva's second choice: defence, combat. And thereby, she secured her sanity. *The Mystic Leeway* was an overcoming. It was a fight for recognition: for recognition, most of all, by the Mother she did not wish to carry as a 'living corpse'. But recognition, too, by all those 'artists, prelates, and magicians' who once had spoken her name. (I think it is problematic that John Cowper Powys made no mention of it, and it seems unlikely that Julia ever read the text.)

If, as I suggested, her writing was combat, defence, even offence, did it take her anywhere?

Frances's comments on her own cursed sexuality are followed immediately by recollections of her visit, with her mother and Hilda, to art galleries in Manchester and Birmingham to look at Pre-Raphaelite art. The 'Rossettis and the Watts and the Burne-Jones', formerly admired, had become 'cheap sentiment', and because of this experience — a 'revolution' she calls it — her life turns round: 'I ceased, at this point, to be a nice woman. I was bitter, scornful of my betters, and determined to be a spy. Myself was my nearest quarry. For better, for worse, I determined to follow where the wind of my desire listed, denying nothing, formulating nothing, but knowing, at least, one woman naked as Eve' (157). This I would call combat. In this search, art generally fared no better than the Pre-Raphaelites: it was 'wishful thinking', and 'cheap sentiment'. It was made by men, who were soft, or women who imitated men. She had already said: 'The male is only capable of a terrific, short-lived effort mentally and emotionally. After that he repeats himself for what it is worth. Take any man that you know, he exhausts himself in the first effort, whatever it may be, a life pose, or an art.' And somewhat more maliciously, 'he becomes an old poseur clinging to his youthful fancies, as Ezra clung to his beret and his velvet jacket and the flowing tie when a round paunch and a ruddy countenance made them pathetic — to those who loved him, and just ridiculous to the young who saw him for the first time in his age' (145). As for women artists: 'Show me a young woman artist and I will show you a stealer of man's thunder' (145). That she has a project in mind, and not just a release in spleen, becomes clear in her assertion: 'I am probably the first real woman artist' (146). But that is qualified immediately: 'If they ever have a beginning, they die young, like Emily Brontë. Not Charlotte. Any man could have written her stuff. But could aught but a woman have conceived *Wuthering Heights*?' (146).

Among the wastes of her time, art revealed itself as illusory, having nothing to do with life, a product of male weakness masking as power: 'Artists did not seem to me the vanguard, but the rear-guard in life. ... They were the cosmic journalists, a noble profession but, as far as creation went, they were sterile and impotent' (121). If this overcoming were to take place, then art might be tried again, and in this re-ordering of the human she is 'probably the first real woman artist'. As for the present, she cannot conceal her malice towards a world that had ruined itself and still, in the winter of 1940-41, would not give up trying: 'never has the world struggled in such contagion as this' (169).

But where has her writing taken her? What did the mirror show?

> I am alone in a void. Here, incorporeal, stripped of the phantasms of the senses, reft of imagination, knowing that I know nothing, here I find the thing that I am. It is cold, hollow as a mask, with sightless eyes. (163)

To trace her arguments towards an ending, as set out in her final chapter, is outside my purpose here. But there are some problems to settle. She discovers that it is she, herself, who is uncanny: 'cold, hollow as a mask, with sightless eyes'. Yet, she saw many things that others do not see. The malaise of a world drawing itself into war took a toll. Auden tells us about it: 'a low dishonest decade'. Frances's appeal for a new leader, who would be a woman and a Jew, surprises us, although the connection between women and Judaism is clear enough: the history of Judaism and the history of woman run on parallel lines — both have been betrayed by a master lover, by a tribal god proclaimed as patriarch. Women have been betrayed and they have betrayed themselves. That betrayal must be overcome.

But Frances Gregg — on this occasion when I have tried to recognise her, and share this recognition — will have almost the last word, a last word directed against a male 'rummaging' through her narrative to find other males, Pounds (or Powyses):

> Indeed, a youthful friend of mine ... rummaging through these

pages for scraps of memories of his hero, Ezra Pound, told me, with that eldrich admonition of the young for the old, 'Some of this is brilliant, but much of it is so unneccessary.' He referred to certain references of mine to 'woollen combinations' and all that I said of Christ. And I am moved to say many spiteful things to this young Merlin — (for whose memoirs are these anyway? and to me all that I am is most necessary). (170)

For Frances Gregg, life was Surprise. Right to the end. Is that Nietzsche I hear speaking? When life ceases to surprise, you are dead.

NOTES

1 F. Gregg, *The Mystic Leeway*, with an Account of Frances Gregg by Oliver Marlow Wilkinson; B. Jones, ed. (Ottawa: Carleton University Press, 1995).
2 J. C. Powys, *Letters to his Brother Llewelyn*, M. Elwin, ed., Vol. I (London: Village Press, 1975), 104.
3 Gregg, *Leeway*, 33.
4 W. Kaufman, ed. and trans., *The Portable Nietzsche* (New York and London: Penguin, 1954-85), *Thus Spoke Zarathustra*, 'On the Vision and the Riddle', III.2.
5 H. Doolittle, *HERmione* [written 1926-27] (New York: New Directions, 1981); published in UK entitled *Her* (London: Virago, 1984).
6 H. Doolittle, *Paint It Today*, C. Laity, ed. (New York: New York University Press, 1992), xx.
7 Laity's Introduction, especially xxvi-xxxiii, is useful on this point.
8 H. Doolittle, *Tribute to Freud* (Boston: David R. Godine; New York: New Directions, 1974), 151.
9 See H. Doolittle, *Bid Me to Live (A Madrigal)* (New York: Grove Press, 1960).
10 Powys, *Letters to his Brother Llewelyn*, Vol. I, 136.
11 Doolittle, *Paint It Today*, xxiv, xxviii, xxxi.
12 Manuscript in the collection of Oliver Wilkinson.
13 *Jack and Frances: The Love Letters of John Cowper Powys to Frances Gregg*, Vol. I, O. and C. Wilkinson, eds. (London: Cecil Woolf, 1994), 4.
14 Gregg, *Leeway*, 61.
15 Quoted in B. Quest, *Herself Defined: The Poet H.D. and her World*, (Garden City, New York: Double Day, 1984), 180.
16 Powys, *Letters to his Brother Llewelyn*, Vol. I, 139.
17 K. Oliver, *Reading Kristeva: Unraveling the Double-Bind* (Bloomington and Indianapolis: Indiana University Press, 1993), 62.

JOHN COWPER POWYS

The Influence of Personality: Who wants his Inmost Self Meddled with and Invaded? *

The appalling influence of human beings upon one another is one of those concealed realities that leap to the surface now and again so suddenly and so sharply that we are rendered aghast at the shock. Our absorption in the mere piloting of our own poor life-ship through the difficult seas renders us pathetically oblivious of what may be going on down there in the swirling darkness; so oblivious, in fact, that when one of the monster-fishes of the dim tide comes up with a splash we are overwhelmed, bewildered, panic-stricken.

For indeed this matter of the influence of personality upon personality is pregnant with the most alarming implications. There are, of course, predatory and sinister persons who draw the very zest and interest of their life from these subterranean complications; but the more natural reaction of the human self in the presence of such things is frank discomfort and dismay. The will to dominate, to mould, to transform, when the perilous stuff of another's fatality is the material, is checked and disarmed in any normal person by the sheer terror of responsibility. No ordinary individual wants to hold the very identity of another's being between his hands; and even less does he want his own inmost self meddled with and invaded.

There is something indecent, something unnatural, one might almost use the word incestuous, about these incursions of one human spirit into the walled-in precinct of another. It is only necessary to drag the occurrence into full daylight to realize the enormity; and this

---

* *First published in the* Haldeman-Julius Quarterly, *Vol. II, No. 1 (1927). It is reprinted here by courtesy of Cecil Woolf. This essay will be included in* The Wind that Waves the Grass, *Volume Three of* The Uncollected Essays of John Cowper Powys *(ed., Paul Roberts), in preparation.*

realization almost always comes suddenly and with the impact of a blow in the dark or a splash in a silent pond.

Even when the 'influence' has been beneficial to the object of its concentration, there still lurks, amid the pleasure with which we recognize the happy chance, a certain obscure distress and uneasiness; as though some primordial sanctity had been violated. And how profound — though it may well remain completely inarticulate — is the indignant grumbling, like the growl of an outraged beast, that rises from the depths of our own nature when the peculiar essence of what we are, our own particular life-illusion, is fumbled at, scraped at, and lugged out of its hiding-place as if at the end of a hook.

The process of influence need not necessarily imply these extreme violences but it rarely takes place without some sort of questionable invasion, some sort of raking and combing and dropping of drag-nets.

Even in a chance company of absolute strangers the thing goes on — that invisible interchange of signals, of messages, of appeals for help, of malignant exposures, of caressing advances, of contemptuous slights, of homicidal hostilities.

In the subway of any city, on the pavement of any street, one is aware of these queer currents of attraction and repulsion, each asserting its own special claim, each giving something, stealing something, rousing or suppressing something. No one who lets go, for the least second of time, his Cretan clue of subjective preoccupation, can remain intact. There is not a single human skull you can encounter but it becomes the focus-point of an immaterial vortex of quivering sensibility, diffusing, dilating, expanding, diminishing, clutching at you, rejecting you, swallowing you, spitting you out! Enter any kind of public place, any kind of public conveyance, and if you are not protected by a veritable armour of self-absorbed concentration, you become conscious that the air is vibrant with invisible influences, some beneficent, some malign, but none responsive in precise reciprocity to your own nerve-edges.

The atmosphere of an enclosed place where human personalities meet, even for the shortest periods of time, becomes nothing less than a galvanized aquarium of vaporous entities; each one of them reaching out far beyond the body of its particular owner, each one of them radiating some curative or some poisonous influence and very often both kinds together.

The curious thing is that the especial modes of influence which are generally associated with sex-attraction, whether normal or abnormal, are as a matter of fact continually being manifested where no direct sex-interest could possibly occur.

Two elderly men, for example, both of them quite unprepossessing, and neither of them in the least neurotic, will catch one another's eye in some crowded room and the most singular 'rapport' will establish itself without the faintest consciousness on either side of what is going on. One mental emanation, hovering around one unobtrusive well-groomed figure, will menace another emanation issuing from a similar figure, with the most extraordinary savagery — or it will fawn upon it and cringe before it with servile abandonment — or it will excite in it some old half-forgotten strain of noble resolution — or it will stir up in it some long-suppressed vice.

Certainly the stuff — whatever it is — whereof our mortal bodies are made is most horribly porous to impressions from other bodies. They seem so solid, these corporeal frames of ours; but in reality they are as fluid as vapour, and there is no skin among them, however tough, no bony substructure even, that does not yield, like impalpable mist, to the magnetic invasion of alien entities.

Conscious influence of one human being upon another, whether for good or evil, is but a small proportion of the drama that constantly goes on. There is some subterranean principle of psychic reciprocity at work among us, according to which the very chemistry of our inmost self takes colour and character from the chemistry of the personalities about us, whether in response to a magnetism that attracts us or to a magnetism that irritates and repulses us.

Not one of us, even the mildest and gentlest, but is continually being betrayed during the most distant and accidental encounter, into some obscure emotion of indignant distaste or subtle attraction. Hardly a human profile presents itself to our attention but something in us, stirred remotely from inaccessible depths, craves the relief of a smacking blow or an impetuous caress. It is doubtful if there is a human countenance in the world whose ears or nose — poor unsuspecting appendages of the inveterate spirit in us! — have not been tweaked and pinched in vicious fury by the invisible fingers of reprobation, as, all unsuspecting, we pursued our innocent way. And these ungovernable, yet well concealed gestures of nervous irritation have, every one of them, a definite influence upon our nature, committing us more and more drastically, as they repeat themselves, or as we rigorously repress them, to the fatal groove, for better or worse, along which we are travelling.

One very interesting mental phenomenon may be noticed and that is, that when any two people meet and engage one another's undivided attention there occurs, from the interflowing of their diverse magnetic currents, an immaterial mirth, a new and intangible entity, so to speak, which hovers in the air between them and has thoughts, feelings, insight, perception of its own, through which, as through an impalpable medium, the two friends interpret life afresh, under a new and exciting aspect, undreamed of by either.

When one considers the primordial instincts, reverting back to incredible bestialities, which snarl and hiss and crouch and growl in the recesses of our nature, it is extraordinary how we retain our decent masks.

It is not exactly that we are unconscious of the perilous feelings we suppress. It is rather that by a queer sort of self-deceiving ritual in our secret thoughts we superimpose on the top of them a whole stratum or layer of more traditional emotions polished up and made presentable and 'appropriate'. It seems to be achieved, this interior conjuring-trick, by the presence in us of a sort of automatic humanizing machine, the evocation, I suppose, of centuries of furtive impulse, the motive-force of which remains mysterious and obscure.

But whatever its origin, this automatic vacuum-cleaner seems to have the power of substituting a complete set of respectable emotions for the growling, snatching, writhing and hissing ones which move about in darkness.

The word 'influence' has indeed a touch of ironic mildness in its sound when one comes to realize what a projection of horrible and beautiful things the wretchedest of human countenances thrusts shamelessly at us as it goes by.

When any two persons meet and look for a second into each other's eyes there is a catastrophic encounter of many universes. 'Deep' does most literally 'call unto Deep'; and faint and feeble are the two timid consciousnesses peering down into those gulfs compared with the abysmal revelations that open up between them.

The more we know of life the more unbounded and fathomless grow its recesses. A man is something much more horrible and much more lovely than the mere case, the mere frame that your senses envisage, that oblong pole with clothes hanging from it, the funny arms and legs that jerk and swing, the fantastic indented knob stuck arrogantly on the top.

Influence! To come bolt up against a monstrous world of convoluted landscapes, each one full of beauty and terror and each one only the scrawled-over window through which another looks out, is an experience that does something more than influence us. It dominates, it pulverizes, it overpowers us. And if it were not that we — even we ourselves — have precisely the same effect upon *it*, there would indeed be the devil to pay.

Children are always a little surprised when they discover for the first time how easy it is to outstare a cow, a dog, or even a panther in a zoo. Stupid people tell them about the power of the human eye. Dear me! It's the power of seven heavens and seventy-seven hells!

Every human face is a granite precipice, at the bottom of which you can discover Leviathans, Krakens, sea-serpents, disporting themselves in waters blacker than night — yet every now and again that precipice's edge is touched by a loveliness more delicate than the most magical dawn, a loveliness that quivers and vibrates —

The face of a man, the face of a woman, is a fathomless hole into which we are compelled to peer, whether we like it or not, when those eyelids are uplifted — a hole that goes down and down and down, through the misty stuff of the universal world and out beyond.

For it is not only the naked skins of serpents and the crimson buttocks of inhuman apes; not only the snarling jowls of hyenas or the drawn-up lips of panthers that meet us down there, along with dead staring eyes of saurian malignity. There are beautiful and tender things there too, lovely moonlit things, like fragments of old tunes from buried cities, from lost paradises — and sometimes, moving wistfully over lawns sleepy with twilight, there are visions in those places that carry unutterable happiness in their shadowy hands.

Those appropriate human gestures, normal affection, normal compassion, normal reverence, are the traditional mask not only of indescribable malignities and perverted obsessions, but of strange, beautiful, super-normal impulses that are like the first quiverings of a new sensitiveness born into the world!

And this is inevitable; because the appearance of exquisite beauty as well as the appearance of desperate evil, is something that excites alarm, suspicion, doubt. What we really aim at, in our traditional moral ritual, is comfort and equanimity, and considering the madness of the swirling forces that surround us we can hardly be blamed for this. An abnormally noble character, like an abnormally inspired genius carries with it through all its days the blighting curse of the mediocrity which it condemns; and even in the souls of quite ordinary people when a wild, strange, beautiful impulse flits for a moment over the familiar scenery there is an instinctive lowering of port-cullises, hauling up of drawbridges, and closing of shutters and curtains.

The psycho-analytical methods, which are so fashionable just now, have undoubtedly done much to push back the boundaries of human nature to deeper and more interesting levels; but by laying stress rather on isolated childish experiences than on the depths of the mind itself they have often betrayed into nailing up again the very door that we want opened still wider.

And they have laid all the emphasis on sex; whereas in reality there are immense gulfs and spaces of the human mind that transcend sex altogether, and yet are by no means free from malignity, cruelty, the will to possess, to torment, to dominate. The truth is that sex is only one aspect of that out-streaming of magnetic energy which is the motive force both of good and evil, and the very electricity of influence.

The conscious desire to 'improve' another personality is almost always attended by some narrow and unintelligent vision of this other's real essential being; and even when it does not imply a secret lust for reducing its object into submission to itself, it too often implies a lack of aesthetic reverence for the organic originality of a life different from its own.

Warily, cautiously, and with infinite delicacy must any beneficent influence go to work! It must be saturated at the very start with a rich, indulgent, imaginative sympathy for the vital essence of the personality it approaches; and its aim must always be rather to liberate from accidental obstacles the true fatality of its patient than to twist or mould this unique thing into conformity with its own taste.

It is hardly realized yet how formidable a part in this fantastic drama is played by persons who deliberately exert influences over others for the mere gratification of their lust for power. There is never any social gathering, whether respectable or bohemian, during which the most amazing orgies of influence do not take place. The most casual encounters of human beings are wrapped about in an electric atmosphere of unseen vibrations; and every one of them is an arena of extravagant confessions — made without words — of penances inflicted, absolutions vowed, seductions consummated, affiliations recognized, abysmal hostilities brought to light.

The part played by sex-attraction and sex-repulsion, whether normal or abnormal, is only one aspect of the extraordinary struggle that goes on when human consciousnesses come together. The lips of the two interlocutors may be uttering the most childish babble; but their souls are peering, probing, biting, stinging, pursuing, retreating, putting to shame or being themselves put to shame.

The only protection from this kind of social rough-and-tumble is itself a startling evidence of the superior importance of the mind as compared with the body. One's body may be completely at the mercy of the invasive chemistry of other bodies and yet the mind within us, intact, immune, withdrawn, inviolable, may be wandering at large over remote pastures, surrounded by infinite solitude.

One of the most curious discoveries into which, as we get older, we are inevitably led is that there goes on under the surface of the most affectionate relations a queer contest — a contest that only death can end — as to which of the two inner natures thus entangled draws most for the nourishment of its own temperament from the temperament of the other.

There are two methods of vampirizing employed in this curious struggle and it is an interesting problem which of the two is the more successful.

The one method is that of flowing like a serpentine mist round every contour and valley of your sweet enemy's inner-self, while with a self-effacement too absolute to be even ironical you pillage the landscape of his identity of its most hidden honey and most delicate fragrance.

The other method is that of using your friend's temperament as a steel plough, against the blade of which you can lay bare the deeper and richer soils of your nature and cleanse yourself in the process of the barren stubble and chaotic weeds that have grown up between the essential quality of what you are and those rains and suns and frosts and hail-storms of the outer world that have so restorative and primal a magic.

Either of these two methods will win its own reward — the reward of a philosophic use of the accidents of influence; but it will probably become manifest in the end, however crafty and subtle your culture-egoism may have been, that the influences that have hurt you most or have enriched you most, as you steered your way through life, were those that came lightly, suddenly, imperceptibly, beyond all premonition or intention; and departed, it may well be, in the way they came — like gossamer seed upon a wandering wind, like wisps of smoke from an unseen camp-fire.

T. F. POWYS

The New Broom

Miguel de Cervantes tells us, though I do not know that it is altogether necessary to go to him for this information, that some families increase in worldly goods and become richer, while others decrease and become poorer.

Mr Peter Maby's household belonged to the former kind.

The Maby stores at Conway had prospered from the first and at length reached up to thirteen delivery cars, and a manager with stern compressed lips whose salary was six hundred a year.

Mr Peter Maby had a fancy for number. He liked to see numbers that lined up well like soldiers. Moreover he thought of his will. He liked to think of leaving something between sixty and seventy thousand pounds when he died. Less than that betokened a common mind, more than that mere presumption and cupidity.

Mr Peter Maby had commenced business in a small way, but in the end he became an example to all Conway. Even social reformers studied his case, and it was said upon the platform of the local conservative club, that Mr Maby had once been an office boy and filled inkpots.

When affairs at the Maby stores had reached up to the second delivery car with Dunlop tyres, Mr Maby spoke to his wife in the same tone that he used to a customer whose bill had run too long.

"My dear," he said, "we are being noticed in the town, we must keep a servant."

Mrs Maby looked down at the carpet. She had swept the carpet herself every morning for sixteen years.

When the fourth delivery car was bought, there were three maids and a daily charwoman. The house wherein Mrs Maby entertained these ladies was called "Glenwood".

THE NEW BROOM

Mrs Peter Maby was forty-five years old by then, she had large wondering eyes, two dimples and the smile of a child. She loved little chickens that were just out of their shells.

A day came when the house was very quiet. Mr Peter had gone to the shop, and all was still. Thinking the moment a chance for happiness, Mrs Maby carried a broom into the dining room and began to sweep the carpet. She swept silently. She had not felt so happy for years.

When she was in the middle of sweeping under the table Kitty the housemaid opened the door. Mrs Maby let the broom fall. She went up into her bedroom and sobbed as though her heart would break. It nearly did. Mrs Maby wished herself dead. All her early married life came back to her, all the many little things she used to do when her house was her own. She called to mind those winter afternoons when after getting the things ready for his tea, she would rest till he came in and wonder whether she would ever have to make long clothes for a baby.

The firelight would flicker upon the wall, and the shadows would dance like little legs playing, until she thought it time to light the lamp, for he never liked the firelight because it made him think the more of the cost of coals ...

Mr Peter Maby liked most men, but not all. He disliked artists. When he had posted the cheque for his sixth motor delivery van, the Mayor of Conway, whose wife painted pictures of reeds and rushes and ducks in a corner, asked a favour of Mr Maby. He asked for the loan of the backyard shed at the stores so that an exhibition of pictures might be given there.

Mr Maby had always used this room for the unpacking of his goods and for the storing of any kind of lumber that was thrown out from the shop. He thought the Mayor very interfering. Mr Maby said in a confiding sort of way that there were mice in his store-room.

This objection was at once set aside, for the lady Mayoress remarked, that she was sure that mice never ate pictures.

Mr Maby hinted about the smell of the shop bacon.

"But it's always the best bacon you sell," said Mrs Dobbs. "We always find your bacon so good Mr Maby."

Peter was forced to agree with this and to lend the room, but he could not help still more disliking artists.

When the first day of the show came Mr Maby took his wife to look at the pictures. Mrs Maby wandered about the room while her husband stood and talked with Mr Dobbs near the stove. The pictures did not interest her in the least though everyone was saying how beautiful they all were.

One thing did interest her however, this was a young man who was looking out of the window.

Mrs Maby was simplicity herself. The young man reminded her of a chick just out of its shell. She went to him and inquired why he was not looking at the pictures.

"Mrs Dobbs says they are lovely," she remarked.

"They are horrid," said the young man.

"Are you a painter," inquired Mrs Maby, "or a chic ...?" she stopped herself just in time.

"My name is Unwin, and I am a painter," replied her new friend.

"I am glad I spoke to you," said Mrs Maby, "you know I do love little chicks just hatched."

Unwin smiled, and pointed out to Mrs Maby a boy in the yard who had placed a hammer on a large box and was playing marbles.

Presently Mr Dobbs remarked in a loud tone, that the police had told him there were robbers in the town, men with creased trousers and pistols.

Mr Peter Maby looked round for his wife. He saw her standing in close conversation with a young man by the window. He supposed the young man to be one of the robbers Mr Dobbs had mentioned. Mr Maby called to his wife and took her away with him. In the shop yard the same boy who had played with the marbles was now opening the large box with his hammer. Mr Maby ordered the boy "to be careful about the jam ..."

The Mayor of Conway was so troubled about the robbers being in the town that he caught a chill and died.

Mr Maby went to the funeral.

As soon as he had gone Mrs Maby walked out into the town.

In a dirty by-street she came upon a young man standing by the open door of a studio and holding in both his hands a new broom as if it were a pitchfork. He was looking sadly at the litter upon his floor as though uncertain where to begin. Mrs Maby remembered him very well, he was young Unwin and he still looked like a chicken.

Without speaking a word, Mrs Maby took the broom. She swept happily. She swept every day. Unwin's studio became like a new pin ...

When Mr Maby petitioned for a divorce his counsel said that a woman who leaves a good home in order to sweep up litter for an unknown artist must be guilty of everything alleged.

The case was undefended.

Before many months were passed, Mr Peter Maby and Mrs Dobbs were married, and Mr Maby bought his fourteenth delivery car.

The new Mrs Maby never wanted to sweep, but she covered the walls of Glenwood with paintings of reeds and rushes and fat ducks, and filled Mr Maby's safe with title-deeds and bonds.

The manuscript of this previously unpublished story by T. F. Powys and a slightly variant typescript are both in the Bissell Collection. We have made use of each for the transcription.   *Ed.*

John Cowper Powys (left), with T. F. Powys and his son Dicky

Llewelyn Powys as a schoolboy in Sherborne

LLEWELYN POWYS

Hedgecock

Although in the familiar outline of the Montacute hills, Hedgecock, sheltered as it is between Miles Hill and Ham Hill, takes a somewhat inconspicuous place in the landscape, it is an eminence by no means to be despised. This shaggy mountain, though no less prominent than its two neighbours, is, as its name implies, wilder than they and for all that it does not flaunt its presence, its bosky conical shape is sufficiently familiar to West Country people; to bagmen coming down over Babylon Hill into Yeovil; to shepherds crow-barring hurdle-holes on Corton Downs; to back-door hen-wives on the Polden Hills; to eel-spearers on Sedgemoor anxious for the end of their water-net work; and to clod-weary ploughmen turning a final furrow on the airy uplands of High Ham. Miles Hill, it cannot be denied, has played a far more notable part in English history than ever Hedgecock has done. Around its manifest earth-trenched summit there has been gathered, through the centuries, a wealth of legendary lore only rivalled perhaps in the West by that of Glastonbury Tor and Cadbury Camp. The distinction of Hedgecock is not such an obvious one, its romantic appeal resting less upon popular fame than upon the secret grace of its own sequestered dells and leafy unvisited hollows. Even as late as a quarter of a century ago Hedgecock Forest flourished in all its original woodland glory. To the right of the mud track that leads to Ham Hill, at the top of the first dip, there used to grow one of the finest beech trees I have ever seen in my life. Towering up and up, branch above branch, in all the splendour of its maturity, it had played for generations the part of a faithful trysting tree for all true lovers. 'Come, woo me, woo me; for now I am in a holiday humour and like enough to consent.' The timber of the forest of Arden was all scratched about, so it is rumoured, with love messages, and the silvered coating of the smooth white bark of this giant beech presented a kind of palimpsest Doomsday Book of the names of all the sweethearts who had trodden over the dog's mercury and primroses of the wood since Queen Victoria first came to the throne. Often I have wondered into whose possession that huge trunk came after the wood-cutters had felled it. In what lumber-merchant's yard did it lie unhonoured, except perhaps by humble rural working men whose imaginations had never been dulled by the deceits of gain? Skeat instructs us that the original books were 'pieces of writing scratched on a beechen board', the Anglo-Saxon word boc meaning book and also beech tree. What a book that huge bole could have been for a wise man's reading, a text that offered an infallible testimony to the mystery of life, with love-knots and arrow-pierced hearts uniting the parents and grandparents of half that Arcadian locality!

When I was a little boy it was a common sight to see red squirrels in the trees of Hedgecock, but in later years these active chattering arboreal little animals disappeared altogether, perhaps hunted down with the stones and catapults of Bishopston urchins, or destroyed, for all I know, by one of those sinister pestilences that periodically infect the rodent world. The following rhyme suggests the plentiful amount of timber that used to grow along this easterly salient of the greater Ham Hill promontory in the old days: 'From Ham Stone to Dogtrap Lea, a squirrel can leap from tree to tree.' The Ham stone referred to was a colossal projection of oolithic sandstone [sic] that stood, I believe, a little southward of the Prince of Wales Inn. This remarkable natural monument —'the girt Ham Stone' as it was called in the district, had survived since the original geological formation of the ancient leonine hill. It must have been known to the early Britons, have been as familiar to the Roman soldiery as to the mediaeval quarrymen. Indeed, it was not demolished till almost within the memory of man; sold, so Dr. Hensleigh Walter informed me, to a common road-contractor to be broken up.

But if the trees of the hill have sheltered together with squirrels, hawks, rooks, and sentinel jays, the ground beneath their roots has provided excellent dens for badgers and foxes. With enormous platforms before each earth, platforms heightened and broadened by the renewed excavations of successive breeding seasons, these cunning four-footed creatures dwell in relative security at the very top of Hedgecock, having need to give attention to few sounds other than the rustlings of rabbits, the crowing of cock-pheasants, and wind in the trees.

As boys, my brother Willie and I would sometimes be invited to go rabbiting in Hedgecock with Captain Chaffey. Followed by Crook, the coachman, with a bottle of Burgundy, chicken sandwiches, and bread and cheese, we would start away full of eagerness from East Stoke House, destined often, as it fell out, to do little else than to keep watch and ward for what seemed interminable hours outside rabbit holes in the hope of recovering a truant ferret that was regaling itself at its leisure, or perhaps even sleeping, at the further end of some inaccessible subterranean gallery. Bob Chaffey was a character not easy to be matched, a lovable sort of Uncle Toby, with an innocent dry humour of his own private invention as natural as it was droll. He was indeed a typical product of the English countryside, an old-fashioned gentleman — stubborn, sympathetic and proud, modest, egocentric and kindly.

Only on one occasion do I recall his straying from the *Tao* natural to his amiable temperament, and this happened under my own ill influence. We had been out one afternoon and *shot nothing*. It was a mild day towards the end of January and we were resting on a fallen tree trunk in the very heart of Hedgecock, idly listening to a cock blackbird that, at the first hint of softer weather, had begun to sing in the rays of leaf-level sunlight, with the full-throated ecstasy of the spring-time.

> Hither my love!
> Here I am! here!
> ......
> This gentle call is for you my love, for you.
> Do not be decoyed elsewhere,
> That is the whistle of the wind, it is not my voice,
> That is the fluttering, the fluttering of the spray,
> Those are the shadows of leaves.

The whole wintry wood was held under a glamour by the bird's passion, not a branch stirred, not a twig trembled. And then Satan whispered slyly into my school-boy ear to persuade Captain Chaffey to shoot this winged creature that thought itself safe so high above our heads. At first he would have nothing to do with so dastardly a plan, but I pleaded and pleaded with him until the moment arrived when the harmless happy hedge-fowl lay at my feet with red blood upon its golden bill. I do not believe the ancient mariner was as conscience-stricken over the killing of the albatross as was my companion over the death of this common cock blackbird. "I ought never to have done it," he kept repeating, and the remorse that he showed all the way home imprinted the incident upon my memory, together with a sense of shame that I feel to this day.

No one was more sensitive to, or indeed quicker to appreciate the peculiar qualities of the people he had to do with than was Captain Chaffey. There are those who would like all the world to be of one fashion. The inhabitants of Stoke and of Montacute never subscribed to this; rich and poor alike, they have always been renowned for their singularities, for being, shall we say, a trifle "out of the ordinary"; and the eccentric landowner relished these eccentric ones as much as they did him. The Yeovil-Ilminster road used to be at the beginning of the century enlivened by the presence of a little jobber named Hawkins. This man almost every day could be seen driving from his cottage somewhere beyond John Walter's house, with its Fives Courts and stag in the garden, into Montacute. His conveyance consisted of a home-made cart, scarcely bigger than a goat-carriage, which, pasted all over with Bible texts, was drawn forward by a donkey and usually filled to the brim with laughing children, whom the jolly little good poor man had taken along with him for company's sake.

Another character who was an especial favourite with my friend lived in a cottage near the gates of his drive. This was an octogenarian labourer named Denman who understood life, and the poetry of life, better than many who were far more learned. He had indeed a pure and most original genius that broke through the crust of the commonplace every hour of the day. All those shallow importunate surface impressions that render most of us as stupid as stock-fish he looked upon with an illuminated God-given imagination. His every day talk was thick with poetry, with poetry that sounded as natural as wind and water. He was a man with hands that were horn-hard from a life of toil. His hair and beard were snow white, and standing under the copper beech, a tree always so eloquent of well-to-do garden securities, he would speak to me like one of the ancient prophets, like the prophet Amos under his wild sycamore. "His word was in mine heart as a burning fire shut up in my bones, and I was weary with forebearing and I could not stay." After I had left him I would sometimes write down what he had said. One of those far off mornings reads as follows: "Sixty years agone today come two months, I were a'trapsing along this here turnpike to ploughing match. Yes, we know as much of life as they that cross the ocean, *we that live on the deep soil*. We have *our* waves, as well as the rest of 'em, we quarry men and ploughmen, come fine, come sleet, come cold, come het."

This essay was published posthumously from among Llewelyn's papers by Alyse Gregory in The West Country Magazine *I, No. 2 (August 1946), pp. 73–6. It survives in a typescript in the Bissell Collection, entitled 'Hedgecock and Hedgecock Memories'.*   Ed.

Sketch by G. M. Powys, showing Montacute Hill with Hedgecock on the right, from A Baker's Dozen *by Llewelyn Powys (1941)*

KATIE POWYS

Brothers and Sisters:
A Selection from the Diaries 1927–41

7 May 1927 Read Pater. Sat for Gertrude. After dinner we started off on our excursion with Josephine to Arish Mell. It was very nice, certain moments exquisite though my spirit was damped for I felt curiously as if I was selfish and like Father making Gertrude drive past horses and past bulls. Going down to the sea we passed a deserted old barn and beyond the new houses Gertrude so quickly spotted cattle and a bull. She fled to nearest hedge. We came back by an unexpected path through a wood which reminded us of Stoke Wood, the Kissing Gate and all. The beech was just out and looked lovely. We returned by the Wool Road. On the shore I read Jack's review on Doughty.

29 October 1927 Wind and gales with heavy rain. Lulu and Alyse leave for America tomorrow. I don't want Lulu to go. I want him near me to caress me, to advise me. I feel I shall tilt over in the mill-pool if he is not near to steady me by the hand. Yet when in real life Alyse managed that last meeting together I know he does not want me nor my will to lavish love upon him.

5 November 1927 Lulu has gone, he and Alyse, to New York. Sailed from Southampton on November 1st Tuesday 4 days ago. Willie saw them on to the Ship. We waited for the car that took them the night before to Dorchester. We had our last tea with them. Willie sitting where Jack sat, I sat with Lulu on the sofa next to Gertrude while Alyse was in her usual place, pouring out for us as if she was never about to leave. It is pretty to see her dependence on Willie consulting him ever about every small matter. I have never seen her behave so with any one before save maybe at moments with Gertrude. It's generally she who takes the weight and responsibility of all. I know I will always make straight way to her regards any unhappy matter.

19 November 1927   Lulu has left us now for more than a fortnight. Today we had a letter from Isobel and Phyllis speaking of their arrival. To read of it makes me just quiver to be there. What a truly blessed spot is Patchin Place. But properly be there in person would mean misgiving and nervous tension. But I should love to see Phyllis once again. Dearest dearest Phyllis. Joy of more than one person ... But it makes me sad to hear how fragile Alyse was looking but we have noticed it here the same. I am sure it is the result of Walter's death.

28 November 1927   Willie's last day here at Chydyok. He is packing and I am writing inventories of what the boxes contain. Gertrude has chiefly been painting him but I have got in an hour or two with him and

The Powys sisters, Dorchester, 1947
from left: Marian, Lucy, Gertrude and Katie

Josephine and her saddle. Otherwise mostly driving him backwards and forwards from Wool. It was pleasant to see him peering over the cliff edge to search for a fox. I like seeing him walking about the valleys with Gertrude. He enjoyed his visit with Lucy to Norwich: Aunt Ellen gave him a saddle. Dear Willie I love him. Gertrude is going as far as Paris with him which I am glad of. They leave tomorrow by the early milk train. Gertrude and I went down in the afternoon yesterday to West Bottom where G. read two pieces of poetry but it is a terrible place. May the soul of Walter have peace. They say Lulu is better, but does not go out at all to dinner-parties etc. Gertrude and I talk and talk. It is strange how much and yet how little she knows me and the other way round it is the same. Only at times I have a sudden glimpse into her real sensations.

January 1930 More I see of Lulu the more I love and appreciate him. He is indeed the Brother of Brothers, the lover of lovers and more I gain in the knowledge of his friendship the more I value and rejoice in the blessedness of it. To me he is the one of all the family that responds with that particular quality of sympathy to each separate one. I feel that if it was put to the test that Lulu would hold the favour of us all maybe except Marian and shall I say Lucy. I know I am right about Jack. Gertrude would if it was not for her great great love for Theodore which is founded from even earlier stages but she comes very close. Of course Theodore raises an entirely different affection. I like best to be with him when walking under the moon alone. He satisfies a profounder and a more mysterious part of the soul. I feel I can never really reach him and yet I feel I am more truly myself stripped of all pretensions when I am with him. Still I am often nervous from fear I should in any way destroy the peace that exists between us. His words are those of a prophet and of a philosopher; they should be considered and not made light of. He should be venerated and when the gaiety of his mood appears it should be taken as the glory of a day between storms, to be treasured and remembered. I tremble and bow before him and it annoys me too that strangers do not value him in the same serious light. He is one who should live where it is even more difficult to get to so that pilgrims who do go should have it hard and tedious so that they may become to regard him in the manner they should. I say, curse those people that treat him lightly and those who write of him should write concerning the Priest of darkness and Wisdom. He touches nearer the philosophy of Nietzsche than any I know. Blessed is his Name.

April 1930   Gamel and Alyse have been through my last story. Gamel appeared quite to like it though probably it is not her natural style, but Alyse was full of objection — why I could not at first make out thus I was wounded and hurt. But since she came and looked the writing over with me and I realized certain of her reasons, I began to understand and instead of being painful our hours were extremely pleasant and greater love than ever spread over myself for her personality. There is a force in Alyse that no one can combat with. How I admire. How the things in her I criticize become nil before her greatness and singleness of purpose. Really and in truth I adore her. To me, if you can get beyond her sting, you are far rewarded. How indebted I am to her help in my writing. For without her I could never have launched my books. She and Lulu were the first to encourage, except my own great friend Stephen Reynolds and Gertrude.

I have been once or twice out with Theodore but what I did value were those days when he crept up to Chydyok before Gertrude returned from Norwich and we had some moments together in my room and walked down the Valley again. They were moments of great value. First to feel he came of his own accord, next to enjoy him without the presence of others and then to listen to his words and above all to hear his praise of my book which to me seems really impossible knowing how he never likes the ordinary novel.

June 1930   I had a happy walk with Theodore over High Chaldon with the Valley beyond, where we sat on the short turf of a small pit in the light of the evening sun. It was afterward that I saw our shadows moving forward together. Perhaps that is how we know each other best. Shadows of the earth, but not living. It did me good to be with him. Strange how immortal become those moments when I sit near Theodore. Though often I feel absolutely dull and uninspired, he seems to make my eyes attend and increase the importance of sitting in quiescence.

6 December 1931   Lulu and Alyse seem to like their cottage. I love them next door but yet I feel eclipsed by them. It was too terrible for words when I broke down before Alyse. How I blame myself after those scenes. How I feel I want to hide: to escape. I feel it were better for me to live amongst strangers than that I should come in contest with the best and most beloved of my relations.

I shall never forget the strange chance of meeting Alyse the same afternoon when I was still depressed and sad. She ran to meet me, a thing I have never known before. She was full of concern and kindness. It seemed the Gods had ordained it. It appeared a forgiveness, a new understanding.

Sunday Bertie was here. Rain heavily at night. Disappointment. Bertie was kindly. I enjoyed teasing him for a change. My relationship with Bertie seems a strange one; I feel more familiar with him than even with Lulu or Theodore. I like to tease him over little things. I like to hear his advice over my money affairs. But when he is gone he is no longer present like Lulu or Theodore. He supports the reality but not the spirit.

3 May 1932   I have just come back from seeing old Bertie off so far as Wool. It was extremely pleasant. I really felt myself. Very happy with him. I always find I can talk with Bertie. It may be because he explains so often in similes.

January 1934   Once more we set sail upon the seas of a New Year. May the God Poseidon be favourable to us. May Llewelyn find his strength again. May his illness no longer weigh heavily upon him. Bertie arrived for the New Year. I shall never forget those opening moments of the year when Lulu wished to hear the Lulworth bells: we all became silent and stood around the shelter in solemn silence. My soul shook. I felt like crying, particularly when Lulu said in a very faint voice: 'They are not very clear' and Gertrude answered in the tone she would use to comfort a child: 'No, not very clear.' I had to retreat. Nor shall I forget the appearance of Willie's profile as he waited in solemn seriousness. The full moon lighting all, falling alike on us, the grass, the shelter, all shining with the hoar frost. Afterwards Willie and Bertie walked away. Gertrude and I after seeing Lulu alright walked for a minute or two beyond the railing amid the gorse — Alyse crept back to Lulu. Before that I had heard the crying call of a vixen. Did a dog fox hear her or did she wander in the heath in vain? The next morning, having walked as far as Chaldon with Willie, I visited Theodore since Littleton had already called. 'Renunciation and contentment' is his wish for the New Year. I was happy to be with him and hear him for even a moment or two.

Summer 1934 They are here: Jack and Phyllis have arrived. Jack's postcard arrived the same morning when Alyse had an agitating letter from the lawyer. The Vicarage people are determined to continue the case. I first saw Phyllis at Wool Station. It was cruel waiting for the train but it was emotional meeting her. Why are such meetings so often fated to be in public? We saw Theodore a moment on the way up to Rat's Barn and then when we walked up the iron road Jack amused himself by counting the iron pieces. It was bright sunshine and Phyllis was enchanted by the distances over Dorset. Gertrude we met below as we approached the house. She had all things ready. We had tea together and then left to hurry back to Lulu where they soon joined us. Since then they have been over and we have been over there. One night I had an all too happy ½ hour there, while they ate their supper and I sat on a chair by the fire. It seems for ever a miracle to have them there, to behold and still more to hold Phyllis in my arms and feel those frail willow bones as if they were the slender frame of a bird. It is a miracle, an everlasting miracle. I find it is almost dangerous; it is upsetting. One night I had to fly to the cliffs to reassure and reason with myself. I want Phyllis. I want to tell her all and everything, and yet I dare not seize her from the others. I fear of pushing myself, I tremble at keeping aloof yet I want her to be with Alyse and for Gertrude to like her, but to have this happen, I have always to hold myself back from her. Lulu and I shiver as over thin ice with the joy of having them. Phyllis would have me come there for lunch the day after Gertrude had been but I did not feel at ease. I was conscious of my horse-like body. I was uneasy at seeing Phyllis cooking and preparing a dinner for me. I could not bear to feel I was interrupting Jack at his letter-writing, yet a quivering delight ran in and ran out of me all the time to actually see him use his pen on a letter which so often has given me such joy to receive and to

Gertrude, Marian and her son Peter, Theodore and his wife Violet, at East Chaldon

watch Phyllis moving with her pans and her dishes preparing so delicately the food which she laid before me. Jack afterwards walked on the cliff with me. I enjoyed to see the butterflies and the swifts and to have the sense of the sun and the wind-blown hills. Still I felt I could relax better when I sat behind a gorsebush with Gertrude. Why is it when one's emotions are most alive one always is so full of doubts and queries?

August 1934   Lulu very ill again, unable to move; we watch him all the time. He was taken with a haemorrhage on Wednesday night before his birthday. I had just come back from an evening at Lulworth, helping with the boats, drinking in company with the fishermen. Hardly in bed when we were roused. Agony, agony. Poor Alyse to begin all over again. Sunday night I was sent hurriedly down to Winfrith for Dr. Anderson to give him morphia. Brenan obtained a nurse from Bournemouth, a worthy woman reminding me much of Ellen, a Methodist or a Buddhist, all too ready to do good deeds. I see her excellent qualities, but for all I want more often than not to dodge her presence. Have read some pieces of *Zarathustra* to Llewelyn before breakfast which I have much enjoyed, but yesterday morning he could not bear reading. My theory is ... it is the excitement of seeing too many and the cursed libel-case, of talking too excitedly with Jack. Theodore says: 'Dullness, monotony and melancholy have never killed people, only despair.' Surely melancholy and despair run very close. I rather have Tom Paine's character than Coppard's: only we did not altogether care for his *Age of Reason*. Coppard is puffed out with conceit. His egoism is as powerful as A.R.P.'s but lacking his supersensitiveness. I seem to see less of Phyllis, but when I see her and Gertrude sewing on two chairs opposite me my spirit rises in revolt and I have to fly to Alyse. Why is it I hate seeing two persons contentedly sewing 'a fine seam'. After the hatred of being shut in a church service, it is the next fundamental hatred of my life. I am a zebra that never really yields to domestication. I loathe, I hate it. I got the same feeling when I once saw Lucy and Gertrude doing so. It brings them rest, it does not do so for me.

September 1934   John Cowper appeared one afternoon in great distress and real rage because I had carried over boxes to him to burn, and he had cut his fingers with them; then Gertrude had ordered coal for him. However I felt at last I had secured him from the clouds: I saw all at once someone besides myself in a needless rage with fate, spiteful as if it was the work of devils, stirred up to fury. I felt strangely delighted for I felt like children, but this time not me but someone else had suffered from lack of treacle.

10 October 1934 Phyllis and Jack have deserted the Barn cottage and have fled for shelter from the winter darkness and storms to fortify themselves in High East Street in Dorchester. Gertrude and I crossed the downs the last morning to see them off. I felt sad but I was conscious that Phyllis's instinctive urge to go was right.

Gertrude put Lulu to bed and it seems harder than ever to have confidences with Alyse at night. I spent an hour or two with Theodore one afternoon. We crossed to the grange dairy for milk. I had again as we waited for the milk to come that annoying impression which I sometimes have when I am with Theodore: the look of the Elms, the dark blackness of the hedge and the very wings of the rooks as they crowded on the dead Ash up that side of High Chaldon looked black. It seemed as if he introduced to me the eternal sadness and sombreness of winter like the ever-hanging knowledge that death will as assuredly throw over us eventually his cloak one day.

27 October 1934 The last week or two have not been exactly happy for me. Fate has cruelly sported with me, even making me have words with Alyse when I expected her sympathy, this in nervous distress; it seems I had not fastened Lulu's hot bottle right and consequently it absolutely soaked the bottom of his bed. It was terrible and all my plans for the evening were frustrated. I could not bear to have harmed Llewelyn.

That very night Jack carried me away with him to Dorchester, where Phyllis did indeed with her sweetness and understanding restore the anguish of my tortured spirit. I felt quietened and calm.

30 October 1934 What harmony and comfort lies in that abode of Phyllis. How contented I watched her every moment and took in each arrangement of her rooms. How the fire shone in the night and the sun shone in the day. How excellent it was to hear Jack read Dostoievsky. I slept the night at the Antelope and met Jack first at the bottom of the London Road while I was wishing to buy Phyllis a rose. Afterward we followed the little stream at the back and Jack showed me the different things which had impressed him such as the Balzac House and the doll's terraced garden. The view from their little backroom is most attractive, of a little thatched cottage in the middle of the meadows backed by high Elms with pure white sheets blowing on the line. I was thrilled by it all and we spent a happy two hours in Weymouth. How strangely at ease I am with Phyllis; in some ways it is more like being with Lucy than with anyone. She says she loves Weymouth. We walked on the hard sands and picked up a few shells. Our cliffs looked most noble. I should have liked to have walked with her on the Nothe but it turned suddenly cold and I preferred her to catch the high bus back. I returned by Osmington Mills.

November 1934   Gertrude has had a cold and Alyse gets weaker every day. Lulu spent a week indoors giving up all writing, all talk, all reading. At first his temperature seemed better but he appeared to me depressed and there seems a different look in his face now he is back in his shelter. Poor Alyse is sicker than ever. I have felt very very worried about her, but her neurotic state makes her very difficult to understand at moments. She refuses to give up but clings to her life here yet the effort of forever attending to Llewelyn becomes more and more difficult. She and I are not made for that kind of life; it kills the spirit and then the body. I should like to drink, drink, drink and she should sleep, sleep, sleep. Gertrude is the most efficient of us all. The week when Gertrude had her cold was a great strain, some day I never felt anything, another day my nerves were a thousand stinging flying ants. However Gertrude persisted I should anyhow go to Lucy's. Lucy and Hounsell and Mary were wonderful. How they put themselves out so that all would be well. The meals were excellent with wine and particularly did I enjoy my Monday dinner though it was hot mutton. Lucy had done it to a turn with hot baked potatoes. Bless her. I was also much touched by Hounsell's concern about Lulu and his advice as to what to give him to eat.

April 1935   I have been twice to Weymouth to see Lulu. The first time I met him coming along the parade with Alyse in brilliant sunshine. He looked so distinguished. I could have cried out with delight. But then I learnt that he had not been too well again, however he was better the last time I appeared. I found him in bed by the bow-window reading Walt Whitman. He spoke so highly of him — Such joy it gave me. We soon ate lunch. I liked to sit so I could watch his profile. Alyse was eager to please but yet evasive. I longed for her yet I felt fearful of her displeasure ... I certainly felt happy to be with them again after having spent the day before with Littleton & Mabel, for I can never feel myself really honest before them & the strain of it wearies me beyond words. It is because I must accept all Littleton's maxims & dare never to disagree when I just long to do so.

The last time I went to Weymouth I returned by Dorchester where I had tea with Jack & Phyllis. A pleasant tea with eggs and bread and butter and her copper kettle hot beside her. How clever she is at making things look nice.

12 August 1935   It is long since I have written in this book. Much has passed. Visitors come and go, Marian & Peter among them. Marian is a marvellous personality. She has been in a happy mood. I read her my poems one morning, the first listener I have had except Phyllis for a very very long time. May has a marvellous force of character. Her courage & her bravery amaze me. Nothing apparently can sink her either the attack of burglars or the loss of her money. She is undefeatable. She is like some great tidal wave which bares all before her — her own fate in particular. I can talk with her, only she is more keen to assert her own opinion than to listen to yours.

29 November 1936   We have gone through the agitating but important event of Lulu going to Switzerland. We trembled for days for what the weather might be on the morning of his chosen departure, but fortunately it was good. Mr. Webb could come right up with the car and all the terrible ideas of wheeling Lulu down in his push chair passed to nothing. As it was all went well. Gertrude walking ahead as she was going as far as London with them and I and Lily walked behind Lulu as Alyse took him in the push chair through the Old Warren. It was a dramatic moment. Poor Lily breaking down into sobs as she saw them get in and I feeling not much unlike her. I did not in the intensity of my feeling give Alyse the goodbye she deserved, yet how often shall I sadly miss my secret waves to her and the many secret sights of her as she hurried to and fro to Lulu or searched some vegetable she wanted. How I shall miss above all seeing her lovely figure making for the top to get one eager moment of suspense from her anxieties. On Wednesday at dinner time we had this cable to say he had reached Lausanne 'well and happy'.

I managed to catch Theodore over at Rat's Barn on Friday. It was one of those rare days of sun and no wind, which we obtain occasionally in the winter. I chanced to see him disappearing toward the gate when I looked through my window at Chydyok. I flew across and in my keenness to search for him in the pit I never noticed he was walking with Susie up along the railings in the same field toward the sea. I experienced one of those happy times which are always so precious. We sat in Rat's Barn by a small fire I lighted, Theodore producing from his pocket a medicine bottle of cold water which he and Susie drank and from which even I took a sip. Theodore talked to me more as if he was thinking aloud to himself — some of those revelations which he discovers that exist behind man's behaviour. He declared that it is through ambition and through the desires for gain and reputation that people lose each other's friendship and love, that it is better not to strive to accumulate fortunes but to be friendly and sure of your affection. Also that melancholy was the most fitting attitude in life to pertain for then you knew where you were with your feet planted on the ground and not in the unsatisfactory air of exalted happiness. I could see what he meant, but it seems hard to acquire always the love of dull days and murky skies. Susie climbed the armchair but I liked her best when I saw her sitting solemnly upon the little stool staring in the fire. I was late for dinner but I made up for it by helping to wash up afterwards. Today I met them in the valley again with Gertrude as I was making home but it was a short moment together as he was anxious not to keep Violet waiting. But he said how a family should always live in different houses — so just to see each other at times but not to live in too close contact with each other —— I agree.

A studio photograph of Will and Llewelyn Powys, 1927

A SELECTION FROM THE DIARIES

7 February 1937   Gertrude on the 27th of January went up to London, driven by Mr. Webb with the car full of her pictures which she is going to show at the Cooling Gallery. I walked down to the village with her and so did Mrs. Lucas who had come to assist carrying things down.

12 March 1937   Back I am from my happy jaunt to France. On my way there I stayed in London just in time to see Gertrude's pictures hung in the Cooling Gallery for their last day. It was great to see them arranged so splendidly in that Gallery. I felt much pride in beholding them. Those many pictures which I was so familiar with hung so finely. It gave me indeed great satisfaction and pleasure. 'Chydyok' is gone to Willie; Herbert and Isobel bought that lovely one of Mr. Diffey's chrysanthemums — a really beautiful thing. It is a picture I will never forget. How beautifully Gertrude has done the reflection on the table on which it stood. All liked her work who ever saw it. The first day when the private show was on must have been very like one of Jack's own scenes in his stories. I did hope he would have written a description of it to me but perhaps, at least I hope, he sent one to Lulu.

Mary fetched me away after tea and I had a happy evening telling Lucy all my adventures. She really does seem interested always in what you do and see. We had a very pleasant walk together on the hills. We even found a cowslip out which we picked. It was on the 5th March. We never repented picking it as it snowed like the devil afterward. When we found it, it looked almost frost bitten, so I hoped the warmth of Lucy's room would revive it. I had a very happy hour as well on Sunday with Lucy in my big room by the fire she had lit there, while Hounsell was talking to someone downstairs. I read her all the way through one of Hazlitt's essays. She enjoyed it I think. Mary and I too enjoyed our walks together. I felt very grateful to her for taking me all the way to Southampton by car so as to catch the afternoon train home. Oh the pleasure I get coming back again to Chaldon and these hills. I feel like a child in my excitement and pleasure — to tread Tumble Down again and mount the Mound and pass into the Warren. Yet after my talk with Gertrude and tea in spite of it there arose an ominous sensation when she told me what her reactions to the place were so much so that I got a feeling that it was almost a death which was separating us — finality.

Gertrude finding her talents hampered here instead of as we all supposed that she really was contented with her sofa and her present endeavours. In a strange way it shook my own outlook. Though I rejoiced at being home, her words dug deep into the future, forwarning. Though often I am perturbed at her more careful way of running the house, yet to feel she wants to forsake her days here seemed to me as dreadful as a familiar tree being transplanted. Yet I feel myself that when I get too old to walk far on these cliffs I shall no longer want to stay. Yet the announcements of her sensations alarm and terrify me. Yet why? I like to be alone. Is it because as one grows older a change of living is always ominous. Let it be. I wonder perhaps as my writing seems to remain so far in the offing and is becoming more difficult to do, that I have not the ambition I should, that the imperative which once I had to do it left me and so to hear Gertrude that night — with that urge of painting crying out, double dumbfounded me ... I know not. I glory in her wants and wishes.

August 1937 Jack and Phyllis have been here staying in the village while Bernie was with us. It was wonderful to see them again. But oh how I longed for a closer communion with Phyllis. How again and again I longed to seize her from Gertrude's side and carry her alone to my room. But no — she seems ever content to remain by the shore of Gertrude's lake-like disposition. I am too wild, too passionate for her reed-like sensibility. Yet who understands me more than she can?

5 August 1937 Littleton and Mabel's sudden visit for the day passed better than usual. It was not till we were walking on my way to Lulworth that he roused my spirit into revolt by telling me how you should attend to things 'spiritual'. How his remarks changed the whole appearance of my beloved world. Damn 'Spiritualism' as he would have me know it. Theodore knows, he doesn't. He reduces all to morals. Why didn't he talk straight of Christianity or of being a christian — instead of making me wish to destroy the very poetry of my being. How I wish I could hear what Theodore would say about it. It makes me crave to see him.

23 August 1937 When I did see at last Theodore and had told him what Littleton had said, he at once said how I should have answered him: 'That it was Lulu who had taught me to be an atheist, to drink and to be lecherous —' What would Littleton have said if I had? I knew his remarks would entertain Theodore so indeed they did. Alas to say I haven't seen him since, but there is something about my friendship with Theodore that whether I do or don't our understanding is the same. He receives me the same and asks no questions. He knows me without being told.

Summer 1938 Jack and Phyllis's visit with Bernie here as well part of the time passed successfully in a great measure. We had a very interesting discussion one evening, which was mainly between J.C.P. and Vanda over Communism and Anarchism. J. defending Anarchists and Vanda Communists. Jack made a great oration about free speech, but to my mind he got too excited, waving his arms and almost shouting. I could not help thinking of what Tom Woolley always said: that argument has no weight when you get too emotional. The next morning at breakfast John Cowper began the subject again. He said how the man in the street would rather be free with a mere crust of bread than be dictated to. The minority might but I don't believe the mass of men would particularly when they had children to feed. I spoke then hotter than I have spoken for a long time. Gertrude thought I was loosing control but I was not for I remembered Tom Woolley and I knew it was Jack I was speaking to and not Littleton.

When I got back [from a visit to Lucy] May was here with Peter. Marian was wonderful; she could put her energy to everything and anything. She was very forbearing and looked magnificent in her cape and evening-clothes. She could not get on very well with the way we cooked but was anxious to help whenever she could. But I often wished she would not utter certain remarks. They very well could be true, but under the circumstances one would not want to admit them and it made me feel uncomfortable. I found it hard to accept her as an intimate sister but I found over certain matters I could discourse more freely with her than I can with many.

How through all this summer I wish I had had more of Gertrude's nature ingrafted in me. How she instils me with admiration. Rarely, if ever, showing the least sign of impatience. Ready for anyone and anything to happen. Cooking meal after meal when she ought to be painting. Keeping her control when I would want to run away. Seeing good in all, reserving her criticism, only revealing it when truth desires it. Her love for flowers and their scents so that you can see her carrying a favourite vase with a picked choice of scented blooms to bed with her, then bringing them down in the morning with her candle and her empty glass which had held her orange juice. Her room that has the charm of a lovely drawing-room yet possessing the relaxation of a studio. Not worried when visitors surround her and fill her room from morning to night. Giving her love to all making all appreciate her, even the cats. Seldom complaining, ready to deal with the difficulties of a house with a sureness of knowledge. Apparently never happier than when gardening among her flower-borders or when she observes some bird. Reserving her mind and will whenever she can in lying reading on her sofa or when the sun is warm enough outside on a deck-chair with her cushions and wrap, either under the gorse-bushes, over the top, or below the shelter of her fruit cage — ready to carry her chairs and coffee anywhere as long as she can rest and read. Yet in an instant ready to take up some sewing or knitting when someone arrives. Enjoying to be read to by Littleton or Bernie, yet going to any length to go with them anywhere or like the day when we heard how Mabel was faced with her terrible ordeal, leaving all her Monday's work of making bread and cooking a duck, to go and see her. Appreciating May to the full, realizing her wonderful 'aplomb' and declaring 'she was like a rose in full bloom' — only criticizing the way she wiped plates. Giving way to everyone's whims and fancies: always having ready at hand things to please children, treating them as living units and not as cumbrances or as an amusement, just to watch. Making Nellie feel important as she helped her make a cake or Stephen satisfied when she found him nails and a hammer. How can I praise her enough — from Jack to Willie we would all say the same. To me she represents the calmness and beauty of a lake, where stillness and unknown depth enrich the shades of all who come near. She takes sorrow and joy with the wonderful grace of a balanced and full nature. She is partial to none, yet through my inconstancy I can be teased and tormented by certain of her ways, such as when she covers the back kitchen-table with dirty ware or when the chest of drawers in the kitchen becomes covered with things. Often I wish she kept a diary which told of her feeling and reactions but instead it is a diary of when visitors come and go. I love it when I look out of my window and see her form in the garden and when she is helping Willie to paint. After she had set him going, there was no abating Willie. I believe his happiest moment in England was when he was painting portraits in Gertrude's studio. And like a child, when Gertrude told him anything, he would only answer 'Why?' It was wonderful how well he did them, considering how he had never touched oils before. He was very strict with those who sat for him.

16 November 1940 How constantly grateful that she [Alyse] preferred to remain next door to us instead of seeking more intercourse with other friends. Yet in spite of the frequent reminders of her past here with Lulu she prefers to stay, to write in solitude in the little upper room. I love nothing so much as to go up through the trap-door and have a talk with her about whatever is rising from her most fertile brain. I only wish I could satisfy her wants with greater sufficiency, but alas I often feel I am unable to stimulate or soothe the restless movements of her thoughts when agitated or down-pressed. But my mind is alert when she reads and speaks of any philosophical ideas pertaining to our present daily lives or to the great truths and doubts which uphold the world. How often I leave her, restored in mind and spirit. Oh! her companionship is great to me. It increases in strength and depth, in a manner which I have never obtained with anyone. Yet I often feel I don't half see her enough and I often lament to think how really lonely she is. Living there, eating alone, reading and writing alone. Hour after hour alone, except those quick moments when she comes in to watch for Mrs. Lucas or to listen to the wireless. It makes me value all the more the half-hour or more when she comes to my room to read aloud the great classics such as *Don Quixote* or Rabelais. Then how it makes me weep in anguish for her life now is like being in a pit, for each sign of spring or line of poetry makes her all the more realize the lack and loss of Lulu. How can we make the sunshine warm again for her? It seems that in no way I can do it. Then it makes me feel such a hypocrite in my love for Lulu for I can enjoy the snowdrops, the clouds and the first spring sunshine without his fellowship. But there!

I have never had the hourly and daily companionship of Llewelyn. Gertrude always says there was no companion like unto him. And she missed it badly when he and Alyse first appeared together for after having experienced it at Montacute (when I was at Witcombe with Willie) and at Weymouth, though there Lulu went through his worst time of frustration and depression before he finally crossed the Atlantic and met Alyse.

April 1941 Do what I will I seem never able to get my diary up to date. Though I am writing this in April 1941 I have still to recount the most important event of last year and that was how finally and at last Theodore has left Chaldon. It was undoubtedly through the scare and distress of the Bombing Germans. It happened all very suddenly — through Violet seeing an advertisement of a furnished school which had been converted into a bungalow by Mrs. Jackson of Mappowder. She at once called Gertrude up and asked her to go with her in Mrs. Webb's car to view it. Gertrude left all and went. They liked it, took it and Violet decided to carry Theodore and Susie there the very next day. I would have known nothing about it, as I was at Rat's Barn, if Gertrude most kind had not turned her steps that way to tell me that they were leaving at 11 o'clock. So the next morning I hurried down for I had to see Theodore, whatever happened. I wished I could get there before any sign of a car was there, but of course it was not so. Alyse was already there and Mrs. Webb and Violet were bringing everything they could lay hands on into the car. It gave me a horrid sensation of a funeral, so that I nearly burst out weeping when I went into Theodore's room and found him sunk in his chair, not dead and stretched out, but still alive, though dazed and confused. I knew exactly his feelings at that moment. The misery of being so suddenly transplanted from our Chaldon Hills and great grass spaces, with the great untrammelled breath of sky over all. I knew what it must mean to him to relinquish it all. Relinquish covetousness, relinquish Chaldon after so many many years of familiar devotion. I knew the anguish of his soul. He spoke, but said little. Then I hoped to have got to the Foot Bridge beyond Mrs. Legg's before they passed in the car but I met Mrs. House and as I had to say something to her about some plants the car passed. Oh it was not what I wanted to see, that vehicle taking

Theodore away though alive for ever from Chaldon. Luckily I did not see Theodore clearly as my back was turned, but I had a sort of vision of Susie and other shapes. After which I fled to the Inn for I felt I had to swallow drink so that I better could smother my remorse. Tom Lucas was there and Florrie. I declared the End of the World was come now that Theodore had departed from East Chaldon after his many many years of living here — over thirty years since George and Jack Jacob fetched him and his furniture with his books from Studland — to settle in the Cottage near the Green where Dicky was born. And never shall I forget that I and Lucy should be the ones who should first hear him read out the advertisement of the Double-fronted House in the *Western Gazette* that brought him here. I remember it well. It happened in Montacute dining-room, he was seated in Mother's armchair which is the one I use now always up in my Room at Chydyok. There with us before him, he read it out and made up his mind that very moment to go and see what it was like, and when he returned from his day's adventure, he told us he had not taken the Double Fronted One but had found a smaller cottage which stood with two others and each had thatch. Also that there was a green and that all water had to be dipped from a well. What more he said about it I don't remember. Only I know what he had said greatly excited my imagination. So fresh, so different from what I was used to, living the life of a well-regulated Victorian Vicarage with servants indoors and a gardener outside. Yet now the cruel day should come when I myself should witness Theodore's departure from this Place of his chosen home. Oh! it has left a deep deep rift in my heart. Oh cruel to think of those happy moments when together Theodore and I would sit a few minutes near a gorse bush or by the Old Hedge in those wonderful secretive small copses which as no one he knew to find, to hide.

ROBIN WOOD

Owen Glendower: Powys's Faustian Prince

On the surface John Cowper Powys's first historical novel *Owen Glendower* seems remote from the horror and agony of the war years, when it appeared in print, January 1941 (USA), and February 1942 (UK).[1] As early as August 1933, while living in up-state New York, Powys had contemplated composing in Wales, 'a real Masterpiece with the traditions of Wales behind it',[2] so that it is not surprising, that a few years after moving in 1935 to Corwen, North Wales, 'in Glyndŵr's patrimony', where he found 'that particular psychic "aura" towards which ... [he had] been groping [his] way for several years',[3] he should write about Wales's great, patriotic Prince, and his failed struggle, in the early fifteenth century, against the English for Welsh independence. All this might suggest that the main imaginative sources that shaped *Owen Glendower* were, first, Powys's enthusiasm for things Welsh, which he ultimately inherited from his father, and which led him to settling permanently in Wales, on return from the United States, and, second, a desire to emulate in Wales one of his favourite novelists, Sir Walter Scott. There were, however, other significant imaginative forces at work.

Powys was also interested in exploring the parallels between the past, the late-medieval world, and the present, and in the 'Argument' Powys suggests a parallel between Glendower's time and his own: 'the period that formed the immediate background to the dramatic events related in this tale — 1400 to 1416 — saw the beginning of one of the most momentous and startling epochs of *transition* that the world has known'.[4] He also refers to it as an age of 'social upheavals', and one in which 'the whole organism of medieval Christendom was breaking up' (xii, xvi). (In *Porius* — set in the Dark Ages (AD 499) — Powys is similarly interested in a transitional age that is comparable to the twentieth century).[5]

While the recorded history of Owen Glendower's time is obviously a major influence on the novel's structure, another important element is the Welsh medieval romance, *The Mabinogion* (c. 11th–13th centuries), in which Powys suggests is recorded, in the form of myth, the history of an even remoter Welsh past.[6] *Owen Glendower* is full of allusions to this work, and when Glendower makes his first appearance in the novel, Rhisiart is reminded of the Welsh mythological hero Pryderi (146). Although Glendower is also associated with the deities Brân and Manywydan, the dominant mythological identification is with Pryderi, and the other southern gods defeated by the Celts, 'the cruel "magicians" of the Age of Bronze' (563). Powys's use of an obscure mythology may present some problems to readers, but no more than in reading a major Russian novel, with its gallery of strange sounding names, or the works of the major modernists. *The Mabinogion* is clearly as important, imaginatively, for Powys, as is his settling in Wales.[7] Powys in the pursuit of what he conceived to be his — and in his view most of the inhabitants of Britain's — ancestral roots, was seeking an alternative mythology to the dominant ones of twentieth-century Western civilisation, capitalism, Christianity, science, and the totalitarian systems of communism and fascism. A central part of Powys's Welsh mythology is the idea, that not only the Welsh, but Britons as a whole, are descended from the Welsh aboriginals, the Neolithic Iberian inhabitants of Britain, and that this is the main racial and cultural ingredient of the British, rather than that supplied by the Celts or Anglo-Saxons. Powys sees the mythology of *The Mabinogion* as a record of the conquest of the essentially pacific Neolithic Welsh aboriginals by the Celts.[8] Associated with this is the idea of a civilisation that preceded the arrival of the Celts, 'some great, long-lost, peaceful civilization that had been destroyed by force and enchantment' (563).

However, *Owen Glendower* is as much a psychological as a historical novel. Powys's concern with the psychology of violence, and the relationship between cruelty, sadism and sexuality, arises from lifelong preoccupations of the author; sadism was always a temptation, at least to his imagination:

Without any question, from earliest childhood up to the

present hour, my dominant vice has been the most dangerous of all vices. I refer to Sadism.⁹

The central psychological concerns of *Owen Glendower* have direct relevance to the years 1937-42 — during which it was written and published — and beyond, and it is interesting to compare the novel with Powys's book of popular philosophy, one of his lay sermons, *Mortal Strife* (1942), which was written to boost war-time morale. Both works are concerned not only with war, but significantly also with magician figures, for Powys describes Hitler in *Mortal Strife* as a black magician,¹⁰ and while Glendower is no fifteenth-century Hitler, he is a Faustian figure, with a strong sadistic streak in his nature, who falls under the influence of black magic. (In *Mortal Strife* Powys links the black magic of Hitler with materialistic science (90-1, 188-9)). Powys's particular achievement in *Owen Glendower* is, amongst many other things, his imaginative presentation of psychological insights into war, violence, sexuality, and the nature of the human imagination.

If the main events of the novel closely follow recorded history, Powys's Glendower is very much the creation of his imagination. Indeed he cannot but be, for Powys is concerned with Glendower's inner thoughts, feelings, and motivations, about which he could only guess. Powys identifies with this magician-figure, both embodying autobiographical elements in Glendower, and presenting aspects of his philosophy through him. Glendower is shown, not as the heroic leader of an oppressed people — the traditional historical view — but rather as a man who eventually turns from the battlefield, to free himself from the cruel, war-like, Celtic side of his nature, and so discover his true Self: that is, his pacific aboriginal Welsh Self.¹¹ (In *Obstinate Cymric*, however, Powys describes Glendower as the 'Normanized Celt' (12).)

That Powys should have taken up the Shakespearean tradition, that Glendower was a magician, is hardly contrary to expectation, because a dominant desire of Powys himself, from early childhood, was to be a magician: 'a magician not yet seven is able to call up but few protecting spirits from "the vasty deep".'¹² Another idea Powys found in Shakespeare is that Glendower was in league with the Devil. Speaking to

Hotspur, in *Henry IV*, Part One, Glendower says, 'I can teach you, cousin, to command the devil' (III.i.56–7). The Devil tempts both Glendower and Powys, in the form of sadism. Not surprisingly the central theme of the novel is Glendower's struggle with himself, rather than with the English.

When Glendower first appears he is a Faustian figure, with his 'enormous crystal globe ... [and] great square board ... upon which ... were inscribed a series of astrological symbols' which suggests 'the abode ... of some Nostradamus or Albertus Magnus engaged in the arts of black magic' (179).

Prior to beginning his campaign against the English, however, Glendower smashes his globe. This marks a major turning-point in his life, because with the destruction of the globe, Glendower rejects one system of values — modern, Faustian, scientific philosophy, with its emphasis on the power of reason, and the factual accumulation of knowledge — for the lost wisdom of the aboriginal Welsh, a choice of the white magic of St Brân the Blessed — who according to legend first brought Christianity to Britain — as opposed to the black magic of St Derfel.[13] Glendower is led to his decision to smash the globe, by his recognition of the one thing which makes him ashamed; this is his desire to do things

'... not as the elements do things, not as the Spirit of the elements does things, but as priests and druids and magicians and fortune tellers go to work, *by meddling with the future!*' (393)[14]

Before destroying the globe Glendower makes the following voiceless prayer:

'Oh Unknown Spirit of the Universe, build up before me ... like the rampart of an unassailable fortress, the unbroken, the undisturbed, the absolute darkness of your impenetrable purpose!' (393)

Glendower has decided to accept Nature's way, the way 'the Spirit of the elements does things'. With this decision to accept destiny Glendower begins to turn from his previous Faustian, ego-dominated attitude to life, gives himself up to 'the Spirit of the Universe', and "follow[s] his demon" in the old irrational sense of trusting the impulses and urges that came from the depth of his being rather than any rational motive' (810–11).

The way that Glendower gives himself up to powers outside his conscious self — "'I'm a medium of the gods for something'" — closely resembles mystical experiences in many religions. In particular Glendower's psychological device of exteriorising his soul, which becomes more important for him after he has broken the globe, is, according to Mircea Eliade, a crucial aspect of shamanism: 'the idea that the magician can leave his body at will ... [is] a strictly shamanic notion'.[15] Another motif of shamanism — and of many forms of mysticism — found in *Owen Glendower*, is the crossing of a very narrow and dangerous bridge: "'My life", [Owen] thought, "is like crossing the *Eel Bridge* — every step's between fatal alternatives!"' (718). It is the bridge, 'only a foot wide', that Gwalchmei in the *Seint Greal* has to cross in his Grail quest.[16] The following comment of Eliade throws additional light on the way Glendower has chosen:

> The bridge [narrow as a hair] symbolizes passage to the beyond, but not necessarily to the underworld; only the guilty cannot cross it and are precipitated into the abyss. Crossing an extremely narrow bridge that connects two cosmic regions also signifies passing from one mode of being to another — from uninitiate to initiate, or from 'living' to 'dead'. (203–4; see also 482)

Glendower may have smashed his Faustian globe, but he has not given up magic.

Despite these parallels, Glendower cannot strictly be called a shaman, for shamanism is a phenomenon existing within a cultural framework, with an accompanying ritual. Glendower's gifts are an isolated phenomenon, within his medieval context, unrelated, for example, to Christian mysticism. In a society where shamanism was a cultural phenomenon, Glendower's trances would have been recognised as a sign of election, and would thus have been 'followed by theoretical and practical instruction at the hands of the old masters'.[17] Both John Cowper Powys and his character Glendower, in their search for such masters, turned to the ancient Welsh writers, to the Welsh aboriginal wisdom of magicians and shamans like Merlin and Taliessin.[18]

When Glendower first appears in the novel, he is a novice in the shamanistic arts, and unaware where his soul goes, when it leaves his body:

> He would have been puzzled to explain in intelligible words ... what happened to his conscious soul when these fits took him. He knew one thing about them, however. They always left him with a feeling of power and confidence and serenity. (410)

Glendower's choice of the word 'fit' suggests that the experience is initially unconscious, resembling epilepsy. By the end of the novel, however, he is like a true shaman, and both more aware, and more in control of the process: 'our souls from the beginning ... have been able to escape into Annwn, into ... into the world *outside the world*' (916–17). As Eliade comments, in the course of his trance, '[the shaman's] soul is believed to leave his body and ascend to the sky or descend to the underworld' (5) — Annwn is the Welsh Otherworld. The idea of exteriorising the soul is an important constituent of Powys's own technique, for 'playing the part of a Magician', and gaining the greatest possible happiness in life.[19]

Appropriately, directly after destroying his globe, and thus choosing a new direction for his life, Glendower visits Mathrafal. Glendower associates Mathrafal with the 'first people', that is, the Welsh aboriginals, who 'must have known secrets beyond the understanding of our fathers' (413). In medieval times Meifod, a village near Welshpool, in Montgomeryshire — now part of the new county of Powys — had been the centre of political power in the Principality of Powys, and the Princes of Powys, from whom John Cowper believed himself descended, ruled from their castle at nearby Mathrafal. His journey into the forest is like a pilgrimage, and though it is a chance suggestion that brings Glendower to Mathrafal, he is profoundly moved, and identifies with these Welsh aboriginal ruins:

[A]s long as *this name* [Mathrafal] lasts on the lips of the people of this land there will be one beat, one pulse, one motion left in our blood that neither the good nor the bad nor the worst nor the best of our crafty conquerors can ever blot out or destroy! (414)

Shortly after this Glendower suffers one of his fits. Fortunately, 'Owen's soul returned to him almost at once' (415), and largely addressing the air, rather than his two companions, he makes his enigmatic statement,'"*The Past is the Eternal*!"' The crystal globe was of course associated with 'meddling with the future'. In connection with the visit to Mathrafal it is worth recalling, that the establishment of a relation to the ancestors is important in many initiation rites. (Powys himself was deeply moved when he made his own pilgrimage to Mathrafal in 1937.[20])

Somewhat surprisingly directly following Glendower's own identification with the Welsh aboriginals at Mathrafal, Morg Ferch Lug identifies him with the Celts, and puts a curse upon him:

'As long as you *destroy* you'll succeed; but try building up again, Owen ap Griffith, try building up these homes and these lives you've laid waste, and you'll see what you've done! For this land, Owen the Accurst, Owen, the pure-blooded Brython, belongs *not* to you, to your evil strength and your weapons of steel, belongs *not* to your talk of good and evil. It belongs to us, to us who have been here from the beginning, to us the *old people*!' (433)

Although Morg is, perhaps, wrong in describing Glendower as a pure-blooded Brython, or Celt, she is right to curse him in the name of the old people, for as yet, in his outward actions, he has not turned from the path of war and destruction. The elemental nature of Morg's curse is noteworthy, in view of Glendower's decision to do things, the way 'the Spirit of the elements does things' (393). Morg says, '"I lay upon you the oldest curse in the world, the curse that is stronger than iron or brass; the curse of the water and the wind!"' (433)

Glendower may be moving in a direction which will finally lead him to the pacific wisdom of the aboriginal Welsh, 'the old people', at this stage of the novel; however, he still finds sadistic satisfaction in the waging of war. Glendower's sadism is most obviously revealed in the way in which he thrusts the half-alive Hywel Sele into the hollow oak. He had begun his revenge on his treacherous cousin by breaking his back against a fallen tree, but this was not enough. Then, on seeing the hollow oak tree Glendower feels that he can still satisfy this sadistic urge for revenge on the dying Hywel Sele:

> It was then, *as he realized what he was going to do*, that he began to tremble with an unholy excitement. His desire that the man should *know* before death snatched him away that he was mastered, his desire that there should be an exchange of realization, 'You have lost' and 'I have won,' was now replaced by a totally different feeling, a darker, more inhuman, and much more agitating feeling. (439)

The 'unholy strength' Glendower possesses at this point is that of a black magician.

Sadism in *Owen Glendower* does not only involve its two main protagonists, Glendower and Rhisiart (the affinity between them has its roots in their shared 'viciousness'), but also Lowri, Sibli, the vivisectionist Gilles de Pirogue, and others. In Glendower's case it is an important factor in his revolt against the English, although certainly not the only one.

Another important factor that leads Glendower into his rebellion against the English is his genuine desire to make the lives of the Welsh better, because Glendower like his author, desires 'to play the part of a Helper'.[21]

Thus in arranging the marriage between his daughter Catharine and Mortimer, a possible claimant to the English throne, Glendower can rightly assert, that he is only accepting what destiny offers him for the good of Wales, and that the sacrifice of Catharine's own personal feelings in this matter, is to be justified in the name of a greater good for Wales. Yet here again, behind all this points Glendower's sadistic nerve, and the satisfaction that it gains from the wielding of power. This is made clear with the visit of Glendower to Pryderi's Tree, shortly after the marriage of Catharine to Mortimer. Broch comments: "'He's at Pryderi's Tree. He's punishing himself for this marriage'" (608). There is a further explanation for Glendower's masochistic self-wounding at the tree, in that his 'conscience ... had protested in the matter of Catharine's marriage' (647).

Accordingly there was not a complete eradication of the sadistic element in Glendower's nature with the destruction of the crystal globe, and he is further tempted by the prophecy of Hopkin ap Thomas:

> 'The divine Hopkin' treated the Prince not so much as a ruling potentate as a fellow-magician, and this brought back, in one great overpowering wave of temptation, all that dangerous dabbling with the unknown future, which Owen had shaken off when he destroyed his crystal. (637)

What has a particular effect on Glendower, is Thomas's prophecy 'about the victorious "virgin in armour"' (638). From this evolves Glendower's plan to dress Tegolin in golden armour, and have her lead the Welsh into battle, something that Rhisiart sees as 'damnable and lecherous wickedness' (687), and which leads him to oppose his Prince. Rhisiart provides the reader with the clue that Glendower has again chosen the devil's way, the way of black magic, the way of Derfel Gadarn, who appears to be a Celtic deity about whom we are told little other than

> '... that not only was the deflowering of young virgins a definite part of the worship of this ancient Welsh god, but that certain unscrupulous men made use of this dark tradition to satisfy their unholy desires under the guise of priests — no! I mustn't say priests — under the guise of *disciples*, of this singular Personage and his Horse.' (242)

Unlike Brân the Blessed, Derfel is not a god of peace but war, for what Rhisiart sees of Derfel in his 'curious hallucination' is 'a gigantic figure, in the armour of the ancient days, mounted on a huge warhorse' (257). Also, the fact that Lowri and the Scab are numbered amongst his adherents, makes it safe to assume that this ancient Welsh god is to be associated with lust, violence, cruelty, sadism, rape, and black magic. In Glendower's plans for Tegolin, he is very much a disciple of Derfel Gadarn, unscrupulously attempting to make use of the 'dark tradition' to satisfy his 'unholy desires'.[22]

The conflict within the Welsh ranks, caused by Glendower's scheme, is resolved when he changes his mind, and decides that Tegolin will marry Rhisiart. This might seem a defeat; however, Glendower sees himself not as having been forced into this action by the opposition, but rather as having exercised his free will:

> 'What I'll do,' he thought, 'shall be without cause, without reason, without motive. I'll do it just to prove to myself that I *can* do it. If I let her go they'll think I do it because of them. If I take her they'll think I do it because of my pride. But they'll be wrong. I'll take her because I want her *more than my free will*. But if I don't take her I'll prove to myself that my will can do — in a complete void — what it chooses — without cause or motive or reason!' (703)

A somewhat puzzling episode becomes clearer, if 'will' is taken to mean the fundamental core of Glendower's identity, his Self as opposed to his ego, and the 'void' as complete freedom from such influences as lust, sadism, fear, or pride. The Christian finds freedom, can exercise his free will, in his spiritual union with God; and in terms of Jungian psychology, a man can only be truly free, if he is fully integrated, that is, finds and recognises his true nature and being. Glendower, as has been indicated, is deeply engaged in a spiritual quest, one involving not a Christian union with God, but rather a descent into Annwn. There is also a relationship between the way Glendower has given himself up to powers beyond himself, and the exercising of his free will: for true freedom entails the acceptance of destiny, both in terms of a person's own nature, and his place in the world. In exerting his will and resisting temptation, Glendower gains in inner strength and knowledge. This involves aboriginal Welsh wisdom, as found in the enigmatic writing of bards like Taliessin:

> 'And until these last days you've not even known what the bards *meant* when they talked of unreturned love! By Saint

Francis you know what they meant now, and a good deal *more* than they meant!' (720)

That is, in resisting the sadistically lustful feelings he had at the thought of Tegolin leading the Welsh army against the English; feelings that are similar to those of Rhisiart, when he sees the arrows pointing at Tegolin's bare shoulder at the beginning of the novel. Glendower puts his new found wisdom to further use in resisting the sadistic temptation represented by the imprisoned Gam and, thinking of *The Divine Comedy* and Dante's Beatrice,

> ... he struggled against his impulse to visit Gam [and] tried to imagine himself mounting, as this Tuscan pretender declared he'd done, by the help of his sainted mistress, through heavenly circle after heavenly circle, towards the Empyrean! (722)

Glendower at this point believes not only that he exteriorises his own soul, but that of Tegolin as well, and imagines their souls being drawn 'across the firmament! — until they were — *mirabile dictu! — outside Space altogether.* ... Yes, it was with Tegolin's soul that he was striding now along the spheroid back of the whole cosmic orb, feeling the wind of outer space on his face' (722). (The journey is of Glendower's soul to Annwn, through the power of unrequited love, an important recurring idea in Powys's works.[23])

This growth in self-awareness, an awareness of the wisdom of the 'oldest of all the races', leads Glendower's decision, during his campaign against the English, not to storm Worcester, and so effectively end the rebellion:

> His chance had been given him; and something in his own nature had balked. ... the impression came over him ... that he and his people *could afford to wait*, could afford to wait till long after his bones were dust and Henry's bones were dust. He knew how his own soul could escape, escape without looting cities and ravishing women. (821)

Glendower has not, however, made a sudden change of heart, because for a long while he has had nagging self-doubts. When at Meifod, near Mathrafal, he had thought: '"It's no good going back on this business

... even in my thoughts. There *was* a time for that — but that time is over."' Then his thoughts had dwelt on 'the first people', who had '"no princes, no rulers then, but only men of the land, living at peace together and worshipping peaceful gods without sacrifices and without blood"' (419).

Furthermore, when Glendower was at Harlech, his conscience had been troubled by the results of his rebellion:

> But he had a strange feeling ... that all these blackened towns and ruined villages were the result of an enchantment, like that flung by the magicians upon the persecuted Pryderi; and that if only the clue-word, the exorcising word, could be uttered on such a night as this, all the waste-lands of ashes and blood would grow fresh and green again! (644)

The enchantment in Glendower's case is the illusion that his destiny involves this violent rebellion against England. Powys seems to be alluding to the mythology of the Waste Land here, Glendower's (the Fisher King's) sickness being a mental sickness, his sadism. The idea of a relationship between sexual impotence and the Waste Land is also implicit in Powys's Fisher King, because Glendower's sexuality is linked with his sadistic vice; and the satisfying of this through the exercise of sadistic power has produced the 'blackened towns and ruined villages'. The restoration of fertility is here equated with Glendower's conquest of this evil impulse. In psychological terms we can say that the enchantment or illusion — which is of course very real in view of the action it precipitates — is the result of one element in Glendower's nature, his sadism, dominating his vision and thus obscuring his real destiny which implies his whole being. This self-conquest, leading to *Self*-discovery, involves his strange fits, or shamanistic trances. On the march to Worcester Glendower has another of these fits, just before he rides down to stop his French allies pillaging the English villages. By escaping into Annwn — which is what happens when Glendower loses consciousness — he finds the inner strength to resist his sadistic nerve, and so follow his conscience and rescue the village.

Now come the final stages of Glendower's life, his retreat into the

Welsh hills after the defeat at Worcester, and his mysterious disappearance and death. Glendower's spiritual growth and the discovery of his true *Self*, entails the acceptance of Death — initially the death of his ego, with the relinquishing of his political and military ambitions when he retires to the cave, but eventually his actual physical death. Powys's presentation of Death as a positive spiritual force is in keeping with the idea found in 'the primitive mysteries of initiation' of 'the symbolism of death as the ground of all spiritual birth — that is, of regeneration'.[24] In his acceptance of death, Glendower, the 'life worshipper', accepts the way of that 'death-worshipper', his friend Broch. Glendower's death, however, is not associated with final annihilation, but rather with the symbolism and mythology of rebirth. The idea of rebirth is found in the legends associated with the historical Glendower, and is most explicitly brought out in the novel with the reference to Glendower's final, Merlin-like, disappearance and promise of a future return. Just as on the symbolic level Glendower moves inward, into the secret cave, and into Annwn, so on the psychological plane he talks of the power he has found 'by sinking inwards':

> If, by sinking into Glyndyfrdwy and Dyfryn Clwyd and into all the land of Edeyrnion, I increase rather than lessen my power, why shouldn't the whole race of Welshmen increase its power by sinking inwards, rather than by winning external victories? (914)

Despite the background of the approaching war, the ending of *Owen Glendower* does not advocate pacificism, as Rhisiart's opposition to Glendower's 'damnable and lecherous wickedness' indicates (687), for Powys did not doubt the need to oppose dictators such as Hitler: 'Hitler has roused in us the same feeling that Philip of Spain roused in his day and Napoleon in his ... not to stop till we're dead, or our enemy is done for.'[25]

Powys is imaginatively working with three distinct historical periods in *Owen Glendower*: first, the age in which the novel is written, Hitler's time; secondly, the fifteenth century, the time of Owen Glendower's rebellion, and, thirdly, an earlier, unspecified time that is recorded not in history but in the mythology of *The*

Mabinogion, the time when, as Powys suggests, the pacific, Welsh, progenitors of the twentieth-century British were defeated by Celtic invaders. Powys's rejection of the more traditional historical view of Glendower has troubled some readers,[26] and the kind of self-identification between Powys and Glendower, that has been considered here, may also make a reader pause. Powys is not, however, indulging himself in the writing of this historical romance;[27] the traditional historical view of Glendower is just as subjective a myth as is his. Powys is rejecting a romantic and nationalistic interpretation of history, for one based on a plausible psychological re-interpretation. Powys is, of course, equally ideological and subjective in his imaginative recreation of history, as are more traditional approaches. Likewise a historical novel more openly acknowledges its *fictional or mythic* dimension than does the traditional approach of historians. A novel, however, must by definition be more than biography or ideology; it must have an imaginative life of its own and characters that hold our attention and about whom we care. A purely ideological novel would be tedious, though ideology obviously influences everything.

Powys's achievement in *Owen Glendower* is not in the arena of self-revelation, or history, but rather in the imaginative use of history in fiction, the imaginative creation of a world into which a reader is drawn; along with this go the psychological insights that he brings to bear on recurrent human issues such as violence and sexuality. The novel is also concerned with the limitations of the dominant twentieth-century ideologies of science and rationalism.

Powys does not deal directly with the contemporary urban world, which he knew well from his extensive lecture-tours in America, as well as his earlier lecture-tours in Britain; and his use of myth and history, and the romance form of the novel provide a powerful imaginative means of escaping the present at one level. However, as he is both a 'romantic ... and ... realistic-minded novelist',[28] his novel grapples realistically with the subject of evil. Above all Powys confronts 'the need to acknowledge the seeds of violence ... in every man',[29] the need of every human being to recognise his true Self with its capacity for both good and evil, instead of repressing the latter or projecting it onto *the other*, the scapegoat, the enemy. Thus *Owen*

Glendower is both a historical and a contemporary novel, a novel about late-medieval Wales and the years that led up to the Second World War.

NOTES

1 The texts erroneously show dates of publication as 1940, and 1941 respectively.
2 J. C. Powys, *Letters to his Brother Llewelyn*, 2 Volumes. M. Elwin, ed. (London: Village Press, 1975), Vol. II, 166.
3 J. C. Powys, *Obstinate Cymric* (Carmarthen: Druid Press, 1947), 46, 56.
4 J. C. Powys, *Owen Glendower* (New York: Simon & Schuster, 1940), x. The 'Argument' prefaces the American edition of *Owen Glendower*, whereas the first English edition placed it at the back of the text. It is also interesting to read in *Obstinate Cymric* Powys's comment that 'the thing that most stirred my own imagination about the land of my fathers [Wales] ... [was] the obliteration of the last four centuries! ... The way in which, in innumerable casual remarks from country people, I am confronted with the Middle Ages is not less than astounding' (45-6).
5 J. C. Powys, *Porius* (London: Macdonald, 1951), xi.
6 In *Porius* the Henog, a 'chronicler' (xviii), is presented as the author of 'The Four Branches of the Mabinogi'. See also J. C. Powys, 'The Characters in the Book', in *The Powys Newsletter* 4, (1974-75), 18.
7 For Powys *The Mabinogion* was a product of Welsh culture — not Irish, as many scholars have suggested. He saw it as a major source in the shaping of British culture through the Arthurian and Romantic Love traditions.
8 See R. Wood, 'John Cowper Powys: Gods and Manias', *The Powys Review* 22 (1988), 3-13.
9 J. C. Powys, *Autobiography* [1934] (London: Macdonald, 1967), 8.
10 J. C. Powys, *Mortal Strife* [1942] (London: Village Press, 1974), 90.
11 'In modern psychology the notion of the self has replaced the earlier concept of the soul. ... According to Carl Jung the self is a totality consisting of conscious and unconscious contents.' *The New Encyclopaedia Britannica*, 15th edition. I have capitalised to emphasise the special use.
12 Powys, *Autobiography*, 39. In Part One of *Henry IV*, III.i.53, Shakespeare's Glendower says: 'I can call spirits from the vasty deep.' In *Autobiography* Powys also says of Theodore Dreiser and himself: 'The Truth is [we] ... are both Magicians'(553).
13 St Derfel is associated with the village of Llanderfel, which is near Corwen where Powys lived while writing *Owen Glendower*. According to Glanmor Williams, in *The Welsh Church from Conquest to Reformation* (Cardiff: University of Wales Press, 1962), Derfel Gadarn ('Derfel the Mighty') was one 'of the 20,000 saints buried in Bardsey'. In medieval times there was a shrine to St Derfel in Llanderfel, which was subsequently destroyed by Oliver Cromwell. (495) Morine Krissdottir in *John Cowper Powys and the Magical Quest* (London: Macdonald & Janes, 1980) also comments: '"St. Derfel" is Darval Gadern or Hu Gadern, one of the chief gods

of the Druids. Hu Gadern dragged the Avanc or monster of the lake from his watery abyss. The rites of Darvel survived at least until the middle of the sixteenth century' (195, note 30). The reasons Powys has for presenting him as devilish are not clear — though it may simply be the spelling! In both *Maiden Castle* (London: MacDonald, 1937), 432 and *Morwyn* (London: Cassell, 1937), 87 Derfel is a beneficent god.
14 In *Autobiography* Powys states that he had 'a mania ... *against knowing the future*' (465).
15 M. Eliade, *Shamanism* [1951], W. R. Trask, trans. (USA: Princeton University Press, 1974), 415.
16 J. Rhys, *Studies in the Arthurian* Legend (Oxford: Clarendon Press, 1891), 56.
17 Eliade, *Shamanism*, 33.
18 Powys, *Owen Glendower*, 389: '[Owen] could see ... the most precious of all his books ... It contained poems and prophecies reputed to have been uttered by Taliesin, Llywarch Hen, and others — one or two claiming to be from the actual mouth of Merlin himself!'
19 In *Autobiography* Powys gives an example of his own power of exteriorising his soul: 'it was possible by a concentrated effort of the will to imagine yourself so vividly in a particular spot that you could touch it with your hand.' In *The Art of Happiness* (London: John Lane, The Bodley Head, 1935) one of Powys's psychological techniques for finding happiness, the act of 'de-carnation', is described: 'It consists in thinking of your soul as something separate from your body, something that exists in the air ... by the side of your oppressed and persecuted body' (25).
20 J. C. Powys, Diary entry for 25 June 1937. Unpublished MS, National Library of Wales, Aberystwyth.
21 Powys, *Autobiography*, 7.
22 See note 13 above.
23 J. C. Powys, *A Glastonbury Romance* (London: John Lane, The Bodley Head, 1932), 112: 'The strongest of all psychic forces in the world is unsatisfied desire.'
24 M. Eliade, *Myths, Dreams and Mysteries*, P. Mairet, trans. (London: Collins, 1974), 203.
25 Powys, *Mortal Strife*, 239.
26 See R. Mathias, 'The Sacrifical Prince' in B. Humfrey, ed., *Essays on John Cowper Powys* (Cardiff: University of Wales Press, 1972), 235–6, and J. Hooker, *John Cowper Powys* (Cardiff: University of Wales Press, 1973), 77.
27 Powys describes it thus in a letter to Iorwerth C. Peate, 22 November 1938. I. C. Peate, ed., *John Cowper Powys: Letters 1937–1954* (Cardiff: University of Wales Press, 1974), 4.
28 See *The Powys Newsletter* 4 (1974–75), 8.
29 R. Miles, *The Rites of Man* (London: Paladin, 1992), 298.

LLEWELYN POWYS

'In his Great Old Age'

In a brand new house on the sea front there lived a retired clergyman. He was so old that he had 'gone dreamy' as village people say, and was quite unable to find words to express what he wanted to say.

His wife was dead and except for his son and daughter who lived with him he was quite alone, quite isolated. Before he had retired he had passed the whole of his life in the same village, succeeding his Father to the living as soon as he came down from Cambridge. The village had been situated on the banks of the Stour in Dorset; and it was here in the very heart of the country known as the Blackmore Vale that he had found the background for his simple, uneventful life.

In the old days he had been never tired of recounting to his children the adventures of his youth in the surrounding country. The twisted mulberry tree at the bottom of the garden where the hollyhocks grew was the first tree he ever climbed; that particular pool in the seven acre field was where he had caught on one occasion a huge pike. That milestone on the road from Templecombe marked the place where the wheel had come off his Father's coach and he as a tiny child in long early Victorian frocks had been lifted through the window of the overturned chaise.

Such were some of his early memories. The rest of his existence in the village had passed evenly enough. Day after day for all those years he had visited the village people, entering each of the little thatched cottages and sitting for a while with them, as his Father had done before him. On Sundays he would preach two sermons, reading them out in a slow monotonous voice and for sixty years making not the slightest alteration in the simple things that he said. Between one of his sermons written at twenty and one of them written at seventy there was no difference at all. His views, and teaching, and doctrine did not alter at all. And it never struck him that it could possibly alter, for after all Jesus Christ had said these things to a world that, as far as he could see, altered very little with the passing of the generations — the sun rising and setting each day, the moon drawing the tides, man going forth unto his labour and the brown waters of the Stour moving slowly each day, each week, each year down towards the sea at Christchurch.

And now everything was changed. He had found it impossible to remember the well-known words of the service, and he had been persuaded to retire and had been brought by his children to this fashionable seaside watering-place. He had never liked it, it had all seemed strange and alien to him but then what could he do? He was unable to speak and he knew that his children considered him unable to think also. At the bottom of his heart he hated the large smart villa looking out on the esplanade.

His study had been arranged for him just as it had always been in the old Vicarage. His bookshelf was there filled with old-fashioned commentaries and theological treatises, the cabinet which contained his collection of birds' eggs was in the corner: and below were the locked-up shelves where he kept his sermons, all written out on blue paper and tied up in separate bundles with red tape.

Everything was there as it used to be, and sometimes as he sat in his armchair he could almost imagine that he was back in the old Vicarage, but then after a little he was *desperately*, horribly reminded of the change. He would hear the crowd of vulgar seaside visitors passing along outside and would see his son and daughter sitting on the lawn in the little garden in front. He was extremely sensitive about his affliction: and because he was unable to find words dreaded lest his children should consider him unable to find thoughts either. For this reason he used to make a point of always holding a book in his hands when he was in his study. 'If they see I am reading, they can't think I am mad,' he said to himself. Of course really he was quite unable to concentrate his attention on the book — he would read the same page over and over again, or sometimes merely occupy himself with turning over the leaves.

His children said to each other, 'Poor Father, it is sad to see his mind giving way — I suppose his arteries are hardening and he will soon have a stroke.' In a vague absent way the old man knew that they were saying this kind of thing. Twice a day he would go for long walks into the country away from the sea. Sometimes his son would go with him, but he avoided doing so as much as possible as he found it tiresome walking by the side of an old gentleman who was unable to say anything.

As a matter of fact the old man liked very much having someone walking by his side on such occasions. He would feel that he was still part of the everyday world, just taking his favourite hour of exercise, that was all.

He would do his very best to say things now and again. When they passed a flock of seagulls on the wide flats, he would stop and point at them with his stick and say 'birds' or perhaps 'white birds'; when they passed a sheepdog in a field, he would again stop and say 'dog'. He was always on the look out to see something before his son, so that he would be able to point it out to him and by so doing prove that he was still in his right mind.

One day in April when the two were walking together the son plucked a simple spring flower and thought to himself, 'I wonder if Father remembers what this is?' He showed it to him, saying innocently, 'do you remember the name of this flower, Father?' The old man dreaded a direct question more than anything else; he hated being unable to answer. So he made a terrific effort, he knew the little flower perfectly well, he had known it for eighty years ever since he played in the orchard where the walnut tree was, on the banks of the river Stour.

He now looked at it, and his old brain struggled with the task of recapturing the name which was put away somewhere in his memory. For eighty summers he had seen it. It came at last — he uttered one word 'cuckoo'. He did not say 'cuckoo flower', simply 'cuckoo'. It was enough, he thought, to prove that he recognised it, and it was the only thing that came back to his mind.

Continually as he walked he would keep looking behind him, as though he expected to be run over. When he did this he would often forget to look where he was going and stumble catching the toe of his boot on some stone.

It was after the cuckoo flowers had faded and given their place to the buttercups, that the old gentleman one day failed to return at the usual time from his walk. The son and daughter found him after luncheon by themselves ... [*Fragment ends here.*]

This fictionalised memory of Charles Francis Powys was written in 1919 and exists (together with other fragments and reviews by Llewelyn) in a blue quarto softback notebook (No. 86) in the Bissell Collection. By 1919, the Revd C. F. Powys had retired from his living at Montacute and moved to 3 Greenhill Terrace, Weymouth, where he was cared for by his daughter Gertrude. Llewelyn had returned from Africa in the summer of the same year, and lived for a while with them, before moving into his shelter on Jordan Hill above Weymouth, taking breakfast at Greenhill Terrace. He would often wander around the back streets of Weymouth or in the neighbouring countryside, sometimes in the company of his father. I have reconstituted the punctuation of the fragment somewhat and corrected one or two spellings. For a further account of C. F. Powys in his 'great old age', see the essay 'Stalbridge Rectory' in Dorset Essays *(1935).* Ed.

The Revd Littleton Charles Powys, Rector of Stalbridge, 1837–67, wood-engraving by G. M. Powys

Montacute Sunday School, c. 1906
Charles Francis Powys with his daughter Katie (centre left)

CHARLES FRANCIS POWYS

A Sermon for Montacute Club Day, May 1894

Look not every man on his own things, but every man also on the things of others. — Philippians II.4

Selfishness lies at the root of very much of the strife and envy and jealousy which brings forth such bitter fruit amongst us. It would be far better if we all followed the advice of the Apostle Paul "Look not every man on his own things, but every man also on the things of others".

We must not be always seeking our own interests and our own advantage — but rather consider the interests of other men, and seek the mutual good one of another. And this is the principle of our provident and mutual benefit Society.

We desire to help one another in times of sickness & of need — by means of securing the services of the Club Doctor, and by sick pay, & by the members' subscriptions towards the funeral expenses in the case of the death of a member or of his wife.

We also wish to promote good will & kindly feeling one towards another — not only by our social intercourse on this our annual festival, but by friendly acts and mutual regard shewn one to another when ever we meet each other thro'out the year.

The fact that we belong to the same Club should be a recognized bond of reunion & good will upon every occasion.

We should be always willing to take our share in bearing one another's burdens with a ready mind (& with a willing heart)!

And I wish you to consider with me this morning the meaning of the words of our text, that we may apply them to ourselves & carry out the principle which they set before us in all our relationships and under every circumstance of our daily life.

"Look not every man on his own things, but every man also on the things of others."

There are other people to be fed & clothed & made happy beside ourselves & our own families.

We must think of others — as well as of ourselves — & those who are especially dear to us.

Our interests must not be confined to our own betterment and advancement, but we must have a care how our prosperity may effect other men.

The words of our text do not teach us to interfere with other men's business — we are not to be busybodies — in other men's matters, we are not to be spies upon other men's actions and manners of life, but we are bound as Christians to think of other men's interests, and to seek their good & their advantages as well as our own interest & advantage.

And we should seek to carry out this principle of mutual benefit every day of our lives. God has not given us life for our own enjoyment only, but that we may benefit others by our work & by the use of the talents & powers which we possess for this mutual good one of another! I believe that we shall find that in the long run, our happiness is in direct proportion, to the efforts we make for the mutual good one of another.

The covetous miser is not the happiest man, that this world produces. The drunkard is sowing for himself poverty woe & death. The Profligate who like the prodigal son spends his money & his strength in self-indulgence & debauchery is hastening on his own ruin, unless like the prodigal he comes to himself & returns repentant to his Father ere it be too late.

True abiding happiness may be found in the heart of that man, who feareth God, and *who loving God loves his brother also* "with a pure heart fervently". The truly happy man is the man whose treasure is not on earth but in Heaven. The man who practises constant self-denial & self-restraint, that he may "have to give to him that needeth". The man, who not only delights to see smiling bright faces around him, but who seeks the real & lasting good of his brethren, rather than their praise & their present gratification. The man, who forgets himself in

A SERMON

his earnest desire to do good to his brethren, because he loves them — & because he sees in them, however debased they may have become, some faint impress of the image after which they were created — & he longs to see them restored to health & life & beauty — & fashioned once again after the likeness of the Son of God.

But let us *notice* & keep in mind the words of our text —

"Look not every man on his own things, but every man also on the things of others."

Let us seek to follow this advice today.

And seek not every man his own enjoyments & his own interests, but rather seek the happiness of others, and the mutual good one of another.

Let there not be an angry or unkind word uttered. Let there be no discord & quarrelling to mar the happiness of our Feast Day. Let there be no excess or riot to leave behind a dark stain and reproach upon this occasion of our social intercourse.

Let us shew today respect & consideration for the feeling & opinion of one another. Let us have constant regard to each other, true happiness and lasting good.

Let every member of the Club have regard to *the character of the Club*, and seek by his own personal conduct to win for it a high reputation for *sobriety*, *good-temper*, and *good-behaviour*.

Let each be willing to deny himself for the mutual good & well-being of the Club. But there is a thought lying below the surface of our text & giving to every word a fresh force and power.

St. Paul, when he wrote this was thinking of one, who has perfectly carried out the spirit & the letter of our text. The Lord Jesus Christ looked not on his own things but on the things of others.

"Christ pleased not himself." "He went about doing good." "He laid down his life for our Salvation." He has opened for us men the Kingdom of God.

May not I say then with the Apostle "Let this mind be in you, which was also in Christ Jesus".

Brothers — *be Christian men indeed*! *Follow the example of Christ*! *Mark his true humility*! no sham humility — a mere cloak of pride, but a real deep sincere lowliness of mind — & of heart, manifested unto all, when "he humbled himself and became obedient unto death, even the death of the cross". *Mark his unselfish love!*

Christ left us not alone in our sinfulness & our folly. He had mercy upon us. He emptied himself of all his glory. He put away his majesty. He came down from Heaven. He was born in this earth as a fellow man. He was content to be known as a carpenter of Nazareth. He honoured honourable toil by the labour of his own hands. And he, when the right time came, laboured in his Father's service — it was his "meat & drink to do his Father's will", and in doing that will, *He looked not on his own things, but on the things of others.* Let us also *follow in his steps* — Amen.

The first page of C. F. Powys's sermon, 28 May 1894

The Sons to the Father:
Six Letters written on the Occasion of the Sixtieth Birthday of Charles Francis Powys

The Train
Between Manchester & Leeds
Jan 31st 1903

My dear Father

Most sincerely do I wish you many happy returns of the day! It is strange to think that you have really lived sixty years on this mortal planet.

Well! you have done your duty by your fellow man and deserve, like a patriarch, to have flocks and herds, children and grandchildren, and the honour of your friends, and coals of fire upon your enemies' heads! I expect your sons and daughters will all join in celebrating each in his own way the worthy occasion of the Diamond Jubilee of your reign over the Powys clan. Long may the clan last and long may King Charles reign over them! Vive le Roi! May "the Lion's gamb between two crosslets fitchée gules" keep its honour as unsullied by future generations as it has been on your shield.

I sincerely hope for all our sakes that at least 20 more years are to be allotted you of mortal span.

I have come across a certain Dr. Richard Baumgartner in Newcastle who claims third cousinship with you. I am to stay with him next week or the week after. Alice's friend Emma Baumgartner is his aunt; and grandmother (your mother) his great-aunt. He talked much about Milton. He has married a Quaker and I met him in his mother-in-law's house. He has a brother another Doctor Baumgartner in Newcastle, whose acquaintance I may also make. It is interesting hearing him speak of the Moilliets and his (and our) Swiss connections. I see a great deal of Quakers in the North and find them very kind and pleasant people. I am now going to spend the Sunday at Meanwood. I was very interested in wandering about the Docks at Sunderland and watching the ship-builders there. The noise of hammering as the men work on the steel plates of the ships is terrific — and a skeleton forest of scaffolding supports the ribs of the new ship-frames. I stayed at Middlesbrough with Socialists who were allied to the working men who work in the blast furnaces there making iron and steel. At night the red fires light up the sky and look very weird. Once again, my dear father, best of wishes for your 60th Birthday.

I am your very affectionate
John

The College,
Llandovery.
January 31st 1903

My dear Father,

I have remembered it is your birthday tomorrow, your sixtieth I believe: & so I am writing to send you all my best wishes for many more very happy returns of the day.

I am sending a South Wales Graphic which came out in the holidays with pictures and a little account of Llandovery.

Still from my point of view there is one photograph not quite satisfactory because it was taken before my friend Inigo Jones & I came to the place. The photos of the Warden are fair; but the one of him by himself was taken years ago and is not very like him now.

It took me some time to get into the swing of work; I felt it quite hard to get started: but now I have an enormous amount to do something like 5 or 6 private pupils and I have got more or less into my stride. Further the first week I was handicapped by having a beast of a cold which now thanks to Llandovery air (in spite of the dampest weather) is much better.

Our boys are playing House Matches and are quite madly excited about them: I confidently expect the victory of my boys though they have one team against them which will take some beating.

It won't be long now before I get my Field Society started: things are gradually moving that way. It is strange how in a big community like that of a public school difficult it is to have one's own way: and I daresay it is a good thing too!

The Warden has been rather laid low by a sore throat — and in addition to that by worries about the School Building Fund. The Governors seem to be treating him rather unfairly, trying to squeeze as much money out of him as they possibly can when they themselves are the responsible persons. Still things will right themselves in time doubtless.

We are as far as numbers go the same — that is absolutely full. We lost boys whom we could easily spare, of the big useless type and I think I have 10 nice kids in their places.

With best love to Mother and much to yourself
    I am yours always affectionately
        Littleton

                Belmont
             West Terrace
              Eastbourne
            Jan 31st 1903

My dear Father
    I wish you many happy returns of your birthday. I was very glad to get your letter, and am trying to do my best here.
    I hope you are all well at home, and that the people of Montacute are also well in mind and body, and are not giving you much trouble, man is a strange animal and often barks when it does not intend to bite, and many people appear worse than they really are.
    Love to all
        your ever loving Son
            Theodore Powys

            Jan 31st 1903
      118, High St Kensington

My dear Father,
    I believe I write this letter on what is actually your birthday though it is usually kept on the 1st.
    I hope you may see *many* succeeding years. Though it is the custom

to give presents on a birthday it is for me to thank you for my books which are very interesting.

I have this afternoon been with Ralph at his Cottage at Laleham. A very pretty place. Ralph is very kind to me.

Last night I went to a meeting of an Art Guild of which Mr Cape is the Secretary. It was he who took me. I met Walter there.

I am very looking forward to see May at Aunt Kate's.

Give my love to any one who wants it especially Mother. Sorry John Frome is ill.

With love from

A. R. Powys

I hope that the First was a fine day and that you spent as happy a birthday as you ever have.

The Green,
Sherborne,
Dorset.
Sat evening
Jan 1903

My dear Father,

Many happy returns of the day. I hope you will enjoy your birthday. I shall think of you tomorrow — especially the class, I should like to be present. I am in V.B. and am working up Pro Sulla and Prometheus Vinctus with a friend who is also going in for the Littlego. I am doing mathematics, with the new master, a little man — but very quick: a great change from dear old Gaffa Wood, but I hope I may get on. R. Barfleet has not come back yet; so I am all by myself in the study. Willie comes in sometimes.

Today we played a house game against Kings, who are the only out house anywhere near us — but they seem to be a little too near us — but I hope in the house matches we will be alright. Tell mother that I will not write to her this week — thank her very much for her letter.

I often think of my drive into Sherborne with Katie. I enjoyed it very much.

I am your most affectionate Son

Llewelyn Powys

> The Green
> Sherborne
> Dorset
>
> My dear father I wish you many returns of the day.
> I hope that you will have a Happy birthday and plenty of presents.
> I feel as if I have been here 6 weeks. Give my love to Mother and sisters I arrived Here savely last wensday [sic].
> We had a good game of Football last Thursday I hope May got on allright at the Dentist, I hope Mothers Headache is allright now, I can see in my minds eye the blue tit entering the coconut and taking a dive in and take a peck and then out again to see if an enemy is coming to disturb it I have not much to say so good bye dear father
> I remain your loving son
> W. E. Powys

The Powys brothers, c. 1902

A. R. POWYS

The Crippled Child

This story seems to be worth telling but you shall read for yourself and judge, and I will not hesitate even to tell you also the exact circumstances under which I heard it, for it may be that without these it will not stir your imagination as it did mine.

In this very year, 1925, a year when children in England are taught more kindly and with greater care than ever before; when there is so much talk of "the milk of human kindness" and so much fuss in regard to the well-being of the sick, I learned this tale of a suffering child. It was at one of those dinners, held at a fashionable London restaurant, where the officers of a county battalion meet and recall to one another the cruel incidents of the war, that this tale was told. They are dull affairs these dinners, very few have any real desire to be present. They owe their origin as often as not to the energy of a pair of subalterns whose activity is greater that their experience and who by their determination make it impossible for the reluctant to keep away.

In this particular case after waiting in the bar for some late arrivals, who had the courage to stay at home though not the politeness to refuse the invitation, we trooped disconsolately upstairs to a room specially prepared for the occassion. I knew very few who were there and found myself sitting next to a solicitor from a northern town none of whose interests I shared. We spoke of those who were not present and asked each other the names of those who were. Everyone was bored save only the two young men who called us together. The only chance of escape from complete weariness of mind was wine, and while I drank this, I very much regretted that my bottle was not shared with some friend with whom to drink is a real pleasure, someone whose company makes wine the richer and more gracious.

The dinner followed its dreary course. My neighbour encouraged by a second bottle indulged in the bawdy stories of a school boy, made on the table strange groups with matches and recited limericks that could never have brought a natural smile even to the face of the coarsest person. The presiding officer proposed "The King". This toast was a sign not only that the proceedings were drawing to a close but also that the guests could move about and by a change of companions perhaps hear a word or two of living conversation. I, who had already drunk enough, believed no change could be for the better and therefore being determined to endure the farce to the end stretched my legs under the table, pushed my chair some inches backwards and waited for the first opportunity to go. The solicitor did the same. He seemed to think my bad manners and surly behaviour the mark of true aristocracy. He copied my every move. When I drank he drank; when I had refused oysters he did the same. It was then with something of relief that a stranger came and sat between us, being introduced to me as an architect from Bristol. I like architects. They are often men who share a fine perception in regard to books and paintings. Besides they usually talk well. I was encouraged to chatter with him and so, to help matters and to keep him at my elbow, I ordered brandy and spoke of Waterloo Bridge, of St Paul's Cathedral, of American Architecture and of the prospects of a modern style freed from academic conventions. I liked his manner; but it was clear that he was preoccupied and only remained in the room in order to save himself from the reputation of a boor. He had come from the country that day, had, so he told me, just returned from reporting on a beautiful church near the Kentish coast. He described its features, and without reference to obscure technicalities gave me the feeling of the place. The narrow lanes deep between the rich grass of the bordering fields, the heavy naked boughs of the great elm trees, the cow-trodden mud at the open gates of the meadows and the smell of steaming dung from a byre against a churchyard all became realities in my mind as he spoke. The place was untouched by modern commercialism. There was no railway near it yet the beauty of the country and the nearness to the sea had drawn to the neighbourhood one or two painters whose names I knew and an eccentric maker of furniture who believed he could in such old world surroundings persuade himself and his neighbours that the Middle Ages were still with us. The village for all its primitive appearances was evidently not without people who in these days we regard as civilised. The Parson, as he himself said, had about him several equals. It crossed my mind that the company I should probably enjoy, were I in that excellent man's place, would be the farm workmen, the wheelright and the postman. I visualised groups of these people telling the gossip of the day beside the evening fire of the inn. But most people, even our mellow architect, would not share this opinion. Something of this I hinted suggesting that the clergyman he had recently left was perhaps lacking in real quality. At this he paused, was silent a space, and eventually said, "You shall decide for yourself". In a rather detached manner he went on to tell his tale, beginning it seemed to me with preliminaries too much drawn out.

He told me that in making arrangements for his visit he had written to the Parson to say he would not be able to reach the nearest station till half past nine in the evening and had received in reply a letter saying a motor car would be at the station to meet him, that the Parson himself would sit up to receive him and adding that he must be forgiven if his wife had retired to bed, for in the country they did not sit up late, as sometimes their night's rest was broken.

My new acquaintance, the architect, told me he had wondered a little why these rather elaborate excuses had been made. A reception of this kind was only to be expected at such an hour in an out of the way village. Anyhow, he travelled by the appointed train, arrived on a dark night with gusts of rain and a devilish strong wind blowing. The road followed the edge of the sea for a mile or so, turned in land, wound rising round a steep hill, passed through gates that had to be opened, sank into a coombe and after many confusing turns through narrow muddy lanes led to the vicarage gate. Even from the car and in the dark the architect got the sense that the garden was well cared for and the drive well weeded. The tower of the church could be seen between the tree tops against the sky and between the trunks a single light shined from the house. At the door he left the car and was welcomed by the Parson. When his coat was removed and his bag set down he was taken into the study and seated beside a warm fire. Opposite him the vicar of the parish, as he provided a drink and tobacco, again apologised for the

THE CRIPPLED CHILD

absence of his wife, adding this time that she retired early as she was often waked at night to look after his ailing daughter. Together the two spoke of the church; and the architect, by way of sounding his client, showed an interest in the parish and the folk who lived there. He learned that the Parson worked hard both as a priest among his people and in his garden. It was evident, I was told, that the clergyman was a kindly fellow, sensitive to human needs, perhaps not very capable in material matters but certainly absorbed by the importance of his mission. "He is certainly a decent fellow and a sensitive", the architect repeated this twice, and paused.

The solicitor immediately seized the opportunity to assert himself. He ordered more drinks, started some story of clerical misdemeanour and subsided gradually into a state of drowsy boredom.

My new friend bore this interruption with polite patience and at a sign of my interest in his story continued. His bedroom, he said, was clean but chilly. The walls were hung with an odd assortment of pictures, on the mantlepiece was a missionary box for navvies or some seamen's mission and beside it was "That picture of Christ with a lantern tapping at a door in front of which grew a lot of brambles". He guessed that Mrs Parson had been at work there. Some dresses hung in the wardrobe and queer elongated boots possibly belonging to the owner of these clothes were beneath the dressing table. A long wire stretched from the eaves above the window to one of the trees hummed dismally in the night.

In the morning the clergyman appeared with hot water, mentioned the hour of breakfast, let in the sunlight and left. He looked as though he had been up for a long time. Had he been serving in his church or digging in his garden?

When my friend got down to breakfast he found the lady of the house and a pretty daughter of about twenty years or so busy about the table. Introductions were affected and after comments on the improved weather the visitor turned towards the fire and observed a second girl of about twelve seated there quietly engaged in lacing her boots with one hand and that the left. He bid her good morning and as he did so became aware that her right side was shrivelled and her right hand a useless thing of skin and bone, while her right leg was a poor weak thing hardly as thick as a baby's. The child's boots were long in the leg and she laboriously pushed the tag of the lace through the hole, let go of it, and with the weak fingers of her poor left hand took it again and drew the lace tight, only to go through the same prolonged task again and again. My friend said he at once wished to help her, but did not do so lest he should make his host and his rather formidable hostess feel that he was surprised and a little shocked at their leaving this delicate creature to complete her painful task alone. They were called to breakfast. The child with difficulty crossed unaided the small space and took the chair beside my friend.

The conversation was not dull, he told us. The elder girl's eyes were brilliant as they spoke of Conrad's novels and life and also of a new book, "Coloured Laughter" he thought she called it. They were evidently an intelligent family. The Mother made him a little uneasy because of her masculine mouth and decided manner. My friend spoke to the crippled child sometimes which evidently pleased her; otherwise she was hardly noticed, that is, after her bread was spread with butter and her toast cut into fingers. When they rose from the table the child still sat on slowly finishing what had been set before her. The cups and plates were carried away the while and my friend wandered off to look at the church before he should meet the village worthies there.

He strolled round the building and noted the evidence of the care bestowed on it, the churchyard grass was well mown and the ivy on the walls clipped, yet as he noted these and other matters connected with his work his mind was occupied with the suffering daughter of his kindly host. He regretted that he had missed the opportunity to help her with her boots, felt himself to have been cowardly. His time he was certain would be better spent telling her stories or drawing pictures for her than in giving technical advice about the arrangement of pews. He imagined how he might have seen in her clear sad eyes and on her sensitive lips the smiles that he was sure seldom played there. I saw as he told his story that he was very much moved at the thought of her.

He returned to the house after about half an hour and in the room where he had breakfasted he found the child alone. Again she was seated beside the fire and again he saw she was still engaged in the tedious task of lacing those tall boots of hers. He did not, this time, miss the opportunity. On his knees he held her poor shrunken feet and drew the loose sides of the boots together. "Please do them tighter," she said, "they strengthen my legs." I can well imagine with what tenderness he obliged the command, and I can see the gentle smile she gave him when he rose from tying the last laces in a knotted bow. "I thank you very much," she said. He longed to make her happy, he told me, to make some pleasant change in the monotony of her existence. He felt clumsy, ill at ease and unable to do or say the right thing. He promised himself he would send her a book to read as soon as he again got among shops. With this in mind and to find out what her interests were he asked her how she spent her days. "Sometimes I go out into the garden when it is fine, but I am often ill," she replied. He thought of her poor crippled little body lying probably in the very room he had used, straining to read in bed. He wondered how ever could she manage to hold the book. As these thoughts took form in his mind his wish grew more definite. And he asked what books were her favourite.

At this point the solicitor yawned noisily, finished his drink and rose, not without the coarser signs of drunkenness, and while he further disclosed his brutality by uttering with indistinct articulation, "What the hell's the point of the story, you lecherous old bugger", I heard the architect say, "You see she had never been taught to read."

As I walked home from this dinner I made excuses for the parents to myself. It must surely have been that her illness and not their indifference had left this poor child without even the solace to be found in books. Anyhow the whole thing was none of my business.

The manuscript of this story, in A. R. Powys's own hand on 12 quarto pages, was kept with other papers arranged by Faith Powys, and is dated by her 1925; it has just come to light. There is a succession of suggested titles: the first three. 'The Cruelty', 'The Clergyman's family', and 'Innocent Cruelty', are struck through. Obvious errors have been corrected and punctuation added to ensure clarity of meaning. The new book 'Coloured Laughter' is clearly an echo of Llewelyn Powys's Black Laughter *which had just been published in America in 1924 and in England in 1925.*

Although A. R. Powys did much writing in his professional work as an architect and as the Secretary of the Society for the Protection of Ancient Buildings, and also published three books and a great many articles in journals as diverse as The London Mercury, The Church Assembly News *and* The Farmers' Weekly, *this is the only piece of fictional writing by him which is known to exist.*

Stephen Powys Marks comments, 'The writing of the piece generally, using the device of a story within a story, has been done with great flow and assurance, giving a very vivid picture of both scenes depicted: if it were not for the ending, which is weak, it would, I think, rank highly as a piece of creative writing, even by comparison with some of the work of his more well-known literary brothers. My mother, A. R. Powys's daughter, observed that he had been a good story teller, but somehow she did not recognise him in this piece. It has certainly come as a very pleasant surprise.'

A. R. Powys in New York, *1920s*

MARY CASEY

Family Portraits:
A Selection from the Journals 1951–53

16 May 1951   Sunday evening, just before dark, the taxi stopped outside the wicket gate of Mother's cottage [in Mappowder, Dorset] and I saw her face at the window. In a moment she was outside and we were together. And in a little while having tea by the fire and feeling so happy and natural.

17 May   After breakfast I walk up the hill to fetch the milk in two cans with pink bows tied on to their lids so that I can distinguish them from other people's. Then letters arrive. This morning Mother went to the village shop to buy the 'rations'. From 3 o'clock in the afternoon we walk with Theodore. Such is the regular order of the day. On these daylight summer evenings there is a compline service at 8.30 which Mother and Theodore always attend, sitting side by side, kneeling and standing together, in a short pew rather at the back of the church. Almost adjoining the churchyard wall is the three-roomed stone house with green painted door where Theodore lives. From the stylegap in the hedge at the end of Mother's garden one can look across a hayfield and see this unusual house which was built, it is said, for a school. Treasures of books and china as well as all the necessary furniture of a living room fill to over-flowing the outer room. Books weigh down the shelves so that they curve downwards in the middle, other volumes are stacked up on the floor. A large fire, kept going all day, makes the air heavy and dense. Theodore, with his white hair and rosy face, moves round the table and between the chairs to greet us when we arrive at 3 o'clock.

19 May   An owl has begun to hoot in the May dusk. Treasures are showered upon me so that I cannot hold or perceive them all. This owl

Gertrude Powys with her niece Mary Penny, 1925

voice touching me as closely as any. The white scar of a chalk pit in a distant hill side lit by a passing gleam of sunlight. How I miss chalk in Africa. 'You don't mean to say, my dear, there is no chalk in Africa? I could *never* live in a country where there is no *chalk*' said Theodore. His utterance is singularly expressive, and certain words or syllables of words are distinguished by an emphasis that makes them very formidable. He has a way of frowning, drawing his bushy white eyebrows together until they hide his eyes, when he is wrestling with a thought hard to speak in words. But in an instant they shoot apart revealing two deepened lines on his brow and a pair of grey-blue eyes set rather near together. His hair is snow-white, thick and long at the sides but growing thin on the top. His face is broad and rosy, pleasant to look at as are the fresh clear cheeks of the old; the upper lip is given to certain tremblings and twitchings when his nerves are agitated. Just now he is reading my favourite of all stories *The Daisy Chain*, and each day he tells me what he has read. He said tonight: 'Ethel there says,' with a wave of his hand towards his house, 'that all anger is pride and temper and she is right, by Jove she *is* right.' And then he said how characters in books are *more real* than people we know, and that is what I have so often felt: making of these story-book friends my imaginary and close companions. When he spoke I had a vision of Ethel emerging from the green door and turning her steps towards the church. Yesterday Theodore conducted us to a certain swampy place where marsh marigolds and cuckoo flowers grow that we might pluck the leaves of a scented willow.

22 May Gertrude and Katie were to come this afternoon: Mother prepared the tea as of old I have known her prepare for so many different tea parties. Then we sat near the fire with ears a-listen and I read aloud the beginning of a story by Thomas Hardy called 'Strangers at the Knap'. Just as I finished the second chapter the jeep drew up outside. Gertrude and Katie. How long they have lived together, how good they are to Mother and me. I am glad to have seen them together and heard their voices — four, nearly five years, since I have seen Katie.

31 May Piano music of Schumann; vista through one doorway of mother's sitting room touched here and there with evening sunlight; and the outer door also standing open showed the clusters and sprays of honey-suckle that embowers it and are ready to enter the house, the bluebells on each side of the path. Mother and I sat together at the table listening and looking through that quiet interior to the world without through that sunlit arch of leaves. Music, and Mother's face — her hair, the shape of her head — the last May evening.

1 June During the walk with Theodore this afternoon through fields of buttercups and daisies I consulted a rye grass (as I learnt to do when I was at school) and the rye grass said yes to my question whether Gerard would come back this evening with the jeep. And just as we had entered Mother's room after church he arrived. We drove up the hill together and parked the jeep in Mr. Kelly's farm-yard. When we were in 'Violets' again there was a supper tray ready set by Mother's hand. And the letter from Uncle Jack which came this afternoon for Gerard to read. What a thing it is to stay with Mother in this quiet village and walk with her and Theodore by green hedge rows, through meadows unbelievably golden! Words of fear, and wisdom, and strange original philosophy, mingled with village gossip curiously coloured by passing through his mind, he utters: often, man-like, absorbed by his thoughts while Mother in a transport of delight over the shining buttercup realm can hardly endure that he should talk so walking as though blind to the glories of early summer. Not that he isn't much of the time aware of where he is, most nicely observant of trees and flowers, hills and sky, and peculiarly sensitive to the quality and atmosphere of each field-corner, clay, trodden track, barn and hazel copse. And how gravely he considers the particular direction of each day's walk, which green field it would be wisest to cross or to encircle; following round its tangled hedges or making straight across it to the gate, or to that certain corner where he knows it is possible to *get out* — where there is a *way through* which he is well acquainted with and has proved many times before.

2 June *Cottage Shadows* is the title upon the cover of a grey exercise book lying on the table by my side. Three more exercise books are in my drawer. Together these four paper-covered books contain a story written by Theodore between thirty and forty years ago. This story was discovered by Phyllis when she was spring-cleaning, and read by John with the greatest excitement. From North Wales to Mappowder travelled his letter to Mother telling her of this thrilling discovery as that she might prepare Theodore. This afternoon, twenty-four hours after Mother's letter came — the registered parcel reached the Lodge. We went for our first drive in the jeep onto the hill called Bull Barrow. When we returned to the village it was church time. Theodore was in his place, his white head clear against the wall. I went to him and he whispered: 'Is your mother coming? I have a book for her.' And held under his large red prayer book was *Cottage Shadows*.

6 June   Chydyok today, my first visit there for nearly six years: and there was no change save for the growth of trees in Gertrude's garden. But how could there be change in those long green valleys running between the hills, with unnumbered rabbits scuttling across them and disappearing down their chalky holes on the slopes; in the great white sea cliffs, terrible in height and majesty, in the cry of gulls flying on strong wings up the Seagull Valley; or in the welcome given to us by Gertrude and Katie. It was a blessed thing to be with them again sitting in warm sunshine and listening to their long, desultory, vague, sensible converse. They even, for all the years, have changed little, only, as old people must, grown smaller and more bowed about the shoulders. Katie has less passion and vigour.

8 June   After Montacute where the air feels full of blessings we went on to Whitcombe. Forty years ago Will farmed here and for one summer my mother, then nineteen years old, housekept for him. Thither in those summer days came my father and in the farm house they became engaged. Then to the village of West Pennard. There in a room in a guest house we found Uncle Littleton prisoned to the chair in which he sat by arthritis, all the shining world remote from him, the country he so dearly loves. But still for all he talked with no mean energy, his blue eyes lighting enquiringly upon one or other of us questing for a responsive glance, and more rarely his upper lip lifting in the old, remembered smile. Oh Mabel, Mabel, he is brave.

9 June   Theodore's rosy face with its spiky crown of white hair had a merry look when he bid us good night at his cottage door, saluting us with a lift of his large red prayer book.

22 June   Leaning against a gate this afternoon Theodore discoursed to Gerard and me as we sat at his feet of the *roguery of nature*. He described how once when he was in the same way standing to rest against another gate a weasel came near and began to sport and gambol for its own diversion. And it played thus before his eyes for five or ten minutes. This natural and instinctive roguery, I think was his meaning, is in us all and is our defence against our minds and against false and stupid seriousness — self-importance — while it may well lead us to the *right kind of seriousness*, for it frees us and lets us laugh at ourselves. Only he, beside the gate, in few words and with certain Theodorian glances said much more than my awkward phrases.

1 July   In the upstair room at 7, Cae Coed on one of the book-shelves is a Welsh Bible. I took it from its place at John's command, and sitting down by the window in his cloth cap and heavy overcoat he read aloud several verses from the beginning of the first chapter of the gospel according to St. John — saying over the English words for us before he read with power and force and excitement the Welsh. For two and a half hours in the close atmosphere of the downstair room where he is all day on his couch he talked to us, growing sometimes so excited his face shone with sweat and the hair on his brow was wet with it, so that in the midst of the glory of his talk my heart was anxious lest my almost eighty-year-old uncle should exhaust himself — and Phyllis, after we had gone, have added concern for him. In the adjoining house 8 Cae Coed we visited Phyllis's mother of eighty-five, the same brown eyes far apart, broad cheek bones, hollow temples and exquisitely slender wrists and ankles ... her voice American. A fearless unquenched spirit. 'We have the same relationship together we have always had,' Phyllis said.

11 July   A quiet day in Corwen with tender skies and light brief sudden rainfalls like April showers: a day of richness sufficient to redeem all the barren and discontented hours of the whole year. In the afternoon we went to Uncle Jack and Phyllis to say good bye and fetch Gertrude's painting. Two and a half hours we were at 7 Cae Coed. The time passed, they stood in the doorway of their sitting room, John behind, a little to one side, Phyllis in front, I looked at their two faces, then we were outside, the door was shut. But it was enough. I am content.

20 July   Another golden orb has gone down below the horizon. Alyse came in the morning and sat a little while under the apple tree with me, talking and feeding a tame cock sparrow with crumbs of a biscuit. Three nights she has stayed in the village at a farm house so as to be with Theodore.

28 July   Katie came in the morning and went off at 3.30 with Gerard to Dorchester. She is very happy with Gerard. Before he came back in the evening Louis and Joan came and stayed for ten minutes. Joan's brown eyes narrowed and sparkled when she shook hands with me, she is happy because she has a companion? Louis's somewhat close-set brown eyes behind glasses expressed nothing. He carried an immense pink and white straw hat he'd been wearing to shade himself from the sun: and spoke in the elegant, faintly drawling, conscious voice affected by Oxford men nearly two generations ago. But his eyes are not bad; though for all he used to make Llewelyn laugh so his face seemed mirthless to me.

1 August   I took mother to the walnut tree today, she broke a twig off for Theodore who had said once he wanted to smell the leaves: when we came to him in church he silently handed me my book of Greek epigrams while Mother placed in his hand the sprig with its sweet leaves.

10 August   Rose's seventeenth birthday. Chydyok: the sea, the cliffs, Gertrude and Katie. Not silence tonight fills my heart but all the loving-kindness I have known today flows through it in long swelling waves of wonder, sorrow, joy, crested with white caps of pride and exultancy in those I love and who give me love so faithful and understanding. I was with Katie in her garden for a little time while she gathered for Mother the kindly fruits of the earth. I was with Gertrude in her fruit cage where red currants hung in rich crimson chains and there were red gooseberries and raspberries. Gerard went onto the cliffs with his father and mother and Anne and I had my lunch with Gertrude and Katie in their kitchen at the Montacute nursery table. Gertrude and I walked onto the cliffs, perfectly happy in seeing before us the ocean, the headlands, Portland harbour all silver in sunlight. Two white sails we saw. 'It is beyond price,' Gertrude said when the whole expanse was before us. Natural and happy as I was with Gertrude and Katie, I still seemed to fail when I was with Alyse to be myself, to prevent a certain cold withdrawing and shunning of any approach at intimate talk. But as Gertrude says, love is all that matters, and that I gave her at the end. Downstairs in Mother's sitting room is a painting of Durdle Door, given by Gertrude, though I can hardly believe it, to Gerard and me.

21 August   Theodore was mellow in the walk this afternoon. Words

Dr Bernard Price ('Bernie') O'Neill

of wisdom slid sideways from the corner of his mouth, his upper lip gave its proud quiver, and a certain expression of cunning was in his grey eye; yet, for an instant, gleamed forth the kind of desperate, formidable, hope-abandoning daring with which a particularly nervous and hyper-sensitive man may on occasion confront the universe. Yet how different, how infinitely cautious is this Theodorian facing of the unknown, from John's. It is no mean achievement to have lived through years of a sort of tragic melancholy and finally emerge with a grasp on life which, at the same time, you defy as NOTHINGNESS.

22 August Oh, I wish for Bernie [O'Neill]; a pagan full of humour, discernment, discretion, fascination, and a most delicate and rare perception of what is beautiful in nature and art. But if I let my mind go free to whatever remembrances of him that it can discover some flash of his earth-ripened wisdom may dart through it — that is the best I can hope. How I'd like to hear him reading 'St. Agnes' Eve', to see him smelling an evening primrose, or examining a moth that had fluttered in through the wide open 'jessamine-muffled' drawing-room window at Horsebridge some warm black August night. Instead I was apt to make sport and mock of his over-fussiness in certain personal matters in those days of my crude youth.

25 August Katie is sleeping in the house tonight and the very familiarity of it gives me a wonderfully safe and happy feeling. Thin she is, in truth, as one of those skeleton-like effigies of very early bishops in Salisbury cathedral. Her tragic eyes are deep sunk in her head and the distinctive lines on her forehead, so well remembered, are yet more darkly graved. Katie, Katie, you are here tonight! A few minutes ago you were sitting on my bed.

26 August The happiness of being at Chydyok; Gertrude with her noble head and perfectly candid blue gaze giving me love; Katie gaunt, her wild passions sunk but still smouldering, her bowed figure at home as ever against the vast sea and sky and inland landscape; Alyse, whom I offend and caress, kiss and render furious the next minute by some naughty word, and who through her distraction is so responsive and sweet to me. But Gertrude is the bond of this remarkable trio, all lean on her, to all she extends love and strength, and wisdom.

27 August This evening I took out of the drawer two small bundles of old letters given us to read by Gertrude. The first secured by a thread of green silk contained the letters written to my grandmother Mary Cowper Powys at the time of her engagement in the summer of 1871. These letters were almost all in envelopes about two inches by four inches with often a coloured monogram on the flap at the back. The second package bound with worn pink ribbon consisted all of black-edged envelopes of about the same size, and their contents were letters written by grandmother herself in the first year of her marriage. Letters to her own mother expressing restrained but most deep emotion and a fearless spirit. Simplicity of wording and a hopeful tone covering the hesitancies of the young girl, her nervousness and tremors at beginning her own establishment; at the earliest sign of her first baby. But most moving of all was the resolution, the determination to be good, to do what she had been taught it was right to do that comes from these pages filled so many years ago. That is fresh and strong as though that youthful, untried mother who was to bear eleven children had but just raised her hand from the paper.

3 September Yesterday we went to say good bye to Littleton. The deaf old man sitting in his room with his dimmed eyes and crippled body is still undefeated and can talk in a loud voice of many things.

6 September Theodore, as we came out of the church porch after litany, began with some eagerness to tell us how he had opened his prayer book by chance at psalm 56 and read there, *sometime I am afraid*; by his expression, tone, quiver of his lip, it was apparent these words had given him satisfaction of a most intimate kind. The first six verses of the psalm were, he assured us, the best — after that it falls away. Sometime I am afraid, he repeated: this was the motif of these six verses which he likened to the theme of a piece of music.

8 September Suddenly after tea the sun came out, illuminating the sad earth, scattering oval seals of gold on the wall near the door as it shone through the leaves that frame the outer door. Gertrude and Katie were in the room, with their wonderful faithfulness they came again to see me, and the time was happy.

9 September   Theodore along the familiar road, pausing by Passion's Gate to watch three separate herds of cows being driven in for milking, then going down into the combe below which is one of Theodore's favourite places. On the way home we picked and ate hazel nuts. Who can tell the wonder of Mother's love for me, the beauty of her face, the courage of her spirit, but the blessing of it may be felt.

24 April 1952 [Africa]   Gertrude is dead. There was a note from Elizabeth on the table when we came home tonight to tell me this: that she died suddenly and peacefully in a Weymouth nursing home. Yesterday I had a letter from Gertrude, and she said she was tired and her eyes were bad. It is hard at first in sorrow to feel thankfulness for the great mercy that she was spared a long illness, the humiliations she had feared of being cared for when she was sick. And her mind clear and unchanged as the letter proves. And there are all her paintings for our joy. May the others at this time of grief be as strong as she always was when people died. The world seems to rock when so strong a tower falls. Oh, how I hope all will go well with Mother in what will fall to her share to do. I can only leave my mind quiet now to grow used to this thing, for it always seems impossible that some one you have known from the very beginning of your life can ever die.

From her last letter, 17 April, 1952: 'I have been sitting out of doors — the primroses and daffodils and cherry trees are lovely.'

25 April   Shrouded in warm damp mist is the land tonight after two hours rain in the afternoon. When rain and thunder had passed for a time yellow sunshine lay on the floor of the room and from this light was reflected onto the painting of Durdle Door deepening and enriching the colours so that sea, blue upon blue, and green cliff tops showed more brilliantly then ever before. 'Because I love the elements,' Gertrude said when some one asked her why she lived at Chydyok. All day long I have been seeing her and hearing her voice and laughter, now a vision of long ago when I was a little girl at Weymouth, now some moment when we were together last summer. She has always been good to me but I felt in the last years that with the extraordinary tenderness, perception and serenity of old age she understood me and loved me more dearly. As she became older her mind grew more fresh and free. Walking hand in hand with her in Tumbledown I felt perfectly content and at peace.

7 August   When Will drove up to the end of the veranda and stopped his new Land Rover there on Monday afternoon he took out his sketch book before he moved and turned to the end. 'Gertrude did this for me, wasn't it nice of her, I like to see her writing.' He handed me the

Self-portrait by G. M. Powys, c. 1905

book. On the last page she had written some notes on varnishing oil paintings, and on the end board she had made dabs of paint of the various water-colours and written their names beside them: also the colours and their complements, a small square of yellow with violet in the middle and so on. His face bore a look of affection as he held the book, and as if his mind freed of the day's cares was restored by the appearance of Gertrude's writing.

9 August   Each night Gerard reads a few pages of *The Inmates* which we enjoy for its John characters and incidents and particular little unexpected details which he has an inimitable way of observing and recounting, but it is a modern tale and so it lacks the huge and liberating and imaginative atmosphere of his historical novels, or a novel like *A Glastonbury Romance* which is built on and over-shadowed by the legendary past. In *Owen* and *Porius* are characters far more fantastic, peculiar, original, startling than any so far encountered in the mental home called Glint Hall: characters more liberally endowed with John's own manias. 'Tis as Gerard says a *tour de force*; now he is back in his true realm of ancient poetry and romance, and this time more distant and more rich with sea-magic than any he has yet explored in a work of his own, for he is writing a novel of Homer's Odysseus.

11 September   Kisima. Grandmother's birthday. I am in the room which was Gertrude's when she stayed here. The last time I entered it she was within, and her canvases and half-packed bags were all about — so that to me it is full of her presence, the tones of her voice, her laugh, almost as if it were her room at Chydyok, or even that bedroom on the top floor of Green Hill Terrace which I remember from childhood. Uncle Willie wanted me to come here to sleep for these last two nights before Gerard comes back because of the activities of these dog-slaying Mau Mau which come nearer each day or rather each night, and I daresay he is right, I shall sleep more soundly.

16 September   We had tea when the Kisima Renault arrived with Charles at the wheel, and Will, Gilfrid, Elizabeth and four dogs. It was to say good bye. But the teaparty was a merry one, every one talked at once, laughed, teased. Elizabeth always looks most happy when she is with her sons. Will was silent, he watched with a look of content the different faces, thinking his own thoughts. When we were returning from the Ngare Ndare at nightfall he said to me that all the time he'd been imagining he was filling large canvases with pictures. Later I reminded him of Richard of Taunton Dene and he sang some of it in an undertone: 'Then Richard he came in to the hall, and loudly for Miss Jean did bawl ... and so if you will marry me now varther will gie us a vine vat zow.' And told me of the old man who taught him the song over forty years ago.

6 October   Gertrude's Birthday. I salute her memory with love. Years ago at Horsebridge she would sometimes come to stay with us for her birthday and mine. What happy walks they were in the dank meadows by the river with the air all smelling of mud and decomposing sedges and weeds. ... And the new wonder of bright stars at night at the first taste of frost in the air. ... So safe and warm and private I would lie in my bed and hear Gertrude's voice and Mother's voice and Gertrude's clear laughter: and I would think, Her birthday is nearly over now but mine is the day after tomorrow.

6 November   A letter from Mother this evening at Timau; she has had another stained sputum. Oh, Mother, Mother. She said Theodore began reading aloud *Herr Baby* to her one day, 'a happy moment'.

7 December   Will played the Montacute Bells on the gramophone after tea at 5.30, the proper Montacute Vicarage hour. They have never sounded better. The sun had gone down behind the hill and he stood by the north window looking at the ram lambs grazing quietly in the nearest paddock. The fine minute bell sounded and he thought of his father. More than once his eyes looked far away and his mouth sad. But the sight of the sheep pleased him, and he made the motion of pulling a bell rope as if he stood with the ringers in St. Catharine's tower as he often did in youth. In the afternoon, so full of clear light one felt awe at its brightness, Uncle Willie drove Gerard and me to see his new trough fed with water from the Wai Mugi spring, his wethers, and ewes and lambs. All the way to the Marania boundary we went and all the way the grass was green. It was a happy time, though there was strangely about those ringing bells something ineffably sad, though whether only regret it was for the past or foreboded future sorrow I could not tell. Both no doubt. But they rang bravely.

20 December   The letter from Mother caused me misgivings. She is in a ward for eight people who cough and talk and sing from morning till night and cough and *snore* from night till morning. If only she could have a room to herself, this kind of thing will do her no good. She has a window in front of her bed, she has heard seagulls calling ... but oh, Mother, Mother, I do not like it for you. It is cruelly hard to learn to live without silence and solitude, and however kind people are that is what you want, that and people you love.

3 January 1953   This day I had two letters from Mother, and with what happiness I read on the back of the second the message from Charles saying 'Katie, Gilfrid and I are visiting Lucy who has *just this moment* moved into a very nice private ward. It is nice to see her.' How thankful I feel to know she can be quiet again.

2 April   Mother said in the letter I had from her yesterday she had begun to get up for one hour a day. In her envelope was a letter from John. What a satisfying thing it is to see his strong clear round handwriting which is easy to read and yet so unlike anyone else's. Well I remember Mother's pleasure over the rare letters which came from him during my childhood, those long American envelopes with a picture of some huge hotel on the gummed flap and the stamps bearing the long-haired or bewigged heads of former presidents. Old Mrs. Playter is quite lost in her mind now and must be fed and cared for all the time. There is a nurse for the night time but Phyllis is very tired and exhausted.

16 April   All day Gerard and I have been on the moorland with Will and Miss Johnson, walking, walking over the burnt land all over which small tufts and clumps of the most brilliant grass has come, vivid beyond words against the bare blackish soil around. Very few flowers have as yet appeared, but Miss J. and I found some tiny dog violets, a white vetch, and one or two others. Will collected a few in his jacket pocket to send to Littleton.

18 April   It often comes in my head how blessed I have been to know my great-aunts: because of their characters, their principles formed by Christian upbringing, their love for and understanding of children, childless though they were — all the atmosphere they allowed me to experience of another age, and which I perceived, small though I was, in the houses in the Close [in Norwich] and in Aunt Emily's and Cousin Marian's houses in Cromer. Not only for their goodness do I love to remember them but also for the look of their faces, their clear cheeks whose skin of exquisite texture had never been touched by make-up and the softness and beauty of their white or grey or silvery hair. You do not, I am perhaps rashly tempted to say, ever see such old ladies today. But though they did nothing to make themselves look young, no one could have planned, carried through and enjoyed some picnic party or excursion more joyously than Aunt Dora. ... Aunt Etta by my bed at Horsebridge saying Keble's evening hymn with the scent of clematis coming in through the window. Genuineness of character is what children always revere instinctively in grown-ups, and the aunts were above all real people, with thoughts disciplined to be steady, hands to be employed — never as young girls were the four sisters permitted to sit in idleness, and in their hearts love and faith in God.

23 April   Mother's two letters were cheerful: she put in a ground ivy flower and that tiny sedge called chimney sweep. The tragic thing is that Littleton Alfred's mysterious nerve ailment is growing worse all the time. Now he cannot use his hands at all, and his voice which was clear only a little while ago is now thick and husky. Yet he said — which is no wonder for John's son — to L.C.P. that he loved life and did not want to die. But it seems there is no hope. I think he is just over fifty.

28 May   What I always desire in my contacts with other people is a touch of Bernie's humour; sturdy yet puckish, unexpected and yet honest were the comments he used to make. Odd they might seem and even far-fetched, but one's mind always complied with their truth. But even lacking his sly and witty words a gleam of the kind of things he would notice and find diverting does I fancy on occasion slide into some corner of my dull brain. But it seems best to say nothing, so heavy and laborious would any description from me seem in comparison with what I inarticulately feel he would have said.

5 June I looked into Llewelyn's letters during my afternoon, glancing over one and another: diverted by a reference in one to Mother to your 'extraordinary clever little daughter, Mary'. That was when I was six years old and my cleverness consisted, I fancy, in refusing to believe he was awake when his eyes were shut. Mother sent me up to the spare room to say breakfast was ready and discerning my uncle with tight shut eyes, though he assured me he was wide awake, I, standing by his bedside, strove in vain with my fingers to separate those obstinate eyelids. But for all the gaiety, brave words, whimsical observation, and happy natural metaphors that are upon every page, I found myself saying, sad, sad, sad, as I shut up the book. Though when I questioned myself concerning this involuntary and unthinking exclamation I met no distinct reply — for he did make his life happy and thirty years of undefeated struggle against disease is not in this world a cause of sadness. It must have been my mood, not his. Was it perhaps that below this gallant attitude and this urgency to live showed so clearly 'the frailty of all things here', even in the speech of a man who spent his days proclaiming the solid strength of earth?

9 July Mother's sad news is that Theodore has had to give up his walks for a time. This she learnt from a letter from Violet. She mentions Theodore's tiredness — but not pain or disease, and remembers how quietly content she was with him for three years.

21 July Two letters from Mother and they said, she was going home on Friday, last Friday. How long she has been away. I keep thinking of her AT HOME after eight months.

10 August Rose's nineteenth birthday. Theodore, Mother's letter told me, is in Yeatman hospital at Sherborne. He is probably to be operated on for cancer in the anus. Not without misgivings can I think of that sensitive man thus *moved* from his home. But as John would say, there it is. He has a room to himself, Mother and Violet have been to see him.

12 August   Now, Mother tells me, the obstruction which is causing Theodore's trouble may *not be* cancer, and that though he may not recover he may be able to go home, returning often to the hospital for attention. She sent me to read a letter from John who has seen his hapless son who can scarcely walk or speak or swallow, but is, through this terrible diminishment of physical powers, undaunted ... strong and of good courage. John told how the Baptist friends of Littleton Alfred who brought him to Corwen were introduced to the 'Father' by their little son, now six years old, who made friends with him when he was very young and brought the priest home to see his parents.

15 August   Mother's letter gathered at Timau made me anxious both for her and for Theodore. He has returned to Mappowder for one month before his operation; if he is fit to have it he will then stay five or six weeks in the hospital. Agitation, anxiety, visitors, constant coming and going are not good for mother ...

24 August   At Kisima today I read letters from Francis, Violet, Littleton and Alyse which told of Theodore's sickness. Will looked bowed and less happy then usual, he cannot stand any of his brothers or sisters not to be well. Elizabeth was cheerful, and told us of their journey to Lake Manyara.

19 September   My father's oak coffer which stood in the dining-room window at Horsebridge — on which mother put a bunch of marsh marigolds in the blue bowl in March — has now on its polished top a shapely pan of thin, I think beaten, brass. Yellow gleams of the metal are reflected in the wood as if those long ago king cups shone again. The pan has been sent me by Phyllis, who said her mother wished me to have it. Also in the carefully packed box were linen — strong old linen — teacloths; two face towels, embroidered with a red J, from the house in the Norwich close; a paper knife; a large handkerchief of softest ancient silk with rich border and pattern of red. With a feeling akin to grief I took out one by one these loved and antique treasures of another country that had about them odours of a forgotten past and were holy with the love of mother and daughter. But Phyllis could tell just where the brass pan used to live in her home in Kansas. On the stool by his bed Gerard has the little box with sliding tray lined with tissue paper in which I found a paper saying — For Gerard from mother's things. When he opened the two minute packages secured with cotton he found a silver figure of a Chinese, perhaps three-quarter of an inch tall, in one; in the other a flat round coin-like piece of unknown stone, part milky and translucent, part with narrow delicate ripple marks and a deep pool of amber.

24 September   Darling Mother's letters — the last two — have made me anxious again for her health. Yet they contain both courage and content in their quiet words. I only pray the happiness of Will's arrival will not make her more tired from excitement. She walks for ten minutes with Theodore, but only rarely now goes for a walk by herself.

29 October   Theodore is weaker, he does not go out, but Mother reads hymns to him now for half-an-hour in the late afternoon.

4 November   Mother in her letter of 29th October says Theodore is feverish and in bed with kidney trouble. She can no longer read hymns to him.

7 November   'I just looked in at Theodore on my way home — he was sitting up a little in his bed with a candle burning (the thunder had stopped the electricity) and he looked very fine — he had had a little blue bowl of bread and milk —' from Mother's letter of All Saints Day.

20 November   A letter from Mother this morning. Theodore has had a fall and is weaker and very quiet now: near, Mother said, the last quiet, that which to Gerard Theodore himself spoke of as his final obliteration.

5 December   Theodore died on the evening of Friday, 27th November. There was a letter from Katie for Gerard, the suffering and poetry of her heart sent to him in a muted cry. Her anguish after the death of her father, her brother, her priest — her longing as of a hurt wild creature, in the language of the Bible, to hide in the rocks at the foot of the White Nore.

T. F. POWYS
Letters to Valentine Ackland

East Chaldon
Dorchester
8 February 1927

My dear Molly

I thank you extremely for the voyages to the Moon and the Sun. I haven't got it. And now that I am trying to experiment with these fables, I expect the reading of this book will give me much aid. I hope you are quite well. I am quite well but rather indolent. You won't take it badly of me, you will be as kind to me, if you leave me out when you take the others to London; if you really wish to be so kind. I cannot manage it my dear. I am faint hearted. Indeed I am best here and can mind the cats. You will be all gone only a very little while and I will wait and pray that you may be happy and return safe. You will all have the benefit of my prayers. Doris is so looking forward to go. And so are Violet and Francis. You would be here for a day or two anyhow and so I should see you. Sylvia left us today. I do think your offer of taking my family to London is a kind one. Only you mustn't do it if it is in the least a bother. Violet is writing.
    Yours ever
           Theo

East Chaldon
Dorchester
26 April 1928

My dear Molly,
    Thank you very much for writing to me and for sending me a present of two books. You said, 'one', but two have come here. I have already read Cain. Doris will be pleased when I tell her that you liked

her letter and that you thought it well written. We are both quite well now, though Violet gets tired rather soon. We all look forward to seeing you again. You know our ways, and forgive us our trespasses. Doris ran after the goose yesterday and fell over the clothes line with a great crash. Thank you for the cutting. I am glad 'The House with the Echo' will be out on the twelfth.

 With love yours ever
Theo

East Chaldon
Dorchester
11 September 1928

Dearest Molly,

 I was very pleased indeed to have a letter from you, and I look forward very much to seeing you at the end of next week. I haven't sent a story to 'Life and Letters', I don't know the address. But I expect you can help me when you come.

 I shall enjoy to read the book on Witchcraft. No I have not read that book of Freud on religion. I should like to very much. Violet is very excited and pleased about your coming. The Autumn damps are beginning so be sure you dress warmly. I do hope Mrs Rocket will air your cottage properly.

 Yours ever
Theodore

East Chaldon
Dorchester
19 June 1929

Dearest Molly,

 Yours is the first word that I have heard about Genesis, though all the books were sold, except Llewelyn's. Yours is the kindest. Llewelyn thought it a little too old fashioned, too pious. I tried to explain ... You stand up and look one way. You turn and look another. Then you think what you saw first is not true. What you see the second time when you look away may not be true either. And both of these views make the Truth. Violet hopes your mother won't listen too much to Mrs Rocket when she calls for the cat. Mrs Rocket will no doubt say all sorts of things about Violet. I hope you will soon come again. We are so very pleased that your finger is better now and I hope you will soon have your complete health again.

I don't think Sylvia is happy. I think she is lonely. I send you a great deal of love. Llewelyn and I were one day frightened by a Cuckoo.

Yours ever
Theo

East Chaldon
Dorchester
24 June 1929

Dearest Molly,

We are very troubled to think that you have had to go to bed again. You must be very near to the kingdom of heaven to say that you enjoy being in bed, and feel guilty because you do enjoy it. I shall like to feel the same.

But if I don't get out into the fields I feel mournful. I have a kind of itch to prove that I can walk, and so I walk. Do get from some library the sayings or the writings of CHUANG TZU translated by Max Muller or Herbert A. Giles. This Chinaman is a brother to us all. No I have heard nothing more about the Genesis — no review at all so far. I daresay nothing will be said. Sylvia likes you I know. And I wish you would meet. Please get better.

Yours ever
Theo

East Chaldon
Dorchester
26 June 1929

Dearest Molly,

Give strong drink unto him that is ready to perish and wine unto those that be of heavy hearts.

Let him drink and forget his poverty, and remember his misery no more.

I had been a little way towards Chydyok with Gertrude. She

carrying a parcel from Sherborne that was mostly mould. And so I came back a little depressed, to find this good gift of yours. I have just drained my fourth glass and feel a little recovered. Sometimes Satan lays hold of my toe and gives it a nip. I do not like the touch of these fingers. But you and your kindly love did this time defeat the Devil. Doris is still away at her mother's, who has some gay shopkeeping lodgers. She shall have your present when she returns.
Much love
    Yours ever
           Theo

                East Chaldon
                Dorchester
                12 July 1929

Dearest Molly
    I thank you very much for sending me this bottle of Wine. I hope all is well, and that you are not sad. At least I wonder if it is not best to be sad. I am always a little afraid of myself and a little uneasy if I am anything else than that. It's what all country places are. We won't be so very long without seeing you I hope dear Molly. Do come when you can. There is always Mrs Wallis and *where we live too*.
    Yours ever
           Theo

                East Chaldon
                Dorchester
                26 July 1929

Dearest Molly,
    I was never grander than I am now. I look at myself twenty times a day in the glass to see how fine I look in this new pullover that you sent me from Wareham. As soon as it came I cast off my old soiled waistcoat and put it on. I thank you very much indeed. I look now completely well dressed. And if I could get my neck tie to set right, and my collar to button I might lunch with Lord Bullman! Violet and Doris enjoyed themselves extremely at Wareham. They caught the early bus and I saw them walk into the gate from High Chaldon. I had

locked the door. They ran round the house like the chickens to find a way in. We miss you very much, and wish the time to go quickly so you may come again.
With much love from Violet and Doris and from me
Yours ever
Theo

East Chaldon
Dorchester
1 May 1930

Dearest Valentine,
We miss you very much. Violet gave me your letter to read. We all hope it will be all right about the cottage, but we have heard nothing. I think I have the same book as you of George Herbert. The Chandos Classics. It begins with Walton's Life and ends with the Latin and Greek poems. And the Outlandish Proverbs begin at page 358. So it must be the same.

'Where there is peace God is.' Jesus never said that. And they wouldn't even let him stay at peace in the ground.

I read today the VII Chapter of Ezekiel. A terrible chapter. I wonder if Sylvia read that to you in Chaldon Church.

We all hope that you will soon be back again.
Very much love
Theodore
The Sacrifice is a beautiful poem.

JOHN COWPER POWYS

Letters to Gerard Casey, 1937–40

7 Cae Coed
Corwen
Merioneth
N. Wales
9 March 1937

Dear Gerard Casey
Your letter was of the deepest interest to me ... aye! but how I agree with every single word you say about the use of the Mass & the Confessional ... & what you write about the effect of the Crucifiction [*sic*] on your mind impresses me as few things have impressed me of late. Certainly our minds *now* are most singularly alike in their reactions — though Heaven! how you have *jumped over the years*, that I should resemble you so at 64 & you only 19!

I can't get over the extraordinary resemblance of our ways of thinking & feeling.

Your praying to the Moon & to that Stone & yet getting that ecstasy from the Mass! It certainly does prove (what I've had an inkling of before) that if a man has the independence & detachment & the *basic power of scepticism* that saves him from any morbid terror of obedience to supernatural authority, no education (for our sense of awe and wonder & reverence and imaginative grasping of the magic of symbols) can equal that of the Roman Church.

Where that Church does harm is where a soul lacks a certain abysmal scepticism & independence that save it from being totally enslaved & terrified by a diseased conscience into masochistic submission.

I was profoundly *shocked* by the tone of a speech of T. S. Eliot over the Wireless entitled the "Message of the Church".

The whole thing was so horridly scared and crushed & frightened and *negative* — "Let me think of *death* & my *destination* — let the Church instruct me what is *Wrong*"! Such was this Anglican Poet's tone! And with it such a sense of fussy, crushed *unhappiness*! I turned with relief to the exultations & wild half-crazy joys (& even boastings) of St Paul's epistles! and all that St Paul talks of as the "Liberty of Christ" and all his extravagant & *super-positive* definitions of "agapé".

I quite clearly see from what you say that it would be totally impossible for you to even think of becoming a monk.

I can see too — with your nervous imagination — that it would be simply *suicidal* to contemplate being an attendant in an Asylum. There remain therefore (when that Civil Service Exam is over) — but of course *that* may decide your future splendidly if you pass — those two other things ... to go into an office ... or a training college to be a teacher.

Well we'll wait to ponder properly on those alternatives till you know the result of this Exam. What would it exactly lead to if you *did* pass? What sort of a job would it mean? And would there be yet more Exams? But I confess at the first thinking of it that to go into an office would *commit you less* and be a more *tentative* & *experimental* thing and a thing that could be taken more lightly than the training college for teachers. But of course such a college would mean I suppose that your people would be keeping you still & you'd be spared money-worries — but *on the other hand* oh I think a teacher's life is so terribly narrowing & so terribly exacting & if you are not popular with masters and pupils so nerve-shaking too!

Awful as most offices are, I confess it seems to me the sort of thing that, if you were propitiatory enough & hard-working enough, would enable you *to keep your soul to yourself*; & the *off-hours* & *off-days* you'd also have to *yourself*, much more than in a training college for teachers — certainly much more than *to be* a teacher!

Well we'll see what comes of your Exam. I wonder what *kind* of Office it would be? There must be great differences! Well! enough for now ... but oh dear! I do hope you'll be befriended by chance & fate and by the little & the greater Powers too! I do feel so interested in

your destiny now I begin to follow the way your mind works more clearly!
yrs most sincerely J. C. Powys

16 September 1937

Dear Gerard Casey

I think I'll send you — when my American lady has tied them up, for I'm no hand at parcels — "Wolf Solent" & "The Meaning of Culture". But far more important than books is this terrific question of your future.

I've always been a terrible Shirker of Responsibility where Youth is concerned; especially in practical decisions which I always shrink from ... but it does seem to me that you are too young to plunge straight off into a life of such risky devotion as the Asylum work. 'Twould be like becoming a Monk *without a Novitiate* & plunging at once into a leper-colony!

I think it would be very wrong for anyone to encourage you to do so drastic a thing when your whole nature is undeveloped & you've only begun to know yourself.

I do indeed fully understand your longing for some hard ill-paid job without any worldly prospects — but nothing will ever make you worldly or ambitious — *that* at least is sure — and whatever you do & wherever you go you'll always have this longing for life on the simplest barest & most elemental terms with something in it, I'll put it modestly, of the category of a "mystic-saint" Novitiate.

But this Asylum idea would be to risk your own reason & how far a young person is justified in doing that I can't tell. I doubt it. Your gifts undoubtedly — of this I am quite sure — will lead in the end to your becoming a writer — whatever you do now to earn your living — *that*, I feel sure, will be your *destined* line — as Milton would say — as ever "in the great Taskmaster's eye".

But the daily contact with the insane — I tell you I've seen it — is only safe for unsensitive unimaginative people who do treat the patients as "jokes" — but you must remember this — as long as they are not cruelly treated physically (& these "jokers" aren't necessarily *physically* cruel to them — only *unsensitive*) mad people live in a world entirely of their own — their madness separates them from even the most sympathetic understanding — when you've got on your mind a *fixed idea* you forever talk to yourself in a void into which no outsider can enter — *& if he does* — as you would try to do — the mad person only uses you as a sounding board for his *fixed idea* and only turns your sympathy into so much more fuel for his phoenix flame. It's the neurotics who are not in an asylum & who are unhappy in the world that can be helped by imaginative sympathy.

Into the fixed idea of a really mad person such as are in asylums your imagination would plunge only to go round & round in a circle forever sympathizing but not healing & all the while risking your own sanity.

I am astonished that with all your imaginative & intellectual literary gifts you have the power of doing such a thing as that air-craft engine work you speak of; but since as is evidently the case (or you couldn't contemplate it) it seems as if that Bristol job would be as good and in many ways better than most ordinary jobs — *for a time*.

It's all a matter of time. You want time for your self-knowledge — time for growing-up — time for thinking and reading — and for (always I hope) a little practice at writing which will be your real job if I'm not greatly mistaken, and as a writer though of course a knowledge of madness *has* its value, it's a very narrow & limited and *special* value — for it isn't the madness of mad people, but the madness of so-called "sane" people that is so important an aspect of a writer's subject & experience.

I doubt if you ought to let your conscience plunge you ere you have mentally & emotionally grown up into so extreme a form of devotion as that asylum would be.

I think our conscience has to be steered and restrained, as much as our vices, and *not restrained by reason either* (for reason is apt to be as ill-balanced & perilous as the conscience) but by that *instinct of life* in us which has behind it the natural and legitimate *sub-egoism* of the whole vital energy as it secretly feels its way forward.

I think the saints themselves had forever to be keeping their consciences under control but not exactly under the control of reason but of that indescribable unseen urge of the whole nature which turns like a plant to the soil & the light that suit it, avoiding this or that danger.

The conscience is a dangerous thing. Much less dangerous is that *aesthetic element* in our longing for an unworldly life on the lowest terms; but this too has its proud & haughty dangers which are much more outward & much more to do with our life-illusion — or how we see ourselves — on superficial outward & external grounds of the outward way we live.

Well my dear Gerard it would be contrary to my deep instinctive dodging of practical responsibility in youthful lives — I've dodged it in the case of my own son and I am now *oh so glad I have*! — for me to advise you in any very positive way — but I do feel I'm safe in saying, gain time, gain time, gain time & allow your own *slow developing* spiritual & intellectual & moral destiny — the slow quiet secret underway of the Gods — to develop itself in free scope — un-limited & uncramped by any devoted drastic plunge wherever you are pushed by that curious self-lacerating vein in our conscience which we do not *know* for certain to be our real self or to be the real will of the gods.

Well I must stop thinking aloud — as time goes on, anyway, whatever you do, the secret urge of your essential nature will find somehow your real destiny. Yes this *is* an interesting letter of "Colophon". Do you want it back? I expect so.

Well you shall have the two books in a day or two.

Good luck anyway!

yr friend J.C.P.

16 November 1937

Dear Gerard

What an exciting letter! But O dear! I hope your cold & cough has gone by now ... how awful if you started trouble in your lungs by that visit to Glastonbury.

Do for the Lord's sake, lad, take care not to stand about & sit in buses when you are soaked thro'. I pray that your good Mrs Cox is a maternal sort of person & keeps an eye on you whether you like it or not ...

Well I do hope you will find another Job.

This morn I've just received *Somerset Essays* by Llewelyn & I like it even better than *Dorset Essays* — What a lovely old chap St Aldhelm (pronounced he says "Yaldhelm") was!

With all our Celtic & Latin tendencies we must I think allow that for a certain kind of simple sturdy goodness these old Saxons (King Alfred included) were as engaging and winning characters as ever have appeared. So thought evidently Asser the Welshman who left St David's to live with Alfred & wrote his life. A Celtic pen dealing with English characters!

What an experience that time in the Glastonbury Church! To my recollection St Joseph's tomb wasn't by the Pulpit but *on the left side* of the Church as you go in — But do go again — but wait till you are *certain* of a perfectly fine day if that's possible there, but it *ought* to be ...

> Where falls not any rain nor any snow —
> Nor ever wind blows loudly, — but it lies —
> Fair with orchard-lawns and bowery hollows crowned
>   with summer seas
> Where I will heal me of my grievous wound

Oh I am so glad you've got Rhys' King Arthur. I don't know any book that has so initiated me into the mythology of Wales and of my Welsh ancestors. I have read it again & again, and again.

I did so greatly enjoy your account of your own private collection of books and it profoundly delights me that you have a good Rabelais. Mine is the edition published by Simon & Schuster (my American publishers) Urquhart & Motteaux's translation but *without* those Doré illustrations of the Chatto & Windus edition here.

That account of the effect of *Mr Weston's Good Wine* & all the palliatives you tried one after another till nothing but the spirit of The Holy Bottle saved you was thrilling to me. Yes there's *a glow beyond that of the Sun itself* in Rabelais as if it were that *intellectual light* (beyond all understanding or reason) which was the first act of creation. *Let there be Light*!

Yes Theodore has ever been the wonder & respect & awe of the rest of us.

Last summer I had the glory of walking with him — & you may depend how I listened & followed each word! — every day from One to Three thirty including his pot of herbs or to be exact his cold tomato & a bit of cheese — but *this* summer I shan't be able to afford such a stay for lodgings in English villages in the summer are terribly expensive.

Aye! but how I've kept you waiting all this while for one word on *your poem* ... I am profoundly interested in it and so is my friend (Miss Phyllis Playter) from whom I took Christie — you must go on just on these lines for awhile!

This poem does not aim at the poetic — has absolutely no personal pose — none of that incorrigible narcissism & self-consciousness of the "little admirable forlorn too sensitive me!" type. Its sole object is to describe as *accurately* as possible your *exact feelings*. It is a poem of psychic-sensuous experience — with a Catholic-Pagan background — as in the poetry of the Jesuit Hopkins. I like the way you have rounded it off too with those 3 resembling lines. Yes you are *absolutely* right my friend in thinking well of these verses.

Well I must get to work ... but oh dear! The publisher wants (but it's my noble *Cassell* of La Belle Sauvage Ludgate Hill who has now accepted for this book of essays that eccentric & interminable one on St Paul so I feel too grateful not to obey) — wants, I say, Essays on Hardy & Dickens too — so I've got to do these & turn from Glyndwr just when I've got to him — his wone self!

Well! Well ... But *with* the St Paul this "Pleasures of Reading" will be an *enormous* volume & appear in Early Spring.

So good luck whatever form it may take!
  your friend
    J.C.P.

12 March 1938

Gerard my friend! but you ought *not* to have spent so much of your Artillery Captain's Pay on your aged Uncle in Corwen.

However! I'm not one to look a Gift horse in the Mouth tho' this is clearly worth a guinea for which my young sir you could have entertained and *taken for a walk into your sunset* the loveliest Baker's, or even Dean's *daughter* (nay! your own Colonel's daughter) — in Cheltenham!

But, Casey, I am simply thrilled to have this book [Thomas Aquinas' *Summa contra Gentiles*]. It's a scandal that you should have given it to me when I was still — miser that I am! — saving up to send you the "Philosophy of Solitude" by a scurvy lollard.

But there it is. I am too happy to possess this book to make any bones about mulcting an over-generous lad of his rarely snatched pleasures so as to get it! Oh I do like it so! P. & I have been already reading it & she says I'll still read it in my old age & then (later) she'll read it still in hers!

We opened & read in those pages about the *cause of evil* — aye! but how it stirs up the mind — & what a brain by God! the old sod must have had ... making our modern philosophers look pretty thin & amateur at thik little job!

But merely to *see* the *cover* of these 3 great volumes with Publisher to the Holy See & trans. by those Dominicans — I shall think of it on many walks with that sideway dart of exquisite happiness that comes when you contrast a plant or root or pool or stump with the idea of an exciting Book at home & *all life* seems wondrous!

Gerard my friend you oughtn't to have done it: but I *cannot help* being glad you did! It has put me into radiant spirits just to have possess own & look on this book — the 1st *real* mediaeval philosophical book I've ever possessed!

We decided after reading your splendid description of that perfect day that you had a feeling for & an eye for *colour* that'll be one of your assets as a writer. In some ways it is rarer than a sense of form. It *was* a fine letter Gerard!

Well — Heaven reward you & forgive me but I am damned delighted with this book!

Bless you with the best from P.
     yr friend J.C.P.

Chydyok
East Chaldon
Dorchester
11 July 1938

My dear Gerard

Alas! it's impossible! My brother William's mother in law has turned up to stay with him and his wife for a week at "Down Barn" & they have to drive her on the only possible free day all the way to the Quantocks to see some relative. Tomorrow they are having a birthday party for Will's little son Charley who is two. Aye! but he's a darling and this will be a tea-party — so *that* day's gone. Then on Wednesday both my brother Littleton & our old friend Louis Wilkinson (Marlow) are coming here to tea & on Thursday Phyllis & I will be at my brother's (Theodore's) saying goodbye to him. *That* is the evening we might have got Will to take us to Chesil & to you (or to you & Chesil) but alas that day he has to go to the Quantocks — and then early on Friday we set off to reach Corwen in *one day*. On the way down here we stopped the night at Abingdon this side of Oxford but on Friday he wants to do the whole journey in a day. So there it is! It can't be helped. Gerard my friend 'tis a disappointment to me — a double one for I had made up my mind that this time I would see Chesil for I have a peculiar devotion to Chesil Beach above all other natural phenomena. For two years I used never to let a day pass without imagining myself on Chesil & holding up a stone to the light *to see thro' it* — first a wet one & then a dry one! I have a curious cult, like yours for that stone at home you wrote about, for Chesil Beach.

What a thing to be *buried* on Chesil Beach!

Gerard I don't like your having destroyed that MS of yours! I am sure it is good to *keep* what you write even if you give it up and go on to write other things having learnt new methods — for these old things will be one day of such great interest to others as well as to yourself marking the *stages* of your development. Don't 'ee destroy any more I beg & implore!

    your friend

               J.C.P.

Miss Phyllis sends her love.

PS Theodore is in a parlous state; but thanks be he can sleep at night. This having the fear of another stroke hanging over him is a bad bad thing & he has always a dull hurting at the back of his head. O deary I! It is not a joke. Llewelyn is better in Switzerland but terribly indeed ghastly *thin* they say. Back at Corwen on Friday.

4 October 1938

Dear Gerard

Phyllis & I are so pleased that you think you really (if Capt Baker approves) will come & be our guest *yug Ughorwen* for *some days* not too short! What I would myself suggest during your visit is that — only I'd have boldly to tell Will this when the moment comes! — you should hear if you can get it out of him, as one Irishman of Catholic upbringing to another!, what exactly *were* young Gerald Hanley's difficulties with my brother out there. He is now aiming at starting as a writer & meanwhile is living with his brother James for whom Phyllis & I have deep affection & respect.

Gerald is a charming boy & a brave one but he is a born Intellectual and a born Artist and politically a Pacifist & a Red.

All I can get out of my brother — for both he and Gerald are very reserved as to the difficulties that did occur between them — is that Gerald is a fascinating lad but essentially more interested in writing and painting and political theories *than in the actual work of a Ranch* like that huge place out there — and Gerald likes expressing his ideas.

Now my brother Will as you'll quickly see is like one of those *Conrad characters*; if you've read Conrad? — like an older Lord Jim or Captain Lingard; regarding "the boys", as they call the Natives, *and* his flocks & herds, *and* the wild animals, as all elements in a miniature (& not so *very* miniature either) Kingdom, of which he is the just, silent, formidable and ubiquitous King!

Now there's no doubt that Kenya offers great scope for anyone who has a touch of silent formidable statesmanship but you need a touch of Fortinbras in you as well as Hamlet!

An Intellectual with the conscience and ideals of a Red and a Pacifist and a preference for reading and drawing *above* the work of the ranch even if such a one is kindly and willing is not exactly the thing.

Now you are naturally silent averse rather than keen to express your deepest feelings. *Your* conscience which I know is very sensitive is like my own a personal not a political conscience.

I fancy too that Will's somewhat inarticulate formidableness is not the sort of thing that would offend you any more than the massive arbitrariness of some powerful un-self-indulgent Prior who at heart was simple & honourable, just and magnanimous would rouse in you quick feelings of revolt if you were a young monk.

Will has come to have the look of some African Native Chief whose remote ancestor was brought up among Lions!

There is absolutely nothing about him of that crude & vulgar brutality of so many(?) white Settlers.

He has made up his mind never really to leave Africa. But he does like his own ways as we say!

Well! You will see. 'Tis a straw thrown on the stream of chance & fate to get you here — but you'll need all your *instinct* both about yourself and about Will — if anything serious is to come of it.

As to my secret confidence in your eventually writing (if you're not killed by a lion like my nephew who was a bit *too* daring) this is not affected in the least by the thought of an African epoch for you; for like my own family I can see you are one who develops very slowly.

It *might* be that you & Will will take to one another instinctively & understand one another instinctively. You are both dark horses both silent both with a touch of the Quixotic and both a different type from the average expressive artist of the "Intelligentsia"!

As long as in the very depth of your *personal conscience* you "got Will's number" & on the whole *approved* of his methods of governing his miniature Kingdom and felt an instinctive confidence in the man I don't fancy there would arise many difficulties.

But of course no one really can sound the effect of one personality upon another.

I've just read this letter to Will's wife Elizabeth & she is delighted with my picture of him!

The only thing she quarrels fiercely with — so I've put a *query* there!

— was when I said *so many* of the White Settlers were vulgar & brutal! This I got from the books of Brother "Lulu"! — but Elizabeth points out that it was in quite a different part of Kenya where "Lulu" was & of course we know that Brother Llewelyn *has* his quick prejudices, tho' of a "social" rather perhaps than a "political" kind!

But listen — Will will not be here till *Wednesday the 12th* and he will be here till *Monday the 17th* so I suggest — with the approval of his wife who will not be here then — that you come & stay in Corwen as our guest from *Wednesday the 12th till Monday 17th*. You'll then be able to have some walks & talks alone with Will.

With love from P. & me —
your old Meddler with Fate! J.C.P.

25 October 1938

Dear Gerard

Aye! what an interesting letter. First that you really are going to sail before Xmas ... & that your family & the Captain are willing & that none will stand in your way. Oh I do pray everything will go well with you, my friend: & that it really *will* be for the best.

Certainly, Gerard, I'll be pleased & proud to accept this invitation to lecture & I know I'd be happy either under the roof of the Father or of the Poet. I leave that entirely to you & to them.

All I'll need will be Tea and a bit of *stale* white bread — & maybe a raw egg & a bottle of cold milk. I am delighted with that generous fee of Ten Guineas. The queer thing is that your letter came just when I was getting a bit panicky about my finances & when I had been pondering & wondering how I *could* turn a penny by lecturing again; but I couldn't think how to get a start. But this idea of yours and of your two poets *may* prove just the start I need. You see I have to have that particular American "Enema" every 3rd day & I have to be here for that for I cannot manage it myself but this leaves me entirely free *for 2 whole days and one night*.

So that if your poets had friends of our type of mind if I may so speak in many parts of Wales this Bridgend lecture might really be a start for me at lecturing in Wales. And oh what a relief to shake off the panicky sensation I get sometimes; being so entirely dependent on my pen, and yet totally out of my element in short articles or any kind of "writing for the papers".

I'd keep to that fixed fee of Ten Guineas — pay my own railway journey but I expect to be *put up* — just like an old-fashioned "pregethwr" — save that they never got ten guineas & I daresay not always one!

Well, Gerard my friend you'll certainly have played "Tit-for-Tat" with *my* meddling with fate if this *does* lead to a permanent revival of my old lecturing & in the land of my Fathers too!

Why I could go to Cardiff, Carmarthen, Aberystwyth — all sorts of places if your two poets were pleased with my methods of lecturing & told their friends.

Perhaps you'd better whisper to all concerned that I have *no teeth* — & not even for the pleasure of lecturing to Welshmen ever intend to get any more.

But I swear to you this will make no difference to the carrying power of my voice — for I tried it out in Wrexham in my Anti-Vivisection talk there — & *very little* to my articulation of words.

It's when I laugh that it shows worst — you know? — like a Gargoyle Spout! but I never laugh when I'm lecturing.

Aye, Gerard; I may be silly to be made in such high spirits by this suggestion of yours — but I think — if I got one lecture a fortnight on a rough average or even one every 3 weeks all the year round and at this generous fee started by you & your friends, why my railway trips at most would only take 30/- a time out of that sum & if I was put up & could avoid Inns I'd be free of this uncomfortable panicky feeling that I ought to struggle laboriously again (for the 50th time) to "write for the papers". I could settle down happily then & write my long books (like the "Owen") to my heart's content & fulfil all my obligations & not sponge on anybody!

Well, Gerard, as I say, I am probably too elated & too much like Mr Micawber in my high spirits but it was this magnanimity of these ten guineas of your poets set me off — *that* & my pure delight at the idea of lecturing to Welsh people!

"Miss Phyllis" says — how nicely you said that, Gerard, it *did* please her so! — that I ought not to take ten guineas out of the pockets of *Welsh Miners* — the only "proletarians" in the whole world (as I *read in my weekly bulletin from the C.N.T. — Anarchists of Barcelona*) who have really & truly given the help *that counted*.

Phyllis suggests that if it were possible (so that I could get back here without more than one night away) some of your friends in the neighbourhood might arrange for me to give a *free lecture* (in addition to the one I'm so royally paid for) to any group of un-employed.

Think over this Gerard — for the one thing that never hurts or tires me is lecturing. Well, there it is! It *will* be so interesting to me to meet both the Fathers & both the Poets and it goes without saying your own family — So Long!

yrs as ever John C. Powys

[*On the back of the envelope:*] Any day towards the end of November would suit me — tho' if it were possible I'd prefer — but this isn't more than a *preference*, to be at home on the 29th of Nov. I think I would choose the 1st Four Books of the Mabinogion, *Pedeir Keinc y Mabinogi*

19 December 1938

My dear Gerard

Well I suppose this is my final letter before you're off — & you know all I wish for you & pray for you so I will not say much of that or indeed more at all. If it was Romeo who first said "Partings are such sweet sorrow" he certainly was a fool or the most *detached aesthete* ever born; and he wasn't the latter for he plunged into Juliet's tomb & died — so if he was the one — he *was* just a fool for I think Partings are *awful* and the worst are when a person goes by ship & you see the ship slowly leaving the dock! I think you said that there would be *no one* you knew on the dock to see you off. You may thank heaven for that. Tho' it's worse for the one on the dock! In fact, I think in partings it's always worse for those left behind than for those going. I am so glad you've got that perfect edition of Pascal far the best I've ever seen. I am beginning to make enquiries of a tentative nature but they very likely will come to nothing as to the possibilities of arranging some excuse in the form of a reading or lecture or something to induce Huw Menai to come up here during the Winter for a couple of nights. I cannot wait for Phyllis to see him all the months till the summer when he said he would come to the Denbigh Eisteddfod. I was so thrilled by a notice Mr Roberts — *what* a kind man he is *and* a learned to boot! — sent me that said my lecture was like the utterance of the *Head of Bran*! God! for what might be called the *Quintessential Tact of Praise* I have a notion none can beat the South Welsh — eh? Think of a Newspaper Report, God! when I think of certain papers in Alabama — "Mr Cow-pat Loves Niggers" — & so forth ... and down there with you 'tis *"the Entertainment of the Noble Head"*.

It is a Black Frost here and colder than Phyllis & I have known it since we came to Britain 5 years ago. Our Telegraph says the coldest Britain's known for *Ten Years*! These poor dear American ladies! — 'tis awful for them — so *thin* they are, and almost crying from cold & the miss of hot pipes. But the Very Old enjoys it: having been born at Poughkeepsie on Hudson "Up-State" New York!

I *cannot stand* what St Paul says about submitting to the authorities. I *cannot* understand his writing such outrageous lies (*Romans 13*). Was it because he was writing to Jews in Rome who were more critical of the Officials than they need have been? I seem to *miss* that black under-channel of tremulous exaggeration with holy malice & holy madness that I like in him. If it had been written to me I should have said — This is an interpolation. This is not the Paul I know.

Forgive my hand — The Old & I — & P. a minute ago are crouching over our little fire & the very *ink* seems frozen. The *pale gold* sun has now gone down. I have to carry parcels for P. to post. I can't bear for her to go out.

Don't 'ee put aside your Journal to write letters — just send P. & me picture postcards en route so we can follow you — but we shall follow you any way!

Bless you Gerard & so says P. P. sends her love.

Please give my most sincere respects to your parents & a kiss to little Anne.

yr J.

6 May 1939

My dear Gerard

I enclose the photos Phyllis took with her old Camera given her by her Father in America 30 years ago & bought for 16 dollars.

I say all this because Huw Menai wrote — aye! Gerard, but I do so greatly enjoy his correspondence — that his daughters told him as camera experts that these were very good pictures — he added that they accused him of *posing* in the one where he's looking far away.

I reckon he has not much chance of growing *conceited* in the heart of his lively and irrepressible family.

Phyllis was as profoundly impressed with the man as you & I are. He certainly is an astonishing one.

I say he's like the original *Sea Serpent* of the Norse Mythology who embraced some Druidess of Mon in the old days — all the caricatures I've been sending him — these pictures don't show the shape of his head which as you will recall is like *this* — he says are more like him than any picture ever taken tho' I do think that one which Mr Ben Roberts has in his sitting-room — did you see it? *sure* you did! — isn't at all unlike him, but it's like this his head if you exaggerate it ever so little ... [drawing] whereas my own head is like this — [another drawing] all the difference in the world.

Our letters to each other are largely occupied with generalizations about the significance of the different shapes of each other's *skulls*. It does please me to try & catch this difference — his head all going *up & away* mine all going back & in! [more drawings]

But of course it's much easier to draw a parrot or a vulture than it is to draw a whale or leviathan! My difficulty is with his nose! I'm so used to the parrot or vulture curve of my own — His nose is *retroussé* but *massively* so *not* pointedly as I've got it above & all those leathery indentations round his chin are terribly hard to draw. His nose is really like the Snout of a Sea Monster! & what could be harder than that to draw?

I keep writing to old Will to cheer him up — I've not of course heard yet the result of the X-rays and whether he'll be allowed to dodge another operation or not. O *deary I*!

Oh dear I can't do it! [two more drawings: see opposite] I bet *you*

& most certainly *Will* would hit if off better. But this last one of Huw shows improvement!

Yes Phyllis felt just exactly the same as I did about him ... & she liked particularly too — indeed who could help it? Mr Ben Roberts ... aye! but he's *a good man* if ever there was!

Do you know my sister in New York sent me five dollars as a birthday present and all this time I've been wondering what Book to get *for a Pound* & a bit over.

I had thought of Taliessin Llywarch Hen Aneurin & a big printed Welsh Family Bible which I saw in Wrexham.

But now at last I've got the very thing for a shilling or two over what my sister gave me.

The Myfyrian Archaeology of Wales published *1801* on Jan 1st. by

Drawings by John Cowper Powys of his own head and Huw Menai's

Owen Jones   *"Myfyr"*
Edward Williams   *Iolo Morganwg*
& William Owen Pughe *Idrison*
It's a huge heavy book as big as a family bible & it's got *all* in it! It's got Taliessin Llywarch Hēn Aneurin and everything else and a little over!
It has as a motto
                Ammau Pob Anwybol
"Everything unknown is doubted"
and it says this is an *Adage*!

It has notes on the "Gododin" which has some *Brythonic* words in it, ere Cymreig started as 'tis today: this is Prof Williams of Bangor says in his recent book authentic 6th Century poetry & authentically by *Aneurin* who thus is the one whose claim can be established by checked up proof as Sixth Century & the earliest Welsh poet — but personally I have a furtive preference still, me wone self, for *Taliessin* whose poetry reminds [sic] meso extraordinary & in *every* way even to his fluid, oceanic, swampy yet airy, *cosmic* boasting!

But these three Welshmen are the ones! God! or Duw! sounding like "Dieu"! and also like what the sea-serpent would exclaim if it found its head in the air! as Huw Menai always says Duw! what men these 3 are. This book is an Enclypodedia of all that you & I Gerard my friend are most drawn to in Literature! I see I've spelt Encyclopedia rather oddly but never mind. This book is a wonder and a Treasure-trove. It's like that volume of *Michael Scott* in Sir Walter's Lay of the Last Minstrel. Michael Scott the Wizard who in Dante's hell is referred to as having such slender flanks! It's like a folio I've *invented* ere I saw this one to place in Owen Glyndwr's hands! Yes Huw's skull goes out & away & John's goes back & in. Well, *bless you*! and so says my Phyllis who is as ever *in garden*.
                          yr J.C.P.

                                       7 January 1940
My dear Gerard
How be? I long to get a line from you — but don't 'ee *hurry ... wait*

till a *good moment* of leisure over the fire comes & pen & paper &*fancy too* all convenient, and contiguous.

It was I can't tell you what a relief & comfort to my mind for I regard you as a Rock of Defence to hear that you *hadn't* been called up yet ... God! I pray — & it is a selfish *Tribal wish*, as well as fear of accidents for your wone self! — that you'll never be called up!

Do you know what I did over the end of my Owen? I had decided to finish it in the chapter-house of Valle Crucis *where I wrote the first page*, but these journeys in the Black Out in these short days are not easy — well! they're not *really* or *exactly* hard — but for your aged friend who next October will be within 2 years of the start of his 70th year they *are* a mighty effort.

And I wanted the end of Owen to be a *thrilling* effort not a laborious & painful one — so I decided to alter my determination, and give Owen a heathen in place of a Xtian send off — whether this will turn out more lucky or less lucky remains to be seen! It is in harmony with the Mabinogion tho' less so with Morte D'Arthur!

So I set out on *Xmas Eve morning* leaving a note for Phyllis not to worry if I were late for breakfast and telling our Betty (who is like a daughter to Phyllis and me and guards us from all ill, as she also does all her own family — our Ladies at No 5 — *and* the turbulent audience of kids at Corwen *Cinema*! where save for the *operator* she's often left in sole authority & control & has to decide what to do if the lights go out or anything goes wrong!) and I started at ten minutes to nine — 8.50 am — and walked with terrific speed with pen & paper in pocket & also a *rough copy* of my end of Owen which ends with a flight of Crows: *no*! a couple of aged Ravens croaking and croaking as it seems to Meredith ("Maredudd" in Welsh) *Meredith ap Owen Glyn Dŵr* his only surviving son — croaking I say as it seems to Meredith as he leaves his father's body to be burnt on the top of our Corwen "*Mynydd-y-Gaer*" who is wondering if his Father's spirit survives his burnt flesh and *sprinkled ashes* — the Welsh words "Nis Gwn! Nis Gwn! Nis Gwn! Nis Gwn! — I don't know! I don't know! I don't know! I don't know" and they vanish like dots in the sky eastward over the Berwyns still croaking "*nis goon!*" — *towards Mathrafal*! And so I make "*Mathrafal*" the last word!

Well I got to the foot of *the Gaer* in just half an hour, namely at
9.20 — and then I took my time — and it took me just half an hour
climbing up it, and then I settled myself in one of those hollow places
among the stones and just as I'd written about the ravens & the words
"towards Mathrafal" a red & great finger of the rising sun *behind me*
came over my shoulder & made a bit of *quartz* (you know that *white
stuff* in our slate-rock here?) blaze like a huge Diamond! So any way
that was a good omen: & could not have happened in Valle Crucis
Chapter House because I should have been *there* by candle-light about
4 when twilight begins!

'Tis an ill wind that blows *nobody* any good. For a tramp-friend of
mine whose stoical self-respect & neatness & cleanness *I've marvelled
at for 3 years on this highway en route to the Casual Ward* — has been
accepted as a *Welsh Fusilier* for Home Defence (*aged 53*) and has just
spent his Xmas leave in Corwen & we have been going walks together
and his satisfaction in every single detail of his job is pretty to see!

Phyllis has taught him how to make American coffee which will be
a change from the tea they make so much of.

I have never in my life seen any middle-aged man so profoundly
satisfied and thrilled. He has always *wanted order, routine,* and *to be as
clean as possible*. These were *manias* with him (as I saw on the road) and
now he is content. He is like Corporal Trim in *Tristram Shandy*. I'm
sure he'll be a corporal soon!

Oh I forgot to say I got home at *twenty minutes to ten* ten minutes
under two hours & Phyllis with her bad cold was late poor little mite &
never knew I'd gone at all!

Bless you Gerard.

With love from us both —

yrs as ever J.C.P.

Don't forget to keep a full Diary!

26 April 1940

My dear Gerard

What a wondrous letter you did write to me *March 6th* about the
Prelude and about the *Prophetic Books* ... Yes I agree with you entirely.
Blake & Wordsworth absorb my interest the furthest too, for they

both seem to have *longer vistas* down which you can go than any other poets. I can see that row of *Berdyaev books* you gave me here on the second shelf on which at this very second over my head the setting sun strikes! Nothing is nicer in a shelf than to see the sun horizontally falling with that dark reddish gold of its final descent and making the books look like leaves, cut in metals, unknown and precious.

I had great happiness in Bridgend in my lecture on Shakespeare. I went on for 2 hours. My chairman was Mr Eliot Croskay(?) Williams no! I've got his second name wrong but he was the best chairman that ever I have had for he left me his chair to act Macbeth and Hamlet and King Lear with and he moved the tumbler of water that they give *speakers* but which *Actors* do not want and he moved the flowers and he crouched on a stool at the extreme side of the platform so that I could have full swing. Mr Roberts & old Huw Menai talked very affectionately of you & afterwards said there was only one miss in our pleasure namely that you weren't there. There was another miss too; for Phyllis had to go to London to her American Dentist so she wasn't there either. This was a disappointment to me but couldn't be helped. She couldn't do both & she *had* to go the dentist and I insisted she should go when I was away too!

But Mr Roberts drove Huw and me over to your home and by the *very wise & sensible* advice of Janie Roberts we timed our visit so that it would be when your father would be there — and there he was!

But it was very piteous to see your dear mother in bed with a broken tendon of the ankle — waiting to have it put ere long in plaster — but she was I think *rested* by being forced to be in bed & I thought she looked *even younger* than the last time I saw her ... but the fact of her being in bed and our having to talk to her upstairs prevented me from the extra pleasure of making friends with the younger ones tho' I caught glimpses of them but I would have liked to have had more than glimpses! But it couldn't be helped with your mother in bed and your father having such a short free time and us three visitors filling up the bedroom.

Your father showed them some exam-papers just delivered — I mean the *questions* — which were of great interest to both Ben & Huw both of whom have children of the school age. Your father bought tickets for the lecture but if he was there he had to leave for some bus and I didn't expect to see him because it's always such a hullabaloo after a lecture. But I was glad to see him even for that brief time. Then this most thoughtful and kind of all men I've ever met — namely Ben Roberts — took me out to Huw's home and I had a lovely time with his family and they gave us tea. Aye! Gerard, but I was impressed with the stark grim grand beauty of the Rhondda!

I don't remember whether I've told you all this before but I don't think so but even if I have I wouldn't mind myself hearing twice about anyone going to my home. Nor can I remember if I've told you about my Owen being refused by Cassell's as they are not publishing books so long in this trouble. But my agent is going to try Cape with "Owen" & after Cape *Heineman* ...

The *Best news* I have for you Gerard is about Dorothy M. Richardson who has just yesterday written to Phyllis & me to say that by the devoted activity of our old enemy *Richard Church* (with whom you had that argument in that paper — if you recall?) who being formerly in the Civil Service knew how to go to work and got God knows who to persuade the Prime Minister. Anyway she has her *Civil List Pension* (like our brother Theodore) and it'll make *all* the difference to her and that enchanting Elfish Being she married — the best of all Illustrators of Rabelais and *therefore* unprinted and unpublished — *Alan Odle*. I shall always be very friendly *in future* both to Mr Church and to Mr Chamberlain. For I have very strongly with all my vices that virtue which was Shakespeare's favourite — "looks so" — namely Gratitude.

Phyllis & I woke up this morning with that lovely feeling that something nice had happened — & then remembered *Dorothy Richardson has a Pension for Life*!

In New York (Touch Wood! DV!) there seems hope that they will take "Owen" — O I pray they won't cut *it him her or them* whatever it may be thinking of a multiverse of monks and abbots and kings and princes and Piers Plowmans and friars and executioners and demons and gods and saints and sorcerers and warlocks and Norman Knights and Welsh Bards.

But they've just cabled me a huge long cable every sentence ending with the written word "stop", as Americans do cable — "stop" meaning *full-stop*! telling me to compose an article of 3 or 4 pages printed as Preface to Owen giving a Summary or Epitome or Synopsis of the History of the Whole Known World from *1390–1416*.

But I think it's a good sign — D.V. Touch Wood — that they cabled like that and wanted me to rush this Preface off. And at this very moment there lies on "Aunt Etta's table" a huge parcel of books from the *London Library* to which I sent a *S.O.S.* five times longer than the New York Cable describing exactly what I had to do — seeing this huge parcel I really am impressed by their care & concern! for I gave them a job. But after all this sort of thing is exactly what Old Carlyle founded this Library for. They won't send books abroad or out of the country just now; but anywhere in Great Britain in any number if you make a list. My Preface will have to be about 2 Popes Rome & Avignon and 2 Western Emperors *one a Czech* and one Eastern Emperor not to speak of Bazajet (I can't spell it), the Turk; and *Tamburlaine the Great*, the *Tartar*!

Love to all. I hope those lions have been conquered!

yr old friend John

P. is over next door or would add a message I know.

John Cowper Powys

PHYLLIS PLAYTER

'On the Departure of Powys for England'

When Spring descending on these fields again
Shall star the meadow the white horses know
With the Elysian flower the bloodroots grow
He will be gone. He will not be here then.

The night will come — the first the horses stay.
They will not wake him with a muffled whinney
When adder-tongues and fern fronds in the Spinney
Unfold themselves to yet another May.

Longer or shorter may the Red-Fin tarry
Early or late the shallow brook go dry
But he who would not suffer them to die
No more of them to deeper pools will carry.

When the Sweet Apple ripens on the boughs
And the Fall rains flood the Prometheus Stone
He will not know. The Golden Fruit alone
Will shaken be and eaten be by Cows.

The newts are gone and the Newt-Pond no more
Will hold the likeness that it once could seize
Nor even the bright eyes of Chickadees
Discern the form that they are looking for.

Ice will transfix the brook to greenish crystal
And pods of weeds will covered be by snow —
But whose feet take the way he used to go?
Whose forehead brush the mantled Stone of Fal?

'ON THE DEPARTURE OF POWYS FOR ENGLAND'

When from their winter nest comes high and clear
Above the sloping field the hawks' wild battle-cry
No answering echo wakes in earth or sky
He will be gone — He will be far from here.

This poem, 'written by the T.T. in the metre of Mr Masters, May 1934', was copied by J. C. Powys on the fly-leaf of his diary for 1934. For E. L. Masters's poem "On the Departure of Powys for England" see p. 196.

American born Miss Phyllis Playter, 1, Waterloo Cottages, Blaenau Ffestiniog died last week. Miss Playter was for many years housekeeper for author Cowper Powis

Reset from The Cambrian News *of 9 April 1982*

CHARLES LOCK

Not the Lost Generation: John Cowper Powys and American Literature *

'You are all a lost generation', Gertrude Stein is reputed to have said to Ernest Hemingway, in Paris in the 1920s. By a curious inversion, that act of gratuitous labelling provided an identification, and a solution: American literature of the first half of the twentieth century had found its own identity among those who were lost. If the Atlantic were a mirror, we might wish that some English visitor to the States, coming across John Cowper Powys in New York, or Philadelphia, or Chicago, or Los Angeles, should have been prompted to remark: 'You are yourself alone a lost generation.' That never happened, of course, or, more crucially, was never reported to have happened, and John Cowper Powys's presence in America remains an obscure anomaly.

While Powys was flourishing in the States, even as his reputation was stifled, Hemingway and Scott Fitzgerald were, in Europe, creating modern American literature. Of the American writers who stayed in America, only Faulkner enjoys the same prestige. Powys, in America, even had the misfortune to know the wrong American writers, those who, after years of great celebrity and honour, would lose their reputations, and now be forgotten, like Edgar Lee Masters, or if still a name, like Theodore Dreiser, hardly read. Powys's literary friendships in America outline what is now truly a 'Lost Generation' in American literature.

Frequently in reading biographies of Dreiser, Masters, Edna St. Vincent Millay, e. e. cummings, one will come across references to

* *A review of* Elusive America: The Uncollected Essays of John Cowper Powys, *Volume One, edited, with an Introduction, by Paul Roberts (London: Cecil Woolf, 1994; 251 pp., £19.95).*

178

Powys, whose presence and status are promptly explained away as those of an English writer temporarily in America on a lecture-tour. For all his general prominence and celebrity in American culture in the first half of the twentieth century, Powys's particular connections have all been invalidated or cancelled. This may have something to do with the chauvinism in recent American cultural histories which tends to obscure and ignore the contribution of foreigners; an example of this, involving Powys, is the Chicago Little Theatre, largely omitted from recent accounts of the origins of American drama, as I noted in 'Maurice Browne and the Chicago Little Theatre'.[1]

Likewise, it could be shown that Powys's involvement in Margaret Anderson's *Little Review* (also based in Chicago), the journal in which excerpts from Joyce's *Ulysses* were first printed, has been neglected. In the early issues, from 1914, Powys's name is everywhere mentioned and honoured. In Margaret Anderson's editorial of March 1915, readers were told that John Cowper Powys was 'one of the main inspirations behind ... this magazine', and that he should be regarded as 'the LITTLE REVIEW's godfather'. Forty years ago one historian of the Chicago Renaissance, Bernard Duffey, acknowledged Powys's part: 'the Little Theatre ... brought to Chicago John Cooper [sic] Powys whose ideas became perhaps the single most important prop of the *Little Review*'.[2]

Duffey's account of forty years ago has now been 'superseded', and Powys's name is seldom mentioned. This realises the plan of Ezra Pound who in 1914, a few weeks after the appearance of the first issue of *Little Review*, had supported Wyndham Lewis in founding *Blast* in London. By 1917 *Blast* had folded, and the continuation of the War was not encouraging to cultural and literary innovation. In 1917, from London, Ezra Pound wrote to Margaret Anderson offering his services as 'Foreign Editor' of the *Little Review*. The offer being accepted, Pound devoted his energies to the elimination of Powys from the *Little Review*.

Pound's animosity had a background, if not a justification. Frances Gregg had been a close friend of Ezra Pound's in Philadelphia: together they had gone to hear a lecture by Powys in Philadelphia, probably in 1911. At that date Powys would have quite outshone

Pound in terms of cultural sophistication and cosmopolitanism, and Frances Gregg, who had been very close to Pound since about 1908, was much attracted to Powys. She introduced herself, with some of her poems, to Powys in January 1912. It was the beginning of a most fraught and tangled passionate relationship that lasted, with varying degrees of intensity, for ten years. Powys's fellow-lecturer Louis Wilkinson then met Frances Gregg soon afterwards, and he married her in April 1912. That marriage was a mere inconvenience in the relationship between Powys and Frances Gregg, and effectively served rather to ensure regular meetings than to separate them. As Powys's feelings for Frances remained undiminished, so did Ezra Pound's; she and Pound met again in London in the summer of 1912, and in 1913 Powys, in one of his many letters to Frances, attempted to explain his jealousy on her account:

> What a quaint thing jealousy is! The order of my jealousies is as follows —
> 1. James least of all –
> 2. Lulu –
> 3. Louis –
> 4. Ezra –
> in increasing seriousness.³

Frances Gregg was the focus of a rivalry that may seem merely amorous and private, but surely exemplifies in its main contestants, Powys and Pound, the possibilities and contradictions of literature in the twentieth century. In 1916 Louis Wilkinson had published *The Buffoon*, a *roman à clef* about himself, Powys ('Jack Welsh'), and Pound ('Raoul Root'). By 1918 Pound was still expostulating on the topic to Margaret Anderson:

> WHY!!! do you recall that better to be forgotten libellule of Wilkinson's????? Raoul Root INDEED. KHRRIST. Am I a pet pug to have blue ribbons curled in my tail?⁴

One is happy to record that by 1928 Powys could write, again to Frances, 'about the noble Ezra; of whom I have nowadays felt, in my lectures, I can say nothing but good'(*Jack and Frances*, 178). Alas, no such mellowing was to be seen on Pound's side, and the memoirist's and historian's line on the *Little Review*, and on American modernism in general, remains Ezra's version.

One might also adduce, as supplementary causes, the animosity towards Powys shown by Edmund Wilson, the most influential analyst and commentator on American literature of the mid-twentieth century; and the change in management in the late 1930s, at Simon & Schuster, the New York publishers who had taken on *Wolf Solent* in 1929, and remained devoted to Powys while he was living in America. After Powys's return to Britain they continued to act as his American publisher for the major works, until 1940, when they produced the elegant two-volume first edition of *Owen Glendower*. But then all the Powys titles were dropped from the Simon & Schuster list, except for the two most lucrative, *A Philosophy of Solitude* and *The Meaning of Culture*, respectively, by 1940, in their ninth and tenth editions.

In gathering and editing the essays in *Elusive America*, Paul Roberts has pulled off a remarkable achievement. A number of these essays are not listed in the bibliographies of Thomas or Langridge; some of those that have been listed are in journals extremely hard of access. This volume should serve, minimally, as Powys's own advocacy of his involvement in American culture; yet the title makes one uneasy. *Elusive Powys: American Essays* would surely be preferable, pointing as it would both to Powys's invisibility in American culture and to Roberts's skills and perseverance in tracking down some pieces that have eluded other researchers. Indeed the title addresses a British readership, curious to define America, happy to have it left ill-defined. That this book has a British publisher only confirms America's indifference. How much more useful it would have been to have included the essays on Dreiser in the University of Pennsylvania's edition of the works of Dreiser. However, these essays have now been brought together for the very first time, and are available, making somewhat less excusable the neglect of subsequent scholars of American literature. One essay, though, has been overlooked: Powys's contribution, 'The writer and his writings', to a slim volume *Theodore Dreiser: America's Foremost Novelist*, New York, n.d. (1917?). Also not here, but obviously known (for it was reprinted in *The Powys*

Review 6 (1980)), is Powys's 'Introduction' to Dreiser's *Notes on Life*, written in 1946 but not published until 1974.

These considerations in no way reflect on or diminish the editor's labours. Roberts's introductory essay is largely biographical, concerned with Powys's first voyage to America, dated precisely by Roberts, for the first time: the *Ivernia* left Liverpool on Saturday, 24 December 1904, and arrived in New York on Tuesday, 3 January 1905. Powys in the *Autobiography* describes his being met at the dock by Frederick B. Miles, President of the American Society for the Extension of University Teaching. Powys was at once given a tour of New York by sleigh, and it is characteristic of Roberts's assiduity that he compares Powys's account with an item in the *New York Times* of 6 January 1905 about the snow and the sleighs in Central Park.

The volume is divided thematically into five sections, of which two are plain: five essays on Dreiser written between 1915 and 1931, and five essays on Edgar Lee Masters, written between 1920 and 1937. Another section, 'The Arts in America', gathers essays on miscellaneous topics. Part I, 'The American Scene and Character', contains eight essays written between 1924 and 1934, while Part V, 'Farewell to America', has just three late essays, only one of which was published in Powys's lifetime. The logic of this arrangement will be tested by the two forthcoming volumes of *The Uncollected Essays*.

Powys's essays on Dreiser deserve to be reprinted and to be reread, not only by Powysians but by the admirers of Dreiser. Dreiser and Powys were extremely good friends, each the other's closest friend in America, and what Powys admired in Dreiser suggests a degree of self-awareness of his own art:

> A paragraph written by Dreiser would never be mistaken for anyone else's. Dreiser's style is remarkable for the shamelessness with which it adapts itself to the drivel of ordinary conversation. In the Dreiser books ... people are permitted to say those things which they actually do say in real life — things that make you blush and howl, so soaked in banality and ineptitude are they. (83)

The same thing has been said by John Bayley about both Powys and

Dreiser, though quite independently of each other, in a discussion of Hardy: 'With his boisterous, cliché-ridden style, his seemingly naïve and facile absorptions, he [Hardy/Powys/Dreiser] *ought* to be bad — but is he?'⁵

It may well be that Powys and Dreiser encouraged and confirmed each other in the deployment of their common weaknesses — weaknesses which have been held against them by purists, critics of the novel who demand that fiction be written well, in a high style. In the same essay Powys concedes that even his taste is offended by the platitudes and banalities uttered by Dreiser's characters:

> But one knows very well he is right. People don't in ordinary life — certainly not in ordinary democratic life — talk like Oscar Wilde, or utter deep ironic sayings in the style of Matthew Arnold. ... They just gabble and gibber and drivel; at least that is what they do in England and America. The extraordinary language which the lovers in Dreiser ... use to one another might well make an aesthetic-minded person howl with nervous rage. ... Dreiser is the true master of the modern American Prose-Epic just because he is not afraid of the weariness, the staleness, the flatness, and unprofitableness of actual human conversation. (83)

Powys's defence of Dreiser is mimetically based; as people talk, so realist novelists should represent them. We could go further and speak of the quality of discord or polyphony which M. M. Bakhtin celebrates in the novel; from one point of view, the novel is able to represent people's speech much more accurately than poetry or drama; from another, and this is Bakhtin's political point, the novel came into being as a literary form in order to give expression to voices hitherto unrepresented or stylised. According to the first point of view the aim of fiction should be imitation; according to Bakhtin, its purpose is, rather, representation, representing all kinds of people not only as they are, but allowing those represented voices to express their desires and opinions. In this light one finds Powys's parenthetical '— in ordinary democratic life —' rather striking.

Powys and Dreiser are of course very different as novelists, but both would benefit, in terms of critical reputation, from a Bakhtinian understanding of their insistence on allowing characters, including the narrator, to 'burble and blather and blurt forth whatever drivelling nonsense comes into their heads'. Bakhtin's theory of the novel emerged in the late 1920s (virtually between *An American Tragedy*, 1925, and *Wolf Solent*, 1929) from his inquiry into the nature, at a linguistic and stylistic level, of Dostoevsky's 'greatness'. (The first edition of Bakhtin's *Problems of Dostoevsky's Poetics* appeared in 1929.) Powys's enthusiasm for Dostoevsky is well-known; yet he does not once mention Dostoevsky in his praise of Dreiser, even though we learn elsewhere that Dreiser's favourite of all novels was *The Idiot*.[6]

The two gave each other enormous and rare encouragement, and Dreiser, already established as a novelist, certainly helped Powys to curtail his lecturing and devote himself to fiction. Dreiser wrote to Powys, on 9 April 1932, that *A Glastonbury Romance* was 'not at all over long'. Dreiser himself, as a novelist, never again attained the greatness of *An American Tragedy*, which was written in the thick of his friendship with Powys. Much later, on 29 December 1943, within two years of his death, Dreiser wrote to Edgar Lee Masters about his difficulties in writing: 'And yet [being] apart from you, Jack Powys, Mencken and several people you don't know I find myself loath to write.' One could suppose that the separation of Powys and Dreiser that occurred in 1934 with Powys's return to Britain was detrimental to both of them. And it seems certain that the appreciation of one will not come without the appreciation of the other. Here it might be added that, while the publication of Powys's essays by such a small press as Cecil Woolf's will make very little difference, even the ambitious enterprise of the University of Pennsylvania Press, in bringing out a definitive edition of all Dreiser's writings, with textual variants and lavish scholarly apparatus, has not yet had much impact on Dreiser's reputation.

Powys proclaimed in his *Autobiography*, and elsewhere, that Theodore Dreiser and Edgar Lee Masters were 'the two greatest Americans of our time'. Such a claim for Dreiser may still seem within the range of the explicable. But Masters, once as famous as Dreiser, has languished more completely. Constantly Powys compares Masters to

Chaucer; he finds him second only to Hardy in 'first-rate philosophical power', of those poets whom Powys had met,[7] and we may note the familiar hyperbole.

Powys endeared himself to Masters before they had even met, when in March 1915 he gave a lecture on the *Spoon River Anthology* before it had been published. Paul Roberts surmises that Powys based his lecture on some of the poems already published in *Reedy's Mirror*. However, there seems no reason to dispute Powys's own account in the *Autobiography*, that he had 'met Dreiser first, and indeed it was owing to Dreiser that I got hold of the unpublished galley-sheets of *Spoon River* for a lecture in Guthrie's Church on modern poetry' (548). Powys's account matches that of Masters in his autobiography *Across Spoon River*.[8] Far more importantly, though, Roberts has located three hitherto unrecorded publications by Powys on Masters, and one unpublished and unrecorded essay of ten pages which may well be based on that lecture of 1915, though clearly written after *Spoon River* had become famous. (The latest of Masters's books to be discussed in this essay is *Songs and Satires*, published in April 1916.)

Masters was a successful and prosperous lawyer in Chicago, and Powys takes up the question of 'genius' and its opposition in America to 'culture'. An original genius, says Powys, will first be attacked for lacking culture; if that genius persists without acquiring culture, he will be faulted for lacking the proper exuberant freedom of genius. 'That a literary genius is only a super-craftsman in the difficult medium of words does not strike these daring ones' (105). This struggle interferes with literary judgments, and is particularly unfair to those geniuses who are neither extravagantly cultured nor experimental. None more so, argues Powys, than Masters. We might find a similar case, however, in Wallace Stevens, another poet whose successful professional career served for decades as an obstacle to the sort of appreciation freely given to Robert Frost or e. e. cummings.

This essay is subtitled 'An Appreciation' and Powys makes the effort to go beyond a celebration of *Spoon River*'s success:

> *Spoon River* is already a classic. It has already taken its place beside *The Scarlet Letter* and 'Ulalume' and *The Awkward Age* and 'When lilacs last in the door-yard bloomed'. ... *Spoon*

River is one of those tremendous and incalculable inspirations of the human mind which become landmarks in a nation's history. (105)

Powys spends much time upbraiding Masters for not being true to the poetry of *Spoon River*, of succumbing to the requirement and temptation of culture. He also faults Masters for admitting the stylistic influence, in some of his other poetry, of 'the obstreperous and rampant spirit of the boisterous Robert Browning. Browning is just the sort of person one would expect to refuse to remain "quietly inurned". But that he should burst out in Spoon River County is peculiarly unfortunate.' (108) Powys's attack on Browning is rather more precise than his apology for Masters:

> That peculiar Blank Verse, with its self-conscious air of colloquial aplomb, one could just endure it in 'Andrea Del Sarto', 'Bishop Blougram' and the rest. But to have it rising from the dead and entangling the clearest and least affected of all modern poetic styles — it is too much! (108–9)

Powys's objection to Masters, in his weaker poetry, is closely related to his praise of Dreiser. Poetry is conventionally admired for its affection, that is to say for the degree to which it approximates the condition of poetry. Modern poetry was routinely deplored for not sounding like poetry at all, not, that is, like the familiar poetic stylisations of Tennyson or Longfellow. Masters writes poetry in the voice of people speaking: Bakhtin would call this the 'novelization of poetry', when poetry responds to the challenge of what the novel can do. Powys of course defends the 'poetry' of *Spoon River*: 'About all these verses, with their bitterness and their humour and their cruel realism, hovers unmistakably ... the evasive and illusive magic of true poetry' (106).

But Powys is more interesting on the question of 'style': what style unites and holds together the disparate voices of *Spoon River Anthology*?

> For this book has a style, as definite, as personal, as magical and arresting, as the style of Hawthorne or Poe or Whitman, or

as Henry James himself. And yet it is a style, so fused and welded, so merged and lost, in the subject matter, that the subject matter seems, as we read, to be, so to say, *writing its own story*. (106)

The syntax here, mannered in its very colloquialism, beautifully enacts Powys's idea, as if syntax also might tell its own story. Story is precisely, it seems, what is supplied to each of the epitaphs of *Spoon River* by their sequence in the whole, as if by each of them. For the book is almost all that Powys claims for it, a masterpiece and, in 1915, quite plausibly 'the most original single volume of modern poetry'. Eliot's *Prufrock and Other Observations* would appear in 1917; Pound had already made the comparison between Eliot and Masters in 1915, not blindly in Eliot's favour, but simply concerning the three most important modern poets — or the two after Pound — and this in a letter to Eliot's father.[9]

Yet *Spoon River Anthology* defies and resists quotation to an exceptional extent, as if indeed what happens between the epitaphs renders the epitaphs alone and in themselves merely mechanical and void. More than elsewhere in Powys's literary essays, one can here sympathise with him for his failure to address the text itself. One must however mention the quality and sequence of names, names on the epitaphs that double as titles of the 244 poems.

In the two later essays, of 1929 and 1937, Powys does cite one or two poems from *Spoon River*, and apologises for doing no more than that:

> One could, I daresay, analyze the shrewd balancing, in passages of this kind, of vowels and consonants; the cunning assonance, the skilful onomatopoeia! The striking thing about it all is the limpid simplicity. Could anything, for instance, be more to the point than this, of Mrs Kessler, who took in washing:

> For things that are new grow old at length,
> They're replaced with better or none at all;
> People are prospering or falling back,
> And rents and patches widen with time.

> No thread or needle can pace decay,
> And there are stains that baffle soap,
> And there are colours that run in spite of you.
> ...
> And I, who went to all the funerals
> Held in Spoon River, swear I never
> Saw a dead face without thinking it looked
> Like something washed and ironed.   (123–4)

Powys does not confine his praise to *Spoon River*, appreciating a couple of poems from Masters's next volume, *Songs and Satires* (1916), and from a much later book, *Invisible Landscapes* (1935). There he finds "Sandridge", an elegy reminiscent to Powys of Hardy and, to us, suggestive also of Edward Thomas:

> They are not merely forgotten, they are even
> As the unborn, as if their landscape never
> Echoed their voice or their endeavour
> Kept green these fields under this changeless heaven. (132)

The Keatsian suppression of rhyme through enjambment is astonishingly carried through in this quatrain, and one cannot help but suppose that Masters at his best must have taught much to poets of a later generation such as Hart Crane, Allen Tate and John Crowe Ransom. Powys, Dreiser and Masters seem to be held in a joint comdemnation, not only, one hopes, for a deal of mutual admiration and promotion not unknown in other literary circles.

Of the other essays on literary topics in this volume, the most interesting were both written in 1927: 'A Modern Mystery Play' on S. Ansky's celebrated play *The Dybbuk*, and 'The Real Longfellow'. The essay on *The Dybbuk* was written in the summer of 1927 and published in the *Menorah Journal* in August 1927. (Readers of *Jack and Frances* should note that Letter 164, a rare occasion on which Powys mentions writing this essay, belongs to 1927, not 1928: July 10 fell on a Sunday in 1927.) In *Autobiography* (475) Powys tells us that *The Dybbuk* was the only play that ever gave him any pleasure, and in this essay he has explained why.

The performers were the Habima company of Jewish actors from Moscow, directed by E. Vachtangov who was, with Meyerhold, the most distinguished of Stanislavsky's disciples. The play was in Yiddish, and Powys understood only a few syllables; this hardly mattered because the acting was extremely stylised and ritualised, and the incomprehensibility of the words only heightened the ritual effect. For all his involvement with the Chicago Little Theatre, Powys never enjoyed watching plays. Here we have some explanation, that modern plays leave the audience as mere spectators, whereas:

> *The Dybbuk* is so unique a work of art because not only are scenery, music, dancing, fused into a homogeneous whole; but, by means of a deep liturgical incantation, the pulsebeats of the audience — nay the very noddings of their heads and unconscious movements of their hands — follow the systole and diastole of the performance! (177)

This tells us something of Powys's fictional representations of performance, whether they be of the Glastonbury Pageant, the puppet-show on Weymouth Beach, or the various rituals in *Porius*: there is nothing objective or aesthetic about them, and the audience is as participative as the actors, always itself part of the spectacle represented to readers.

Another clue to Powys's own art is found in this:

> And how the physical unimportance of these small objects — the sacred roll ... the sacred rams' horns — enhances their occult quality! They are the true vehicles of that *Deus Inconditus* [*sic*: unformed, rather than *absconditus*: hidden?] of which they are the Shekinah. (175)

One can think of any number of trivial things in Powys's fiction, their occult sense of most precious value derived from their absolute insignificance and, even better, from their condition of complete neglect.

The Longfellow essay comes as a true surprise, for Powys's only mentions of Longfellow seem to be a few routine celebrations of *Hiawatha*. Yet in this essay Powys displays a thorough familiarity with the contents 'of the too well-remembered volume' of his childhood (161), and his critical judgment and advice remains timely:

> As with a similar imaginative element in the far cleverer Tennyson the very popularity of his worse poetry — I am not speaking now of *Hiawatha* or *Evangeline* but of such distressing poppycock-idealism as reeks to heaven in things like 'Excelsior' or the 'Psalm of Life' — has side-tracked many lovers of poetry from hunting out his best verse.
>
> Drowned indeed in this flood of moralistic bathos ... it is still possible to catch ... certain faint, far-off, magical notes that are different from anything else in English poetry. ... The rule I would suggest for any modern reader is a simple one; namely, the deliberate skipping of all passages where the words Angels, Paradise, Life, Liberty, God, Flowers, Death, Truth, Will, Endeavour, Harp-strings, Time and *The Poet* occur. (162–4)

Powys proffers an interesting explanation, similar in tactics to his essay on Masters. He wants, and it is not an uncommon critical ploy, to separate the good verse from the bad, and then to explain how the poet could have written both sorts. In Masters, as we have seen, Powys finds the poet succumbing to the temptations of intellectual themes and to the style of Browning. In Longfellow, Powys sees a different problem: that his verse about Angels, Paradise, etc. is bad not because it is moralistic, or sickeningly cheerful in the way of Browning, but because Longfellow probably didn't believe it himself:

> Was it that, deep down in his nature, he was never really converted to Benevolence and Righteousness, never converted to the energetic ideals of Puritan stoicism? Was he all the while ... worshipping silence, peace, quietness, non-existence, eternal passivity? (163)

Powys's identification with Longfellow, and his identifications of Longfellow's best poetry, are surprising, and refreshingly free of superlatives. Even in one of Powys's favourites, *Evangeline*, he has to fault Longfellow's ear for betraying him into even attempting such a poem in such a rhythm: 'I know well that these easy half-conversational hexameters are forbidden by some baffling restraint in the very texture of our language from thickening and concentrating into firstrate verse' (168).

Powys is a far more interesting critic of neglected or disparaged writers than he is of the canonic and the classic. Once *Spoon River Anthology* is accepted as a great work, Powys can do little more than rave about what it is that all great literature is and can do. But a work that has not enjoyed success elicits from Powys not only a certain sympathy, but a critical discernment and a capacity for argument that one hardly finds elsewhere. 'Elsewhere' means, largely, the three books of literary essays, *Suspended Judgments*, *Visions and Revisions* and *The Pleasures of Literature*.

In his defence of Dreiser, Masters, and Longfellow, Powys seems considerably more interesting, and more challenged, than in his essays on 'classic' American writers such as Poe, Whitman and Melville. It should not be thought, however, that his advocacy, no matter how hyperbolic it may be, is merely a service of friendship. British writers among Powys's friends, such as James Hanley, Redwood Anderson, or Huw Menai, elicited a very different kind of support, and a support almost valueless given Powys's peripheral status in British literary circles.

In American culture, however, Powys occupied a central place, and could make judgments of extraordinary foresight, derived from years of watchful immersion. Powys had not responded very well to Faulkner's early books (just as, oddly enough, Faulkner had written a far from friendly review of *Ducdame*), but when Faulkner met critical resistance with his most difficult and challenging novel, *Absalom! Absalom!* (1937), Powys proclaimed it his best work, and often recommended it. Until quite recently the late novels of Henry James were treated with condescension and even ridicule, yet in 1946, in a letter to Louis Wilkinson, Powys gives his favourite among James's novels, none of which would have been on most people's list at that time: *The Sacred Fount*, *The Golden Bowl*, *The Wings of the Dove*, *The Ambassadors*. We will recall that in 1928 Powys was prepared to put aside personal feelings about Ezra Pound; this was just after the publication of the first two instalments of *Cantos*. Equally, Powys's sense of American literature can be told from a letter of 1948, when Powys had been back in Britain for fourteen years already: 'The best to my mind of modern American writers is a certain Saul Bellow who has only written 2 books ...'[10] One wonders whether any critic in America could, or did, make such a claim about Bellow as early as 1948.

We can be amused and informed by Powys's essays on America which assume the foreignness, the Englishness of their author — 'Elusive America', 'The American Scene and Character', 'An Englishman Up-State' and 'Farewell to America' — but one must protest that Powys was only an 'Englishman' for precisely such rhetorical occasions and purposes. For most of those thirty years his closest friends were the most American of American writers, those who never had to lose themselves in Europe, and who embodied the national self-consciousness of American literature that had been endemic, if not mandatory, since Emerson's essays of the 1830s.

Powys may have used America in his fiction only once, and that, in *After My Fashion*, not published in his lifetime. The settings of all his great novels may have been British, but in American cultural life Powys was an insider, one whose opinions were respected or contested, but whose nationality (or accent) was seldom invoked by way of either praise or dissent.

Through this most interesting collection of essays one hardly expects that many new readers will be brought to Powys. But we can hope that Powys will bring new readers to his favourite American writers, and thus give shape to that elusive history of American literature in which Powys, Dreiser, Masters are present, and given voice: a generation yet to be heard, and found.

NOTES

[1] Published in *Modern Drama*, XXXI, No. 1, March 1988.
[2] B. Duffey, *The Chicago Renaissance in American Letters* (East Larsing, Michigan: Michigan State University Press, 1954), 243.
[3] O. and C. Wilkinson, eds., *Jack and Frances: The Love Letters of John Cowper Powys to Frances Gregg*, Vol. I (London: Cecil Woolf, 1994), 67.

4 M. Anderson, *My Thirty Years's War* (New York: Harcourt, Brace & Co., 1969), 167.
5 J. Bayley, *An Essay on Hardy* (Cambridge: Cambridge University Press, 1978), 4.
6 See M. Tjader, *Dreiser: A New Dimension* (Norwalk, Conn.: Silvermine, 1965), 216.
7 J. C. Powys, *Autobiography* [1934] (London: Macdonald, 1967), 549.
8 E. L. Masters, *Across Spoon River* [1936] (New York: Octogon Books, 1969) 367.
9 See V. Eliot, ed., *The Letters of T. S. Eliot*, Vol. I (London: Faber, 1988), 100.
10 L. Wilkinson, ed., *Letters of John Cowper Powys to Louis Wilkinson 1935-1956* (London: Macdonald, 1958), 254.

APPENDIX

Edgar Lee Masters described John Cowper Powys in his autobiography of 1936, Across Spoon River, *and he wrote two poems about him. In addition, in 1925 Masters dedicated his* Selected Poems *to Powys. We print here an extract from* Across Spoon River, *and the two poems, "John Cowper Powys" from* The Great Valley *(New York: MacMillan, 1916) and "On the Departure of Powys for England" from* Invisible Landscapes *(New York: Macmillan, 1935).*

One day a tall, rather bent man with frizzed black hair, with the manner of a traveling scholastic, was ushered in by Jake Prassel. It was John Cowper Powys, one of the most extraordinary minds that I know, a genius in every sense of the word. He had a way of jiggling when he was excited, of kowtowing so to speak, of laughing with wide mouth, and thus exposing a great row of Piltdown teeth. His eyes were blue and penetrating but a little simian; his forehead above his eyes was ridged, and not very high. His head was small and compact and shapely. His manner reminded me of the friendly countrymen I had seen about my grandfather's farm, as he rubbed his hands, and laughed and exclaimed "my word," and entered into everything I said with joyous sympathy, with deferential agreement. We became friends at once. His understanding of me, his generous appreciation of what I had done won my heart naturally; while our differences of opinion were not of a sort to create any dissension. It was at this time, I believe, that he gave a lecture on *Spoon River*, at Maurice Browne's Little Theatre, which was filled with Chicago people to hear what the Cambridge scholar had to say about me. I sat in a box behind the curtains and was not known, until the lecture was over, to have been in the audience. He went on saying that I was the reincarnation of Chaucer. I am unable to tell how terrified I was as I heard him. I fairly shook with excitement. For here I was: Suppose I was some kind of a reborn

Chaucer, how was I ever to sustain that role which had been thrust upon me? How with my law business, my expenses, my shattered health which a thousand emotions and themes bore down with crushing force?

John Cowper Powys

Astronomer and biologist
And chemical analyst and microscopist,
Observer of men's involuted shells
Where they conceal their hate and even their love
Under insipid ooze or nacreous stuff.
Tracer of criss-cross steps made when great hells
Kept lime as soft as wax
Which thereupon took the imprint of the air
From gnat-like wings of joy or shadowy care.
He makes hard secrets stand in the cul de sac's
Entrance and face him till he lays all bare
That eyes hold or heart of blood contains,
And curious traits in diverse curious brains,
And starved desires in hearts and hopes forgot
Under the sifting ashes of one's lot.

X-ray photographer who flashes
What's in you out of you with sudden crashes
Of wit or oratory in a flood.
He samples and tests the book's, also your blood.
Shows what you are and whence you came,
And who your kindred are, and what your flame
In heat and color is. Poet and wag,
Prophet, magician taking from a bag
Eggs, rabbits, silver globes; the old engram!
Scoffer with reverence, visioned, quick to damn,
Yet laugh at, looking keenly through the sham.
Confessing his own sins, devoid of shame.
He knows himself and laughs,
Or blames himself as he would others blame.

ELUSIVE AMERICA: A REVIEW

A naughty boy who kicks away the staff
Which poor decrepits walk by, nearly blind,
Then hurrying up with varied thought to find
Medicinal clay with which dim eyes to heal.

What is the human secret but Proteus'?
And who can catch the old man but his kind?
He was Poseidon's herdsman, knew the streams
Of early being, sea-filled ponds and sluices,
Where life took birth through elemental dreams.
And Proteus glanced with lightning and divined
The cause of Bacchus' madness. But at noon
He counted his sea-calves and ocean-sheep
On Carpathos where waters made a tune
Following the Orphic sun out of the deep —
Then in his cave he hid him, turned to sleep ....

So runs our life to change! and who can catch
The Protean thought must watch,
And he adept at wrestling, in the chase.
And know the god whatever be his face,
Through roar of water where the porpoises
And extravagant dolphins play, in silences
Of noon or midnight. So John Cowper Powys
You stand before us gesturing, shoulder bent
A little like King Richard, frizzed of hair,
Rolling your eye for secrets, for the word.
The thresher of your mind is eloquent
With hulls and flakes of words, until at last
The kernel itself pops out, not long deferred ....

Here is our wrestler then,
Hunter of secrets of creative souls,
Eluded he may be, he tries again.
His hand slips clutching at the irised shoals
Of rapturous thought. And at times his eyes
Are blinded by a light, or a disguise.

But finally both eye and hand
Obey the infallible senses' brave command —
He catches Proteus then, and with a shout,
The gods shout too, and we who watch the bout
Join in the panic of their merriment!

On the Departure of Powys for England

With Spring descending when the robin's song
About Phudd's Bottom chants the crystal dawn,
And snow, save in the vales, is gone,
And again the grackles throng;

And crows preparing once again to nest,
Fly calling, and race the rising mists,
The master of the landscape lists
These sounds, with dreams oppressed

Of England, which never leave the pilgrim heart,
But hold it as a tide toward the sea
Until the shoreward urge is free
For his return not to depart.

Long will these roads and meadow lands,
These hills with windmills and old sheds,
Houses and barns, and stony heads,
Remember him of Weymouth Sands.

The country folk for many a year will speak,
Passing the little house where long he bode,
Of him, and of the lonely road
He walked to the woodland creek.

They will recount the dog that raced his side,
The walking-stick he carried as he tramped;
All this memorially is stamped
Upon this land wherein he testified

Of earth and heaven and the soul of man,
And of the spirits which infuse them all;
Of soil and souls, and mystical
Comminglings thereof with no plan.

There will be inward vacancy in this scene
When he is gone; the lonelier plowman still
Will glance the sun below the hill,
Lonelier for what has been.

For men impart to houses, fields, and roads
Their spirits, and departing leave behind
Spirits which live, and walk, and wind
About old loved abodes.

*John Cowper Powys with his sister Marian and his dog
at Phudd Bottom, early 1930s*

REVIEWS

Petrushka and the Dancer: The Diaries of John Cowper Powys 1929–1939
Selected and edited, with an Introduction, by MORINE KRISSDÓTTIR
Carcanet Press, Manchester; St.Martin's Press, New York; Alyscamps Press, Paris, 1995, 340pp., £25

It is a truism that, whereas John Cowper Powys's *Autobiography* achieves an intensity and depth of self-revelation that is matched only by such masterpieces of autobiography as Rousseau's *Confessions*, it leaves a great deal to be desired as an account of Powys's life. As Powys himself observes in one of the entries in his Diary (131), it leaves out any discussion of his relations with women — as a consequence of which it tells us nothing of his relationship with Phyllis Playter, nor anything of his passionate love of Frances Gregg, who became the wife of his close friend Louis Wilkinson. Its account, therefore, of his complex involvements with his brothers and with the people in their lives also had to be inevitably — especially in the case of Llewelyn — highly selective. These observations about the limitations of Powys's *Autobiography* — at least when it is considered from the standpoint of a future biographer — are as sound as truisms usually are; but they omit other peculiarities of that book, which at once qualify its usefulness as a source of our knowledge of the man while enhancing our sense of it as a literary achievement.

In the *Autobiography*, Powys brings to the task of self-knowledge the same capacities of clairvoyant empathy and imaginative divination that he applied to thinkers and writers such as Saint Paul, Shakespeare, Nietzsche and Poe in *The Pleasures of Literature*, *Visions and Revisions* and similar works. That he should have appropriated in the service of self-understanding the almost mediumistic powers he deployed as a writer and lecturer on the great books and authors of the past is a paradox, and it creates difficulties in the way of any assessment of the truth of the self-portrait the book contains that go well beyond those attendant on any kind of autobiographical knowledge. We are familiar with the notion that, in any account that a person gives of his own life, the usual categories of fact and fiction are hard to apply, since the purpose of such accounts is the construction of a coherent narrative, and not literal fidelity to events. This is only to say that, with regard to the most important events in anyone's life, the truth of the matter is in the telling, in *how* what happened is told or left untold. Autobiographical knowledge differs from other kinds of historical knowledge in the peculiar difficulty others have in assessing the adequacy of the narratives in which it is embodied. How can another judge to be wanting a person's account of his own life? What sense can we attach to the notion that there is a true account of a life, to which the subject possesses a privileged access? In Powys's case, this difficulty is exceptionally severe, in that the movement between self-discovery and self-invention, which is a feature of any human life and of any biography, is incessant and profound in the *Autobiography*. Powys's personality was itself so prolific in contradictions, so much of an irreducible plurality, his propensity to acting out his life through the fashioning of personae so pervasive and his remoteness from unreserved natural sincerity so great, that any account of his life — and especially any he gave of it himself — could only be one among many representations to which it is subject. At times, the *Autobiography* reads like the life of a character that Powys himself invented, a character, like those in his novels, that had grown from authorship by Powys to become a personality he could not himself fully control.

If the *Autobiography* can be read as the life of one of Powys's characters, *Petrushka and the Dancer* might be read as a fragment of the biography of the single most important character of Powys's life, Phyllis Playter, his creative muse and companion of forty years. She is referred to throughout as the T.T., the 'Tiny Thin', or 'The Tao', 'in a sense, the real subject of the Diary', as Morine Krissdóttir puts it in her remarkable and stimulating Introduction. It must be said at once that, wholly indispensable as it is to anyone interested in John Cowper Powys, *Petrushka and the Dancer* is far more than a contribution to Powys scholarship. It is, in fact, not one, but two literary masterpieces — one of the great diaries of this century, perhaps ultimately the greatest, and a creative editorial exploit. Morine Krissdóttir's selections never limit, but only deepen and heighten, our understanding of Powys and his work, his laborious creation and recreation of his 'life-illusion' of himself as a Magician, his development of a radically original personal philosophy, and his love of his companion. Those who have read John Cowper Powys's Diary in the unabridged form in which two years of it (1930 and 1931) have been published by Jeffrey Kwintner will appreciate the magnitude and the delicacy of the task which Dr Krissdóttir has here successfully accomplished. If John Cowper Powys has bequeathed to us an inexhaustibly rich album of his deepest thoughts and impressions, in a Diary that he began at Phyllis

Playter's prompting in 1929 and which in its totality spans thirty-three years, Krissdóttir has rendered the first third of that Diary here in a form that is immediately captivating and enduringly engrossing, without at any point compromising fidelity to the original. In its own way, Morine Krissdóttir's *Petrushka and the Dancer* is as extraordinary an achievement as Powys's Diary itself.

It is hardly possible to give more than a few gleanings of the wealth of thoughts, sensations, moods, observations, and images this volume contains. We learn that Powys's conception of the 'ichthyosaurus-ego', which can draw on a store of memories that is deposited at the most primordial level of human consciousness and which can attune itself to the consciousnesses of non-human, animal and vegetable life, found its true fulfilment at Phudd Bottom, Hillsdale, up-state New York, where in a backwards unravelling of his life, memories of the places and people of his childhood return to him — 'all my past began to be Retrouvé — Le Temps Retrouvé!' (48). It was here Powys and Phyllis Playter moved in April 1930, just after the completion of what is, in the present writer's judgement, his most original book of philosophy, *In Defence of Sensuality* (1930). In that book, Powys sought to exemplify a way of life in which 'static contemplation' is central:

> an art of divesting the mind of all thought, and sinking down or out and away through any material objects but keeping these (any) objective things in mind and working outwards centrifugally upon these casual little material objects, not getting tied up & numb in a Tight *inward* knot — but forgetting all worry all future all past in a sensation of Being; but not of any sort of Over-Soul or Religion or Unity or Brahma or God — entirely lonely and separate — a hard little Crystal. (97–8)

The 'ichthyosaurus-philosophy' — shamanistic and pluralist, magical and not in the least mystical, heathen and profane in its earth-worshipping reverence for the minute particulars of things — seeks a certain sort of sensation,

> some secret ecstasy in certain things that ... has to do with some marginal sensations *not* of any particularly beautiful thing or pretty thing ... it is non-moral — non-spiritual — *non-mystical* — no it is *not* mystical *at all* — *nor is it poetical* — it is the plenilunar circle of the whole moon of life seen faintly from horn-to-horn of the young crescent moon! That's what it is — *entirely* materialistic and earthy and yet *psychic* — (183–4)

So far as I can tell, the epiphanies of memory and sensation that come to the ichthyosaurus-ego in Powys's conception of static contemplation are not at all akin to the archetypes of Jungian theory, since they are particular images, often of the most inconsequential and marginal things, rather than universal symbols of any kind. The inner life recorded in the Diary has nevertheless many Jungian echoes, for example in its synchronicitous interweaving of mythological motifs, garnered by Powys from his careful study of such books as John Rhys's *The Arthurian Legend*, and events in the 'outer' world.

Powys's relationship with Phyllis Playter is itself rendered by him in the mythopoeic form, or, rather, as Krissdóttir puts it in her Introduction, in the idiom of a fairy story — the story of Petrushka and the Dancer, as that was turned by Stravinsky into his ballet *Petrushka*. Powys saw himself, as perhaps Phyllis sometimes saw him, as her 'Inanimate Doll', Petrushka. In Stravinsky's ballet, Petrushka is a puppet, brought to life by a Showman-Magician together with a beautiful Dancer by whom Petrushka is captivated, and whom he tries himself to enchant by a series of leaps against the wall of a prison cell which she has magically entered. In the fairy story as rendered by Stravinsky, Petrushka fails to impress his Dancer, and ends as a ghost — the phantom of a puppet; but, as Powys saw it, he captured his lovely Elemental, Phyllis the Dancer, thereby becoming the 'Showman-Magician' he had always wanted to be. The theme of the Magician creating a Doll recurs in the Diary, in Powys's references (on p. 242 and elsewhere) to the *Mabinogion* tale of the wife made out of flowers by the Magician Gwydion ap Dôn for his favourite, Lleu Llaw Gyffes, and whom the Magician called Blodeuwedd (Flower-Face). Yet Powys never surrendered to the illusion that Phyllis was a magical contrivance of his. As the Diary shows, he was acutely aware that the danger of magic was that it encouraged him to live in a world of his own creation, and thereby to neglect the separateness of other selves — one of the cardinal precepts of his philosophy.

In fact, Powys thought of his love for Phyllis Playter — of whom he writes that 'All my philosophy came in Being since I met her' (50) — in terms which acknowledged, but sought to overcome, their separateness: as a love between two 'half-born' people (155), two 'half-human things', each of them 'half-mad'. In one of its readings, the Diary tells how these two halves became, together, one sane whole human being, despite — or because of — their enormous divergences in tastes and temperament. Powys craved solitude and rural landscapes, Phyllis Playter 'distraction' and the intellectual and social life of the city; Powys rose early and loved cold and daylight, Playter was a night-bird who cherished warmth; Powys was a resilient and energetic man, despite his ulcers and his chronic constipation, while Playter was frail and elfish, never equal to the task of running a house, yet devotedly committed to looking after Powys and her mother, year after year. Powys had achieved an equanimity in the control of his fears, whereas Phyllis Playter was ever liable to despair, and sometimes talked of suicide. It was as one half of this seemingly ill-matched couple that Powys wrote during the eleven years covered by this Diary four major novels, including *A Glastonbury Romance*, five books of popular philosophy and his *Autobiography*. His prodigious creativity as a writer during these years he owed in considerable measure to his life with his companion, not only through her direct contributions as critic and commentator on his writings, but also, and perhaps even more decisively, because with her he could fashion a daily round in which his animistic, fetishist and mythopoeic nature was given full expression and embodiment. In his devotion to their doll and surrogate child Olwen and to their dog 'the Old' — his account of which in the Diary must surely constitute one of the most moving testaments in any literature of deep love of an animal companion — Powys was able to live out his conviction that the force of personality could kindle consciousness in inanimate things and cross the barriers of the species.

As a selection from Powys's Diary, *Petrushka and the Dancer* is an enduring work of study and interest. It is important for the insights it affords into the medium-like near-automatism in which creative writing sometimes occurs; and for its picture of a man in whom the boundary between conscious and unconscious mental life — represented by orthodox theories of the mind as rigid and impermeable — is fluid and at times non-existent. Furthermore it contains the living essence of John Cowper Powys's 'Elementalist' philosophy; and it shows Powys experimenting, in ways he did not do in the comparatively traditional format of his novels, with a variety of forms in which the diversity and elusiveness of unmediated experience could somehow be rendered. It is most memorable, in the end, for its account of his love of Phyllis Playter, and as a testament to the part she played in the creation of his work.

John Gray

REVIEWS

Sylvia and David: The Townsend Warner/Garnett Letters
Selected and edited, with an Introduction, by RICHARD GARNETT
Sinclair-Stevenson, London, 1994, 246pp., £20
The Diaries of Sylvia Townsend Warner
Edited, with an Introduction, by CLAIRE HARMAN
Chatto & Windus, London, 1994, 379pp., £25

From the publication of *Lolly Willowes* in 1926 to that of *Kingdoms of Elfin* in 1977, Sylvia Townsend Warner displayed a wryly compassionate outlook that was only just not reductive because so refreshing and, in the fullest sense of the term, so humorous. An English original, country-based but with an urban sophistication of style and viewpoint, she has, since her death in 1978, been the subject of two biographies. Wendy Mulford's emphasised her political affiliations, Claire Harman's her personal relationships; yet neither of these aspects of her life can account for the sustained allegiance her poems, novels and stories have inspired, despite a failure to recognise their merits on the part of the arbiters of literary fashion or of the academies. She has been undervalued as were the Powyses.

Her concern is with the perceptions rather than with the emotions or the social conscience; her style is pungent, exact, and displays a command of appropriate yet surprising simile. As a writer she keeps her distance, her affinities being with the eighteenth rather than with the nineteenth century. Since our own popular culture is more interested in its artists' lives than in the nature and significance of their artistry or in their artefacts (unless commercially exploitable), Warner's work is at last reaching a wider public through the appearance of her various private writings. In 1982 her American literary executor, William Maxwell, published a number of extracts from her witty, exhilarating, far-ranging letters. But such a selection inevitably lacked what Warner herself calls (in *Lolly Willowes*) 'the comfortable amble of day by day' that characterises any correspondence in its unabridged entirety. The book proved to be rather too brilliant for its own good.

This defect, if defect it be, is remedied in Richard Garnett's selection from the letters exchanged between Warner and his father David (the 'Bunny' of the Bloomsbury group) — despite a long silence between 1933 and 1954, possibly caused by Sylvia's preoccupation with her companion, Valentine Ackland. This collection improves as it goes on; the exchange between the two ageing friends is genuinely affecting. If, compared with Warner, Garnett seems a trifle humourless, she brings out a far warmer and more likeable aspect of him than did T. H. White (see *The White/Garnett Letters* (1968), often mentioned here); while their discussions of her difficulties in writing White's biography should interest any reader of these three most individualistic authors. But Warner and Garnett were as friendly with painters and musicians as they were with writers: their correspondence exhibits a mental and cultural life of the utmost discrimination and integrity. The letters also contain some of the best writing about cats that I have ever read; but what strikes one above all is the dispassionate interest of both Warner and Garnett in objects and aspects of life outside their own immediate areas of feeling. Their letters demonstrate the saving qualities of an objective outlook, since they both record moments of great sorrow and suffering without self-pity, firm in the knowledge that relief can only come from a concern with the natural world around them.

Warner's own sufferings arose, as did most of her greatest joys, from her lifelong love for Valentine Ackland, whose temperament was so much more wayward than her own. Their story is told most sympathetically by Claire Harman, who now illuminates it further in her selection from Warner's diaries. But, as with Maxwell's edition of the letters, we come up against questions of editorial choice. Ironically, whereas his book was remaindered, the *Diaries* sold out at once, showing that a far lengthier selection would have been justified, even commercially. As it is, Warner's admirers are likely to feel defrauded, especially as the complete diaries are almost as long as those of Virginia Woolf, which were published as a matter of course in their entirety. But now it would seem the pitch is queered.

The diary was kept only intermittently between 1932 and 1949, with more continuous entries before and after those dates. Nowhere in this selection is there a boring page. While reaching its greatest intensity at times of emotional crisis, it repeatedly exhibits the gaiety and delight in giving pleasure which are so marked a feature of the letters. Both letters and diaries contain many quintessential turns of phrase. Thus, concerning Lucy Penny, Garnett is told that 'She is full of Powys piety and quirks ("eggs do not agree with us"), the bouquet is unmistakeable, but with much less body.' Then, as though unable to resist, Warner proceeds, 'This may be because she married when she was a girl and the early bottling took her off the lees.' Such domestic imagery is instinctive with her.

It was Valentine who appreciated Lucy: Sylvia came to do so later. She was especially drawn to Alyse Gregory, whose stoicism and clear-sightedness she admired, remarking of her death that 'People so seldom get the end to crown the work. She has, dying as unvexed and solitary as a blade of grass.' There is much else in the *Diaries* that is illuminating about the Powyses — Theodore,

Violet and Katie especially. With her Bloomsbury connections Warner was able to appreciate the singularity of the family without being absorbed either in or by them. 'True goblin daughter of that goblin race', she comments on a remark of Lucy's, 'it was blood-curdling as anything of T.F.P.'s.'

Although both Garnett and Harman write helpful introductions, the annotation they provide is meagre. Where the *Letters* are concerned this hardly matters, but the *Diaries* call for far more supplementary information than is provided here, many of the notes being casual and imprecise, as though designed for a one-off reading. There are some blunders too, as when Coleshill House in Berkshire becomes 'Carles Hill' (whether this is Warner's error or not should have been made clear). More seriously misleading is the note on page 368 that 'Katie Powys had specifically requested not to be buried in a churchyard.' No authority is given for this statement, which is both refuted by Katie's will and contradicted on page 133 of Judith Stinton's account in *Chaldon Herring: The Powys Circle in a Dorset Village* (1988).

The *Diaries* cry out for the detailed annotation afforded to those of Woolf — concerning whom Warner makes a comment to Garnett after she had read *Mrs Dalloway*, which, as early as 1925, shows her independence of taste and mind. 'What is the use of describing feelings and thoughts, however vividly, if they are all to remain the author's? This is *My* book, this is what I feel about it — It made me feel almost ashamed as I read it to see such gifts made such a schoolgirlish use of.' So bold and clear-eyed an evaluation, however clumsily (for once) expressed, typifies the exacting artistry and outlook of a still undervalued writer who was, so one of her friends recently remarked to me, the most completely loving person she had known. These are the letters and the diaries of one of those rare people who are as kind as they are clever.

Glen Cavaliero

Jack and Frances: The Love Letters of John Cowper Powys to
Frances Gregg, Volume One
Edited, with an Introduction, by OLIVER WILKINSON, assisted by
CHRISTOPHER WILKINSON
Cecil Woolf, London, 1994, 271pp., £29.95
Powys to Glyn Hughes: The Letters of John Cowper Powys to
Glyn Hughes
Edited, with an Introduction, by FRANK WARREN
Cecil Woolf, London, 1994, 80pp., £12.50

Among the many responses likely to be provoked by this first volume of letters between John Cowper Powys and Frances Gregg, which run from their first meeting in 1912 to 1929, perhaps the most lasting will be simple frustration that Powys, 'in a place of rocks and butterflies', as he told her, ceremonially burnt all those which Frances had written during the first ten years of their relationship. In his later correspondence with some of the more peripheral figures in his life, this one-sidedness is no great cause for regret. But with someone as central to his earlier life as Frances, his first significant passion, one longs for more of the particular dissonance and harmony, heard so fleetingly here, of two distinctive voices.

Of the 171 letters in the volume, we thus have only nine from Frances, who doesn't make her entry until 1922. Her impact is immediate — 'it was never your *genius* I doubted, it was your control of it'; 'I have gotten over my love for you, but not over something else unnameable and deeper than the love was. I mean that you are there in my consciousness, I am sure, forever'; 'I never stop thinking of you. There is no single day without my turning to you for something. But you will *never* understand I think. No, you will never understand.' The directness of her honesty, all the more pleasing for its gentle sonority, is a perfect foil for the more rhetorical and declamatory eloquence of his. 'Is there any chance of seeing you? I should be content with a day, or half a day, or an hour. I should so like to walk over a marsh, and hear our two voices shouting about the unimportant verities, an hour out of the clutter of reality would do me worlds of good' — this is Frances in the throes of divorce from Louis Wilkinson, burdened with two children and financial worries, yet capable of confiding 'I get absolutely swamped in misery' without a trace of self-pity. Louis, she says, was 'always a bit blind in his social relations, but if I could tolerate that when others were the victims, naturally I don't flare up and hate him when I happen to be the victim' — and this despite the fact that he threatened to name John as correspondent in a countersuit if Frances pressured him to provide more money than he wished for her and the children.

The peculiar love-hate relationship between John and Louis, exacerbated by the Frances factor, is illuminated by Oliver Wilkinson in his informative and entertaining introduction, which also provides a psychological backdrop to the letters (though possibly makes too much of John's supposed cerebral sadism, as Powys did himself). But that oft-recorded notion, again stated here, that because John was not free to marry Frances himself he thought it 'an excellent idea' to marry her to Louis may strike some as rather more baffling than convincing, especially since the result, as also stated, was instant and long-lived jealousy. This was before Llewelyn too was to learn that 'to love Frances is like loving the fires of purgatory'. Was that really all there was to it? Was John the victim merely of his own blind impulsiveness? If he had wanted to continue his peculiar brand of love-making with her (the occasion for some powerful flights of imagination in some letters), bringing about her marriage to anyone, even within his 'circle', would surely have been folly.

There is a particular poignancy in the repeated declarations of love in his earlier letters, a time he was playing Heathcliff to her Cathy — 'I miss you today. I miss many long hours which were only minutes to the conscious F & J. I want to tell you that under everything and behind everything *I love you*'; and again, 'I have been "infatuated" ... before and I have idealized before — But may God swallow me if I have ever been in love before.' This is a John Cowper we have not heard till now, a man surprised, troubled by his emotions, a little fearful of them. Seven years after her marriage he is still love-sick and has sleepless nights thinking of her on the other side of the Atlantic — 'It was a night of thought — but I held you in my arms all the time and now and then I stopped thinking and made love to you and kissed you and kissed you and kissed you ... and then with my mouth upon your right breast I drank up your soul till our souls mixed together.' Encouraged by news of her separation, he contemplates stepping into Louis's shoes and making a life with Frances, for 'we know now that we are made to fit into each other like a classic knife into a classic sheath.' Encouraged also to greater intimacies he confesses that 'normal sensuality' has become 'a troubling craving for you, for your arms ... for your naked body. Never before have I thought of a thing like that — never before! But you are Frances and I now undress you and kiss you from hand to foot — but only to be so gentle with you in the end, my life, my love —'

Then 1921 came round. Frances found someone else for a while and John is no longer jealous, for John has found Phyllis Playter for life. The passion begins to subside, a poignancy of a different kind. 'I am no longer in love with you a bit', Frances declares in 1925.'That is the smashing of a state of mind that has stood the wear and tear of twenty years.'

The editors, Wilkinsons *père et fils*, have provided an admirably detailed Biographical Glossary of main characters, useful beyond the immediate purposes of the book, and a wealth of notes, designed largely for the reader dipping into the volume at random. The repetition this entails may strike some readers as annoyingly excessive, especially given the book's cost and that notes account for 70 of its 300 pages. One could question the necessity for notes on Dostoevsky or Oedipus or Michelangelo. Unfortunate too is the reversal of Katie's and Gertrude's names accompanying a family photograph, though a study of expressions therein makes this not the least interesting page in the book. But such quibbles do not detract from the main text, which has been thoughtfully and intelligibly presented. The book will be an essential vade-mecum for those who would follow the tortuous path of John Cowper's psyche through the years of his greatest passions. These are letters of many shades, and will need careful reading to discover all they tell of the strange interlocking of two egoistic and magnanimous spirits.

In one sense, perhaps, John did step into Louis's shoes: he often gave Frances money. He gave money to Glyn Hughes too, as revealed in Frank Warren's introduction to the slim volume of 34 letters spanning just four years of Powys's late old age. One of those peripheral figures, Hughes was a musician, actor, jack of all trades, who died when only forty in 1972. These letters have the peculiar charm of a very old man writing to a very young one, though much of their content can be found in other Powys letters of this period (but what are the 'certain omissions' indicated by the editorial ellipses?). They are ultimately perhaps less interesting than the *fact* that Powys wrote them. 'Please let us never stop writing letters to each other' he says in only his second. Which gives rise to the question, why? *Why* would a still active eighty-four-year-old writer, burdened with bad eyesight, who in other letters from these years records the inconvenience of having to write so many and of having so many visitors, enter a plea for correspondence to someone 60 years his junior whom he hardly knew? There are hundreds of unpublished letters from the later Corwen and Blaenau years which say many of the same things to many people many times. *Why* did John Cowper go out of his way to encourage people, often complete strangers, to write to him at this point in his life? Too gregarious to be a hermit in the Theodore Powys mode, was it the only way left, away from the lecture hall, in which he could interact with the outside world and review and propagate his philosophy to a

range of captive audiences — the Preacher of the Platform become the Chronicler of the Couch? Such is one salient impression from this collection.
Both volumes are handsomely produced and together bring to nine the number of John Cowper Powys related books published by Cecil Woolf — and there are half a dozen more in the making. It is worth reiterating, whatever the merits or failings of individual volumes, that no other publisher has done so much for Powys in the past twelve years. That is something for which Powys admirers will be grateful and to which future biographers will be enormously indebted.

Anthony Head

A Net in Water: A Selection from the Journals of Mary Casey
Edited by JUDITH M. LANG and LOUISE DE BRUIN
The Powys Press, Kilmersdon, 1994, 229 pp., £7.50

The outer facts of Mary Casey's life are set before the reader in the 'Preliminary' to this selection from her Journals. The second fact to be mentioned, after her date of birth, is that her mother Lucy Amelia was the youngest child of the Revd Charles Francis Powys and his wife Mary Cowper Johnson. There is no need to justify the priority given to this fact — her Powys blood and her close relationships with her Powys aunts and uncles, especially John Cowper and Will, were important influences upon Mary Casey's life. Some readers, no doubt, will turn to this book for its 'Powysian' interest; and they will not be disappointed, although it is not, in the main, a record of external facts. The Journals cover the period from January 1963 to a month before Mary Casey's death, in January 1980. During part of this period Mary lived with her husband Gerard at their farm in Kenya and made prolonged visits, alone or with Gerard, to Mappowder in Dorset, where her mother lived. The alternation between the landscapes and weathers, the cultures and wild life, of Kenya and Dorset provides a significant portion of the 'colour' of the Journals. Their heart and soul, however, is a passionate inwardness; not a turning away from the outer world, but an acute response to its radiance, to birds and dawn light and night sky, for example, and also to personal relationships. Outer radiance and metaphysical light irradiate the mind, but the inwardness also registers suffering, and pain. The Powys influence — in the blood as well as in the mind — is real and substantial, and has to be acknowledged. But Mary Casey was her own person, and a writer of emotional power and intellectual acuity. She experienced heaviness of heart, and speculated that it might be, 'in part to do with *fin de famille*, the only child of an eleventh child, myself childless, all but the last two gone, dead and gone, of the proud eleven; all of them so strong and real and life-absorbed, before (as it seems to this late-born one) the age of shades set in'. But Mary Casey, in her writings, stands in no one's shadow.

How does one review the record of an inner life? One doesn't, I think, unless it is one's own. Fortunately, in this instance, there is no need for me to try. *A Net in Water* is not a confession. To begin with, it is a selection of a selection. Mary Casey was, as she says of herself, a person of 'innumerable underlying and deep reserves'. She was reserved even with herself, in her Journals, choosing what to say and how to say it; and her editors have worked in her spirit, making a choice of her choices, further condensing her concentrated vision. One important result of Mary Casey's selectivity is that her Journals are a work of art; and therefore can be reviewed. To Mary Casey, words meant 'living and aesthetic perception'. Writing as imaginative shape-making is evident throughout the Journals. It is equally present at the level of natural perception — for example, 'High in the clear air buzzards mew their aubade' — and in her use of the Journals to help her endure periods of emotional or spiritual drought, as in this example: 'My thoughts just now are at an end, I feel as though my skull lies white and empty in the soaking grass, with the soft blind blades pressing up, urgently growing about it'.

There was a Homeric and a Biblical quality about the life Mary Casey experienced in Kenya, alone or in the company of Gerard and Will. But this was also a quality of her mind, which she showed in her approach to writing and in her style, as well as in her attitude towards life. Her Journals meant to her, 'above all a transmutation by poetic thought of grief into some kind of tragic drama; of joy in the elements into song'. The keyword here is 'transmutation'. Mary Casey was, in her words, 'passion-tossed', but she had the 'inward gift of making despair a taut lute string'. Hers was a Homeric 'objectivity', which transmuted private passion, whether of love or grief or joy, into 'the poetic vision of mankind'.

This, it might be said, is *the* Powysian poetic gift. It may be so; but the gift is, first, Homeric; and it is always paid for in experience, and the mark of an individual soul. Alyse Gregory had it, who was one of Mary Casey's closest friends. *A Net in Water* has a tough-mindedness reminiscent of Alyse Gregory's Journal (selections published as *The Cry of a Gull*), and a similar concern for style, for aesthetic shaping, that transmutes raw feeling into vision. But there were also great differences between the friends.

For if both could be described as religious, in the broad sense of apprehending the wonder of being, Mary Casey was a Christian, who combined a theology of suffering and redemption with a Plotinian, metaphysical approach to truth.

Mary Casey's freedom to read and think and write, and above all to explore her aloneness in the core of being, was secured by her stable and supportive relationships: 'Simplicity between the poles of Lucy and Gerard', as she put it. Another story that her Journals tell, integrally but not on the surface, is that of her self-discovery and realisation as a poet. This was evidently set in motion in 1966 by her passionate friendship with Valentine Ackland. Her subsequent development was unified, combining poetry and prose, intellect and emotion, metaphysics and passion. Her conscious preoccupation with style manifested itself in the parallel growth of her poetry and her novel, *The Kingfisher's Wing*, and the extremely sharp critical intelligence which she applied both to uses of exhausted poetic language, and to any kind of subjective excess in spiritual writings. From a literary point of view, one of the most interesting things about Mary Casey's writings, as it is also about Gerard Casey's poems, is their conscious modernism, which arises from the conviction that eternal truth, notwithstanding its 'newness', needs, in the twentieth century, new language and forms. There was also, I would say, a tragic intensity about Mary Casey's thinking about the soul, which profoundly affected the kind of poetry she wrote.

Thus, she writes: 'Love a wave bearing the soul beyond all reason and understanding, all known boundaries and supports of convention, a sense of being "beyond intellect" which yet is folly to say; an awakening to liberty of spirit that would be too fearful without the companion in love, and which yet of necessity is the loss of that companion. *No real loss* — for the companion in love is an illusion, a "lure for feeling" as Whitehead has it, while the love is truth.' By this philosophy, if I understand it correctly, love is a rare communion between two essentially lonely beings, and it confirms the ultimately incommunicable aloneness, that of the Alone to the Alone. It is a philosophy that awes as it chills me, and I would surmise that it denotes a basic tension within Mary Casey's thinking, between Christian redemption, also to be understood as a communion between 'members of Christ's body', and absolute isolation from other beings (although not from the Alone). Whether or not I am correct in my surmise, it is surely some such fundamental tension that produces the piercing quality of Mary Casey's religious poems.

Finally I would like to quote one whole entry from the Journals, which illustrates the qualities I have mentioned in this review, and one important quality that I have not. It is the entry for 6 January 1974.

Continuing brilliance, of stars, sun, moon, for the shining forth of God. A dancing hailstorm in sunshine turning every trunk, branch, twig to silver glisten, glass clear with a living shimmer. Hail, which I always salute as coldest of grain, is a brief-lived dancer. Warm too, wren singing, great tit see-saw; fieldfares and smart jay I saw in my watery walk. Translated '*Auf dem See*'; *See*, feminine, 'sea', *See* masculine, 'lake'. A long reading of that desperate taskmaster Karl Barth last night; I think life is more mysterious than sin and death, sir.

Here are the cosmic radiance which irradiates with the presence of God (Mary Casey is frequently close to Gerard Manley Hopkins with his vision of inscape and instress); and the birds, which are loved winged creatures before they are symbols of the soul; and the reading in literature and theology; and the fascination with words, with both meanings and image-making. But here, too, in the choice and placing of that final word, 'sir', is an aspect of the discerning, sharply critical intelligence — a wry sense of humour, which says to the whole world of masculine learning and intellectual mastery, 'my mind is my own, and as capable of seeing and speaking the truth as any master's'.

Jeremy Hooker

Paint It Today
H.D. (HILDA DOOLITTLE)
Edited, with an Introduction, by CASSANDRA LAITY
New York University Press, New York and London, 1992, 160 pp., $40 cloth, $13.95 paperback

H.D.'s prose fictions can be read as transparent narratives of her own sharply recalled experiences, or as 'distanced' narratives, tracing the mythic journey of a young writer, exiled in a strange land, separated from friends and intimates, discovering new relationships and making new commitments to her art. Neither of these readings is adequate. To read these texts as autobiography is to miss the patterns of mythic discovery that characterise H.D.'s work, but to read them as explorations of the Artist as Subject is to miss the deeply moving struggle of a specific person (or persons) in the turmoil of the modernist period.

These fictions were not published in H.D.'s lifetime: *HERmione*, tracing the adventures of H.D., Ezra Pound and Frances Gregg, was written in 1926-27, but not published until 1981. *Paint It Today* was composed in 1921, but not published in its entirety until 1992. *Asphodel*, also published in 1992, is the third in this series of 'three autobiographical novels exploring H.D.'s love for women' (Laity, 'Introduction' to *Paint It Today*, xvii). The three novels, along with other texts by H.D. (for example, *Bid Me to Live* and *End of Torment*), provide accounts of living in the Modern that extend far beyond the confines of any specific interpretative approach.

Cassandra Laity's introduction is entitled 'Lesbian Romanticism: H.D.'s Fictional Representations of Frances Gregg and Bryher'. It is generous in its scholarship and interpretation, and it offers one of the first detailed considerations of Frances Gregg in the extensive literature on H.D. Laity makes it clear that Gregg's portrayal in the novel (as Josepha, which was Frances's real middle name) is fictional; it is based on myths of 'fatal women' and thralldom (xxv). We shall be concerned here with the Powys connection, and I cannot emphasise enough how important it is for readers of John Cowper Powys to make further connections to the writing of Hilda Doolittle (and Frances Gregg), writing that both draws from and enriches the uncanny world of those writers —Powys included— who began their work in the first decades of the twentieth century, setting out with extraordinary purpose, watching their purposes shattered, shifted, betrayed, and strangely accomplished.

Laity states that Gregg 'figures as the most compelling erotic and emotional love-experience of H.D.'s life', and she sets Gregg against another woman, Winifred Ellerman, called Bryher, who became H.D.'s 'protectorate, "child", and life partner': '*Paint It Today* is a mythic, lyric recreation of H.D.'s love and loss of Frances Gregg, her first woman lover, and her later meeting with Bryher' (xvii-xviii). Gregg is the '"muse" who alerted the young H.D. to her poetic vocation' (xix). Gregg and H.D.'s relationship was a 'sister love' (xxviii). Laity is right, I think, to write her introduction under the rubric 'romantic'. The lesbian world of *Paint It Today* remains a fiction, an elegant fiction, mythopoeic, an expression of H.D.'s own brooding on a world of relations, male and female, that, by 1921, had been shattered. And there is much truth in fiction.

Another of Laity's comments takes us close to John and his likely response to Frances: 'Gregg's ability to draw out the young H.D.'s mythopoeic powers arose as much from Gregg's brooding, "dark" sensuality, her fascination with prophecy, witchcraft, and other supernatural forces (in the novel they call each other "wee witches") as from their mutually sustaining sisterhood' (xxvi-xxvii). If we go back to 1912, with the *brooding, darkly sensual, prophetic, bewitching* and *supernatural* Gregg in mind, we can imagine for ourselves John's response. And if Gregg was the muse for H.D., we can speculate that she had a similar role in the forming of Powys's career. We are just beginning to see the importance of their exchange.

Paint It Today is a story of partings: the parting from America, from youthful aspiration, from romance, from women, from men. Above all else, it tells the parting of Hilda and Frances. H.D.'s writing is always lucid, and it is informed both by the deep feeling of the moment and an ironic acceptance of that moment. The parting at the railway station in Liverpool is an example (this is the return of Frances and her mother to America at the end of their European tour, with Hilda, in 1911; Hilda stayed in England):

> It is a very long story or it is a very short story, depending on how you look at it. I could more or less tell it in a paragraph. I could spend my life on ten long volumes and just begin to get the skeleton framework of it. For every life contains the world and sometimes the world is not big enough to contain one life. (27)

The scene marks the parting at Liverpool, but it sets out the whole story of *Paint It Today*: 'Josepha and Midget were torn asunder with all their little untried babyishness and all their hypersophistications' (27). John would, of course, have written it as a very long story, and he would have liked Hilda's 'For every life contains the world and sometimes the world is not big enough to contain one life.'

From America, Midget received the devastating news of Josepha's marriage. A second parting took place one year later (1912) after Frances had returned to England with her husband, Louis Wilkinson. ('Seaford' is Louis's name in the fiction, based, perhaps, on his East Anglia connections.) The setting is Victoria Station, from which Josepha is leaving with Seaford for his lecture tour in Europe. In the real-life drama, Ezra Pound had prevented Hilda from accompanying them. We now know that John, too, was there: he speaks of having seen Hilda 'on that wild morning of your departure from Victoria' (*Frances and Jack: The Love Letters of John Cowper Powys to Frances Gregg*, Vol. I, 109). It must have been quite a scene.

In *Paint It Today* we have only the aftermath to the parting: Midget's fiancé Raymond (this is Ezra) consoles her over the loss of Josepha but at the same time reprimands her for wanting to join Josepha on the trip to Berlin. In response to the reprimand, Midget says: 'She says she needs me. *He* says she will be lonely as he must be away all day and she has already heard all his lectures' (35). Raymond explains to Midget *why* she must not join Josepha and Seaford on the European tour — the trip is an intrigue because Josepha "*is in love with that Irish dramatist* that crossed with them on the boat"' (35, emphasis added). Raymond is speaking:

'The dramatist, she told me, had arranged the marriage. The fortunate husband is a friend of his. They are to meet abroad later in the summer. Josepha thinks she is clever. I myself have played my little game of chess in my own times. You are the bon bouche [*sic*]. She told me already Seaford is your victim. *Partie carrée*. All very pretty, all very chaperoned, Madame, you see, and her friend, and Madame's husband, and the other person, well, I suppose they will call him the brother of the friend of Madame.' (35)

'Madame' is Frances, 'her friend' is Hilda, 'Madame's husband' is Louis, and the 'other person' is, of course, John. Strange events are concealed under the cover of the lecture tour. "A Game of Chess" from Eliot's *Waste Land* (1922) comes to mind. We may, some day, be able to sort out the intrigue, but until then we have to keep in mind that this *is* a fictional account, based on what *may* be Pound's malicious account (Midget says openly that Raymond 'hated Josepha') of a *possible* actual event in which all the participants were carrying out roles they had *invented*, mostly from reading fiction.

Laity's note on this is only partly correct: the marriage 'was merely an arrangement so that she could be near the man she really loved, novelist Llewelyyn [*sic*] Powys' (93, Note 26). We know, from Llewelyn's and John's correspondence, and from *The Mystic Leeway*, that Frances had a deep affection for Llewelyn, but there are no doubts about John's role as the maker and the manager of the marriage. Why the lover is said to be Irish is not clear. Perhaps there were ulterior motives.

It is 'a very long story'. The portion of it marked out in *Paint It Today* provides only the outline, and the lines are uncertain. Frances's marriage to Louis was devastating to Hilda. *How* devastating it was could only be told in a 'very long story'. But there is little evidence to support Laity's view of a one-sided 'betrayal' by Frances ('Gregg's sexual betrayal(s)', xxxii). If they were joined by 'sister love', neither excluded males from their intimate relationships. Hilda (Midget) was at the time affianced to Pound, and throughout *Paint It Today* there are frequent references to him and to another (male) companion (this was Richard Aldington, whom she later married). Clearly, neither of them had pledged exclusive 'sister love'.

In *Paint It Today*, the shifting between fictions and facts is never clear. It is, after all, *today's* painting. Tomorrow's will be different. Events are seen from

H.D.'s perspective, filtered by her love for Frances Gregg, but filtered, too, by the failures of her relations with Aldington, D. H. Lawrence, by her new love for Bryher, and by the anxieties connected to her determination to become a writer of importance. And Hilda, too, played her games of chess. As Oliver and Christopher Wilkinson have already shown in their editing of the Frances and Jack correspondence, and as the publication of *The Mystic Leeway* now shows, there is another perspective.

Ben Jones

The Mystic Leeway
FRANCES GREGG
Edited by BEN JONES, with an Account of Frances Gregg by her son, OLIVER MARLOW WILKINSON
Carlton University Press, Ottawa, 1995, 150pp., $Can 29.95 casebound, $Can 19.95 paperback

Until the publication of *The Mystic Leeway*, only very modest literary significance could be claimed for Frances Gregg. Her links to some of the privileged names of modernism had secured for her minor anecdotal attention. As a literary footnote, she had been contextualised and circumscribed as Other: as a fringe member of Ezra Pound's circle; as Hilda Doolittle's lesbian lover (recent North American scholarly interest in H.D. has generated this interest); as wife to Louis Wilkinson, and as provocative 'connection' to John Cowper Powys.

The Mystic Leeway makes available a different point of view. Gregg's personal narrative recontextualises not only its author but also its literary period. By refusing anything other than subjective recognition for itself, the authorial voice in this text queries the modernist assumption that the woman who serves as inspiration for great art is the woman completely satisfied. Gregg's observations come from beyond the grave in this posthumous publication. The textual release of her mystic Self entails a radical haunting of what conventional modernism named 'life'. Her enunciation discloses a desiring female subjectivity possessed by a need to relocate Art as art, and in so doing claim Life for itself.

In his Introduction, Ben Jones responds to Gregg's wish to speak for herself. She says: 'So far, in all my life I have met no single Man ... nor has any man encouraged me, or indeed been willing for me, to be a Woman.' Jones says: 'If no man would speak for Frances Gregg, she could speak for herself, and this is what she has done.' There is no editorial assignation of place to the nomadic writer here — and perhaps author *is* the wrong word for Gregg — and no further complicity through Art to objectify Gregg's voice in the name of 'revealing' or 're-locating' the lost and neglected text. The editor's only intrusion is in making available an ideological context that permits a coherent reading of Gregg's sometimes idiosyncratic writing. Jones names her the 'uncanny', but this location outside the socio-symbolic order is of her choosing, not of his. To be reminded of her strangeness, however, alerts the reader to the eccentric perspective of the Gregg text. Its writing is ritualistic, even perverse. Through it, Gregg imposes an order of her own on a world that she finds to be almost unbearably hostile. The editor recommends making 'leeway' for the strange words of Frances.

The Mystic Leeway is the narrative of a Woman intent upon breaking the systems that enclose her. In Gregg's telling, the 'Moderns' are sophists, masqueraders, imitators and inventors of false gods. They waste their substance 'on states of mind that had been done before, and darn better'. Afraid to walk in solitude, they 'run panicking back through the ages, clutching at this gaud and that'. To the author, they are 'not ... the vanguard, but the rear-guard in life'. Like Judas, they are 'all but Christ'. They lack 'that ultimate imagination, that ultimate intelligence, that breeds perfect skepticism'. She wants to proffer herself 'to someone like Christ'. She wants not a god-like lover, but a man-god lover: she wants Epstein's 'Adam' (beautifully photographed in this volume).

Gregg posits her vision for a future of originality in the possibilities of the unique mind, born again, and allied to nothing. These possibilities occupy a space, not a place, and it is here that the nomad Gregg puts up her tent of desiring being. Her son, Oliver Wilkinson, provides an astonishing account of his mother in *The Mystic Leeway*. His word confirms that the tent was never erected twice in the same space. As caravan, as Elizabethan mansion, as cottage, as beach hut, the uncanny and warmly-welcoming 'home' housed the only meaningful constants of Gregg's existence — her two children, Oliver and Betty, and her mother Julia Vanness Gregg.

The presence of the mother is a puzzle. Ben Jones situates this 'formidable' figure in a counter-Persephone myth, where a lost Frances is unable to escape from 'the perennial Mother'. Convention describes this relationship as one of the many 'ambivalences' of Gregg's life, but the measure of conventional mythology cannot be tailored to fit perspectives that are fashioned on what Jones calls 'the site of Nothingness'. In her text, Gregg tells of the afternoon in France in 1911 where Julia 'without a verb to her name' makes sense, while she and Hilda with all their syntax 'could only dither'. Frances admires her mother's faith in the power of the incoherent to rupture 'seamless' convention. In her writing as in her life, Frances Gregg is a breaker of systems. Passages of impassioned and even 'evangelical' prose in *The Mystic Leeway* escape bathos precisely *because* they are syntactically incoherent. By shattering the patterns of syntax, Gregg hopes to break the traditional ideas perpetrated in them.

Gregg's voice is polyphonic. When she speaks through the monologism of modernism, she says: 'I have but one law — I serve.' However, when her writing consciousness speaks from the mystic leeway that is reserved for the authentic expression of will, *non serviam* is its strong message. She labours to undo and to make new. She seeks 'words for the things that are not yet'. She renounces the transcendental 'I', and dedicates her subjectivity to a space outside the centre where 'nothing personal was ... to be considered an end in itself'. Gregg may well have been influenced in this by John Cowper Powys. In 1919 she typed the manuscript of *The Complex Vision* in which Powys discusses the importance of pursuing 'the impersonal element ... so that the soul may find at once its realization of itself and its liberation from itself' (*The Complex Vision*, 134-5).

At the conclusion of *The Mystic Leeway*, Gregg struggles with the unsayable. She posits salvation for the future in a new world order presided over by a Jewish matriarchy: 'I believe that it is again to the Jews that we must look for a leader, and I would hope that that leader may be a woman.' For assistance in understanding Gregg's apparent *volte face* as she moves from this affirmation of faith to a castigation of both Jews and women ('the combined menace of the past'), we must look to Gregg's own metaphysics. Ben Jones recommends that the ending of *The Mystic Leeway* be read 'in the context of Frances's messianic obsession and, connected to this obsession, her philo/anti-semitism.' I would add that Gregg wages no argument against the Other that she does not first direct toward herself. The possibilities that she configures for the human race are the successes she perceives in her own self-love/self-hate struggle — 'I was, I am, a beacon.' The self that Frances Gregg loves is the one that resides (is the residue) in the mystic leeway. Like Jews and other women, she has to find a home. Like her, their possibilities for a born-again selfhood reside in a leeway, outside the socio-symbolic order.

The Mystic Leeway is the work of an original and creative intelligence, and is difficult to situate for this reason. Given Gregg's neglect of such 'female' issues as the oppositional demands of womb and mind for the woman artist, it would be mistaken to claim her as a victim of 'gendered modernism'. Her contempt for the woman artist who imitates the male, and her disgust for the woman that culture has produced ('I loathed all women, and saw them as bulbous and blobby ... completely mummified') are ideological declarations against the modernist way of life. It is not the issue of gender that intrigues and stimulates Frances Gregg's creative imagination, and it would be counter-productive to 'read' the intentionality of her text through the narrow lens of this culturally-generated prescription. The configurations of gender are never absent from her text, but the main force of the author's furies are directed against what she names 'old mythologies'. These are the all-embracing metaphysics of the aesthetic ideology, and for Gregg represent the multiple deceptions of a dominant tradition. Out of the rich residue of the past, Frances Gregg writes a new mythology against the old gods and toward the possibilites in consciousness of a divine, reborn, human subjectivity.

Margaret McCullough

The Supernatural and English Fiction: From *The Castle of Otranto* to *Hawksmoor*
GLEN CAVALIERO
Oxford University Press, Oxford, 1995, 273pp., £18.99

When Horace Walpole published *The Castle of Otranto* on Christmas Eve in 1764, it was presented pseudonymously as the translation of a sixteenth-century manuscript. This romance of thirteenth-century Italy was an immediate success with the public, who consumed its spectral manifestations, giants and feuding nobles with surprising relish. A second edition soon appeared, this time bearing the initials 'W. H.' — Horace Walpole. This edition, however, was received less favourably, at least by the critics. Piqued perhaps at having been taken in by Walpole's deception, their objections are nonetheless revealing. As a reviewer from the *Monthly Review* of 1765 observed:

> While we considered [*Otranto* to have been a translation] we could excuse its preposterous phenomena, and consider them as sacrifices to a gross and unenlightened age — But when ... [it] is declared to be a modern performance, that indulgence we afforded to the foibles of a supposed antiquity, we can by no means extend to the singularity of a false taste in a cultivated period of learning. It is, indeed, more than strange, that an Author, of a refined and polished genius, should be an advocate for re-establishing the barbarous superstitions of Gothic devilism.

It would appear that for this reader to enjoy fully the fantastic events of this tale, one thing is requisite — a comforting distance between the events depicted and the recognisable world he himself inhabits. Take that distance away and the reader is compelled to reconsider his comfortable worldpicture, and imagine, if only for a moment, the possibility of a return of 'Gothic devilism' to this 'cultivated period of learning'. This was the effect of the first example of the 'supernatural' in English fiction, and it is the effect, according to Glen Cavaliero, that this mode still has today.

Cavaliero's *The Supernatural and English Fiction* charts the development of this literary mode from its emergence in the late-eighteenth-century tale of terror, to its contemporary manifestations in the work of such writers as Peter Ackroyd, Iris Murdoch and Muriel Spark. What these writers have in common is their ability to disrupt the 'established certainties' (240) of their respective cultures by evoking suggestions of something which transcends the wholly rationalistic and mechanistic worlds they inhabit. For Cavaliero, the

> history of supernaturalist fiction charts the exposure of nineteenth- and twentieth-century rationalist philosophy to the concept of the unseen; with equal validity one might interpret it as the continued assertion of a previous, less mechanistic reading of human experience, as against the disjunction of physical from spiritual consciousness implicit in a technologically motivated response to life. (234–5)

In short, supernatural fiction, at its best, provides what Cavaliero refers to as a 'refutation of [the] single vision'. This 'single vision' can be exemplified by the narrow adherence to the values of a 'cultivated period of learning', boasted by the eighteenth-century critic, or the 'pre-emptive scepticism' of his counterpart today. The refutation of this 'single vision' opens onto the possibility of access to, or a glimpse of, what Cavaliero terms the 'mysterium', a concept which is fundamental to this wide-ranging discussion.

The most conspicuous aspect of *The Supernatural and English Fiction* is the diversity of the works discussed. Cavaliero's achievement in this respect is impressive and would undoubtedly floor a less experienced critic. Alongside the tales of terror of Walpole, Radcliffe, Lewis and Maturin, are found the works of Christian 'mystics' and propagandists, George MacDonald, Charles Williams and C. S. Lewis. As well as works of the occult and the uncanny by Bulwer-Lytton, Le Fanu, Arthur Machen and R. L. Stevenson, he discusses the 'novels of nature mysticism' provided by such writers as D. H. Lawrence, Constance Holme and John Cowper Powys. He even finds room in his discussion for Grahame Greene's *Brighton Rock* (1938), and Evelyn Waugh's *The Ordeal of Gilbert Pinfold* (1957), titles not readily associated with the supernaturalist mode of fiction.

The inclusion of such works in Cavaliero's book says much about the philosophical subtlety of his understanding of what constitutes the 'supernatural' in fiction. Notwithstanding the distinctly 'Gothic' packaging of his book (the dust jacket sports a quintessentially Gothic monochrome photograph of a ruined castle by moonlight, while the publisher's blurb dwells on ruined abbeys, far-off wailings, and unquiet graveyards), the Radcliffean tale of terror plays but a small part in the author's analysis. Indeed, for Cavaliero, the first exercises in 'Gothic devilism', despite the anxieties of contemporary critics, were still very much a part of the rationalist philosophical context from which they emerged. For him, therefore, Walpole's *Otranto* 'is more like a Gothic folly, the diversion of the rationalist imagination, than a stronghold of supernatural romance' (26); and of Radcliffe's *The Mysteries of Udolpho* (1794) he asserts: 'however much Jane Austen may have ridiculed the taste for which it catered, [it] is in its inculcation of rationality and self-control, a novel of which she must surely have approved' (27). It is, however, with Charles Robert Maturin's *Melmoth the Wanderer* (1820), that 'supernaturalist fiction comes of age' (29). This statement is revealing, and is indicative of this critic's approach to his subject. What he finds in Maturin's text, which eludes him in Walpole, Radcliffe and Lewis, is evidence of what he asserts is essential for 'true' supernaturalist fiction — a 'controlling metaphysic' (36). The work of a Protestant clergyman, Maturin's tale of a man who barters his soul for an extended term on earth, is for Cavaliero, 'Ultimately ... parabolic in effect' (32), and 'verges on theodicy' (33). Beside the dark metaphysics of Maturin's tale, the skeletons and spectres of Walpole and Lewis become just so many phantasmagorical stage properties. This insistence on the 'metaphysical' dimension to supernaturalist fiction is a thread which runs through Cavaliero's authoritative and engaging survey. It is both its strength, and (potentially) its limitation.

This emphasis on the essentially 'metaphysical' nature of true supernaturalist fiction, accounts for the great diversity of the material which Cavaliero discusses. The term 'supernatural' evokes a range of associations. As he explains: 'At its highest it suggests what Rudolph Otto designates "the Holy", but it is an experience open to anyone who for a moment obliterates the thought of past and future. The opening on to the mysterium can be as homely as a garden gate' (19). Whilst such a definition obviously allows the critic an enormous scope for discussion, to be effective, it also demands a coherent philosophical framework, and a degree of imaginative tact. Both are evident in Cavaliero's book. However, notwithstanding his reference to the supernatural's ability to obliterate thoughts of 'past and future', Cavaliero does not neglect the historical dimension in his discussion. Dreams and nightmares always bear the traces of the specific contexts which produce them, and this book above all attests to the *development* of this literary mode. As he observes,

> as the twentieth century proceeded, piety was to commend itself more generally in terms of place, of landscape, and physical and historical rootedness ... In this respect John Cowper Powys is a significant figure, since his handling of traditional supernaturalistic material combines a scepticism concerning previous interpretations with a committed belief in the existence of a transcendental world of the imagination which is rooted in the life of everyday people and affairs, and is thus available for all to enter. (239–40)

Powys's novels, including *Ducdame* and *A Glastonbury Romance*, are discussed in these terms; showing how the latter text, whilst 'not a novel which uses the preternatural to make moral or dramatic points', nonetheless presents a 'view of life as itself supernatural' (151).

Cavaliero's thesis is at its best when, as in the above quotation, it allows even the heterodox and the unconventional a valid contribution to the supernaturalistic fictional mode. Unfortunately he is not always so philosophically 'ecumenical'. While he strives to eschew the doctrinaire, an awareness of the author's theological standpoint is unavoidable, and in the last analysis, potentially restrictive. To be fair, Cavaliero addresses this issue in the 'epilogue' to his book, one of three philosophical sections which frame the eight chapters of textual analysis. As he states, the question whether the supernatural is 'an authentic part of human experience, to be taken seriously [or a] delusion ... can only be confidently answered by the religious believer or the equally assured atheist' (244). In the terms established by his argument, this is indeed the case. However, it is evident that his book is written for the former, and is in danger of alienating the latter. The 'controlling metaphysic' behind Cavaliero's thesis reveals itself in a number of places.

Thus, whilst for him, supernatural fiction 'braces the mind against all that is doctrinaire and partisan, everything that denies the nature of the mysterium' (248), his adherence to this belief does not guarantee him immunity from occasional dogmatism. As he says: 'the more serious writers of supernaturalist fiction point by implication towards a spiritual order transcending human formulations', and 'whether consciously or not [they] *necessarily* proceed on the ground that ... a belief [in ultimate transcendence and telos] is justified' (13, emphasis added). Cavaliero is unwavering in this assertion; for him, the 'mysterium is embodied in the figure of divine Wisdom, at once reflector and articulator of the glory of God. Both theologically and linguistically it is this source of the natural, and its regulatory activity, *which should alone be designated supernatural*' (16, emphasis added). Does this mean that the 'assured atheist' (244) is excluded from any significant enjoyment of, or response to, the supernatural mode? I rather fear it does, for as he states: 'any discussion of the supernatural which does not allow for [a belief in the 'spirit'] and take it seriously is self-stultifying from the start' (15).

For Cavaliero, therefore, supernatural fiction serves as an antidote to 'crass unbelief' (183), effectively a surrogate for, or supplement to, established religion.

The weight of this conviction he throws into a confrontation with the 'preemptive scepticism' of contemporary critical theory. In the book's philosophical passages, he takes on the deconstructionists, and, somewhat provocatively, plays them at their own game. His trump card in this contest is his assertion of the priority of 'traditional religious understanding' over the 'atheistical scolasticism' of the deconstructionists (11). For, as he observes:

> Mystics, saints, and theologians have always been well aware of how provisional all verbal formulations of metaphysical reality must inevitably be, even while conceding that it is the function of poets and storytellers through verbal means such as parable, imagery, and song, to keep alive that feeling of life's illimitable mystery which is metaphysics' energizing source. (244-5)

Thus whilst the deconstructionists deny the possibility of absolute presence, in a move to refute metaphysics, Cavaliero finds in absence and the ineffable an affirmation of transcendence. Therefore he concludes: 'Airy talk about "language games", while fully justified theologically in relation to the ultimate unknowable absolute, is, in an atheistic or irreligious realm of discourse, merely self-cancelling: there is a world of difference between an acknowledgement of epistemological limitation and a carefree propagation of futility' (246). Ultimately, however, the acknowledgement of this 'world of difference', like so much in his analysis, rests on 'faith'.

Robert Mighall

Mock's Curse
T. F. POWYS
Edited, with an Afterword, by E. and M. B. MENCHER
The Brynmill Press, Denton, 1995, 213pp., £16

In the course of the last few years it has become apparent that what used to be thought of as T. F. Powys's output, eight novels and eight collections of short stories and novellas, in no way reflects the sum total of what he wrote. After the publication of two additional novels, *Father Adam* (1990) and *The Market Bell* (1991), we now have from The Brynmill Press *Mock's Curse*, nineteen more short stories which, the publishers explain, 'are part of a huge collection left unpublished at the time of Powys's death'. Brynmill is to follow this with a new edition of *The Two Thieves* of 1932, renamed *The Sixpenny Strumpet* because it will contain an extra unpublished novella of that name in addition to the three tales that originally appeared in the volume.

With a few minor reservations, Brynmill does an excellent job with the text, and as with *The Market Bell* they have supplied the reader with some useful notes and a brief but helpful Afterword. It is mildly frustrating not to have T. F. Powys's tendency to use the upper case in a random fashion, and to overpunctuate, corrected on the relatively infrequent occasions where a sentence seriously suffers. Powys was in the common enough habit of allowing his pencil or pen to rest upon the page in mid sentence while reflecting upon how to proceed. Such moments are easy to spot, but I nevertheless found myself wondering if some of the offending commas might have resulted not so much from errors on Powys's part, as from an editorial failure to read a pause for thought: 'Everything must for a while be in confusion, though under Mrs Titman's care, that confusion, lasted but a little time' (177), or again, 'When the traveller, had satisfied his curiosity, he proceeded to Norbury, where he found his Inn ...' (90) A relatively minor point perhaps, but it is to be hoped that in the future the copy editor will be prepared to act on the reader's behalf.

What *Mock's Curse* does is increase the reader's familiarity with the T. F. Powys that is already known; there is nothing here that gives fresh insight into his character as a writer. Indeed, the collection offers an excellent variety of his story-telling moods, from Powys at his darkest and most solemn, to Powys the gentle comedian. For those who feel they already know the man as a pessimistic, frequently sadistic grumpy old chauvinist, a man who celebrated these qualities in stories about brothers called Mock, farmers called Cockaday and squires called Yollop, this is perhaps not good news. For the

Theodorian evangelist it has to be a somewhat disappointing prospect; with every new publication Powys becomes more like the writer those who prefer to know about him rather than read him have already responded to. He is not a writer who, as a result of new work published, might be expected to attract new readers.

What these new stories are undoubtedly showing us is the committed artistry of T. F. Powys the writer. He did not work up his view of God, life and death, only to experiment with a few novels and stories by way of explication. The evidence clearly is that he wrote through those ideas with what amounts to an obsessive commitment not just to his ideas, his faith if you will, but equally to his art. It is indeed the very familiarity of what is encountered that becomes the hallmark of Powys's unique achievement. How could he work so many variations on what is essentially a single idea? Yet he does, and miraculously each story has, for the most part, its distinctive timbre, a fresh twist to what somehow never quite becomes an overly familiar tale.

One of the best stories in *Mock's Curse* shows us Powys working in a very familiar vein of apparent satire upon the dullness of country folk. 'Two Chairs' is about a miracle, and contains a characteristically Powysian delineation of the rural peasant mind. Jacob Moss longs to convince his friend, John Flower, that miracles truly happen:

> Jacob Moss believed in Miracles. There was no miracle recorded in the Holy Scriptures that he did not believe was true. The opinion of John Flower in this matter was otherwise. John thought that all miracles, that of course included the belief in the Trinity, were invented by Mr Hayday the clergyman, in order that Farmer Lord might not feel that he paid his tithes for nothing.
> "Without thik Bible and loaves and fishes, and little Jesus in manger, what would 'e have to tell folk about!" John would say to his friend, "and who have seen the folk at Weyminster walk along the sea?" (90–1)

Since the age of miracles seems to be well and truly past, Jacob decides to make one of his own. His thinking is relentlessly rational and wholly without imagination:

> Upon a Sunday afternoon in August, a drowsy sultry day, with a continuous though far distant mutter of thunder, Jacob astonished Jenny at dinner time by laying down a fork, as well loaded as any pitchfork had ever been, with the most tender runner beans that ever

woman cooked, and staring at the two wooden chairs that were upon each side of the fire, one that had come from her family and one from his. And Jenny was more astonished than ever when her husband said, "Did it ever happen that two chairs like they, have been set out on a little mound for working folk to sit on in the daytime?"

"Only at Auctions," answered Jenny ...

"If we two folk were to sit in they parlour chairs out on little hill 'twould be a miracle."

"Surely it would," replied Jenny. (91–2)

By sitting with his wife on the hill in their parlour chairs Jacob believes he can convince John of the credibility of miracles, and in this way save his soul.

Described thus, this frankly appears to be the behaviour of an idiot. The miracle of Powys's technique is to elevate such simplicity — simplicity that borders upon imbecility — to the level of profundity. It remains difficult to lose completely the notion that Powys patronises his rustics; they are simple, they are silly, their sense of dignity is comic:

Very Solemnly did Jenny, dressed in her Sunday gown, sit herself beside her husband, feeling the extreme dignity of her place. While Jacob too sat there, though with more ease, as though to become a miracle was no new thing to him. He would not smoke his pipe, for no miracle that he had ever read of did that ... (93)

It is in fact Powys's intention to bring these people as low as possible in our estimation, for his next move is to claim a superiority for them which in turn shames our lack of patience with their behaviour. In 'Two Chairs' he brings it off; he didn't always.

Jenny dies in a fire in her cottage while Jacob is drinking with John in town. Jacob refuses to believe in his wife's death and sets off to find her. It is now no longer appropriate to suggest (as some have been tempted to do in the past) that Powys's ability to change gear in the course of a story, to transform rustic stupidity into heroic stoicism, was in some way an instinctive gift; it was something he worked at with painstaking determination. The same archives that give us these unpublished stories are giving us also an increasing number of manuscripts of work already well known, and the result has been to disclose a meticulous craftsman at work.

In 'Two Chairs' that change of gear is initiated by a relatively rare incursion into overt literariness. This is not the smoothest of shifts perhaps:

Never did Ceres search for her lost Proserpina, or Cadmus for his sister Europa with more zeal than Jacob Moss sought for his departed Jenny. (97)

But it leads into a wholly convincing image of the newly perceived Jacob:

> He was a splendid old man, and as like Honest in *The Pilgrim's Progress* as one pea is to another. He never begged, though he did not refuse what was given to him, and there was something in his look with the great beard that he wore, and his tall staff, that moved many hearts, so that he never lacked food or lodging. (97–8)

In the end Jacob's miracle takes place, the two of them sit on their chairs upon the hill; yet the act is of course transformed into a miracle indeed, because John Flower, now dying, sees Jacob and Jenny on the hill, 'She was dressed in the same gown that she had worn on the day of the fire. Jacob looked like one who had travelled far' (100).

By way of contrast, *Mock's Curse* includes stories in Powys's lightest comic vein. I am bound to say that I cannot understand why simple copy editing procedures were not employed to make 'Mr Pompey Seeks Preferment' — a Theodorian gem if ever there was one — read without a hitch:

> And so Mr Ballard [the vicar] turned his thoughts to the conversion of Pompey. There indeed was a proper task for a good minister, a Sinner, after St Paul's own heart, one who sinned doubly in flesh and spirit. Derided God and worked uncleanness. (24)

'An Odd Convert' is also a story with no death in it, no suicides, and only the faintest whiff of sadism. It is, however, an excellent example of how Powys jeopardises his chances of extending his readership specifically through the way he writes about women, even more specifically when they are young country girls of the plumper variety.

In 'An Odd Convert' the girl in question is Sally Dent, and her lover is Dicky Dillar:

> Miss Sally who had watched Dicky's strong arms cutting the grass, thought how fast her heart would beat if they were around her, for being a young woman of seventeen with skin as soft as sweet moss she wanted to be touched, and that not too mildly.
>
> Even if Dicky didn't hold her as close as she wished, she liked him for his straight forward manners, for he never hid anything that was in his heart that so many lovers do, but declared his passion most openly, saying that the greatest joy of his life was only to look at her, and that

he would willingly die for her every day of the week except Sunday.
"And why not Sunday too?" asked Sally letting her head fall back among the primroses, so that he might be able to gaze a little lower into her neck.
"Because we two do go to Church on Sundays," replied Dicky, "and after that we do walk down the dark lanes and then dying bain't to be thought of." (69–70)

This is Powys's perfect rustic couple, which is to say there are imperfections, '... Dicky didn't hold her as close as she wished'. Watch the hackles rise, and understandably too, '... she wanted to be touched, and that not too mildly'; she wants to be ogled among the primroses. Well, girls like her do, don't they! With the best will in the world, this kind of thing is going to make it very difficult for a good many readers — male or female — to turn the page and read on into what becomes a farcical tale of the rich, cynical gentry made to look fools by the rustic lovers.

When the rich farmer Goathill, who has married Sally's widowed mother (because she makes peerless apple dumplings) comes to decide who Sally is to marry, the allusion to the cattle market is wholly appropriate:

"Come near to me, hussy," cried out Mr. Goathill angrily, and taking hold of her he felt her as if she were a prize heifer.
"Thee'll do for Simkin," he said.
When Mr Simkin arrived and saw Sally at table he agreed that she would, and having once decided so in his mind, he believed her to be his. (73)

With so much more to read now of T. F. Powys's work, and that includes the reappearance of *Fables* (1993) and *Soliloquies of a Hermit* (1993), a seminal text for those who have not properly studied it before, a reappraisal must be called for. A central issue for such a reappraisal must be to reflect on how significant Powys's unregenerate attitude to women is in a general assessment of his writing. In *Mock's Curse*, 'The Widow' provides us with an interesting and appropriate test-case.

This story has as its central feature the mildly unpleasant materialistic nature of Helen Titman: "Mrs Titman was twenty years old, she had the pinkest skin in the world, but her mouth looked artful and knowing, and her eyes though tender were a little small' (170). Powys's persistently misogynist streak is frequently at its most disturbing when it is thus muted. The woman is forever Eve, not to be trusted. Yet in the first glow of married bliss, and thus in spite of her normal self, she is moved by the story of Lazarus raised from the dead to offer up a prayer, 'She prayed that did her dear John die before her, that Jesus would come, she would know him by the marks in his hands, and raise up her husband from the dead as He did Lazarus' (170).

Powys tells us at once that her prayer is answered; Jesus himself briefly joins the congregation in church, though none there know him except a child in the back row. Powys's artistry is undeniable here. In 'Two Chairs' the manifestation of a transcendent world beyond this is reserved for the climax of the story, matching perfectly the pace and mood of the tale. In 'The Widow', our knowledge from the first that Helen Titman has had her prayer honoured casts a spell of gradually increasing tension over the rest of the story.

Helen's father insists that before his daughter is married, John Titman must insure his life for ten thousand pounds. Thus John, an easy going, likeable and profoundly ineffectual being becomes worth far more dead than alive. There is no sinister plot dreamed up to do him in, however; just a gently ironic commentary upon how, as Helen skilfully manages the diminishing family budget to ensure the continued payments of the premiums, mother and daughter reflect upon John's value to them:

> "If any accident were to come to your poor papa," sighed Mrs Titman — she was always begging him to be careful not to fall into the pond — "we should of course be better off than we are now."
>
> "But Papa is not very old," Mary replied, threading her needle, "and always wears a muffler when he catches cold."
>
> "He never used to," observed Mrs Titman. "And you know neither of his parents lived to be old. You never even saw Grandfather Titman."
>
> "Ten thousand pounds is a great deal of money," remarked Mary. (175)

John is eventually knocked down by a car and killed as he tries to save the dog he himself had rescued from a poacher's snare. The dog, who has been named Trap, escapes; and of course Christ appears to work the miracle Helen had prayed for.

Powys's handling of the dénouement reveals once again a master of the short story form at work; this is comparable with the very best in the genre, and it is a good deal better than much that is more widely and frequently read. But that is not my immediate concern. The problem here is not Powys's undoubted craftmanship, it is the extent to which the way in which he genders the issues might be perceived as creating a problem.

This story simply confirms what is well known and understood about its author. Powys's religious convictions were unashamedly yoked to a patriarchal tradition. Satan was the author of evil, Eve was recruited as Satan's helpmate on earth, man was the victim. The disrespect Powys manifestly displays for women in his writings is a stumbling block throughout his work. Where not overtly stated or slyly implied, misogyny is nevertheless detectable, it hangs in the air despite the fact that it frequently seems to be more than compensated for by the inhumanity of the male of the species. It is to the woman we invariably return as the primary instigator of our collective degeneracy and fall from grace. Accept this in Powys, and the rest falls readily into place, including the argument for him as a writer of considerable stature. So is this too much to ask?

At the end of 'The Widow', the priest — who is profoundly embarrassed by the unlooked-for arrival of Christ in his parish — is deputed to act as Helen Titman's envoy:

> Then Mr Maylie entered, having been called from the church; he stepped softly upon his toes as if he approached the Host set upon the Holy Table.
>
> Though he entered the kitchen humbly enough he looked grieved, as though he thought so strange a thing as this untimely visit ought never to have happened.
>
> "You know, Lord," he said, "that the man is truly dead."
> "I am life," answered the Christ. "Take me to the body."
> "Mrs Titman would rather not," Mr Maylie observed hesitatingly.
> The Christ bowed low.
> The dog howled. He pulled again at the Saviour's garment.
> Jesus took Trap up in His arms and left the cottage, and no one hindered him. (179–80)

With Helen Titman having prayed to God at the outset and had her prayer answered, the reader has been waiting with increasing expectation for the dramatic consequences of John being raised from the dead in spite of Helen's subsequent wishes. The economy with which Powys achieves the sudden, unlooked-for turn of events is breathtaking, and focuses upon the central paradox around which all T. F. Powys's writing revolves.

In the brief prologue to the title-story of this volume, Powys describes God as 'all-powerful', as indeed He must be. Yet here, in Christ, we see God ordered around and submissive to the human will. This is by way of proposing that the world we live in is our own making, not God's; and in this world we have created our own Gods to worship. Christ will therefore be sent away, taking John Titman's dog with him. The prologue to 'Mock's Curse' concludes, 'The blessed hope of the New Testament lies not in the will to power, but in the utter renunciation of all vaunted selfhood' (9).

We have here an indication of why this collection of stories is such a successful book. The miracle Helen Titman prays for is waiting to happen, but when the time comes she cannot allow it and has to stop it. This takes us back to Jacob Moss and John Flower, and their dispute over miracles in 'Two Chairs'. Jacob makes the miracle happen. Those of us deriding him at the beginning do not do so at the end. *Mock's Curse* is thus not just a collection of stories, it is a book with an overall thematic coherence that impels us to read on. It will certainly entertain, it will challenge, and it may well at times infuriate its readers; but readers it most certainly deserves.

John Williams

NOTES ON CONTRIBUTORS

GLEN CAVALIERO is a member of the English Faculty of Cambridge University and Fellow-Commoner of St Catharine's College, Cambridge. He has published poetry and critical works, among them *John Cowper Powys: Novelist* (1973), and, most recently, *The Supernatural and English Fiction* (Oxford, 1995).

JOHN GRAY is a Fellow of Jesus Collge, Oxford, and has been Visiting Professor at Harvard and Yale Universities. He is the author of *Isaiah Berlin* (HarperCollins, 1995) and *Enlightenment's Wake* (forthcoming from Routledge).

ANTHONY HEAD works as a news editor and journalist in Japan. His articles appear in several publications, including the *New Statesman* and the *Far Eastern Economic Review*. He has edited *The Letters of John Cowper Powys to Ichiro Hara* (Cecil Woolf, 1990) and the forthcoming Powys to Sea-Eagle, the letters of J. C. Powys to his sister Philippa.

JEREMY HOOKER is Professor of English at Bath College of Higher Education, where he directs the M.A. in creative writing. He has published studies of David Jones and John Cowper Powys. His most recent collection of poems, *Their Silence a Language* (Enitharmon, 1994), is a collaboration with the sculptor Lee Grandjean.

BEN JONES is Professor of English at Carleton University, Ottawa, where he teaches literature and interdisciplinary studies. He is co-editor of essays on Thomas Gray, *Fearful Joy* (1974), and Nietzsche, *Nietzsche and the Rhetoric of Nihilism* (1990). He was one of the founders of The Powys Society of North America.

CHARLES LOCK, Professor of English at the University of Toronto, is the author of *Thomas Hardy: Criticism in Focus* (1992) and numerous articles on the Powys family, as well as on literary theory and aesthetics, Byzantine theology and iconography, and prehistoric rock art.

CONTRIBUTORS

MARGARET McCULLOUGH teaches French, and also lectures in the Department of English at Carleton University, Ottawa. Recent work of hers has been on the politics of H.D.'s language.

ROBERT MIGHALL, Junior Research Fellow at Merton College, Oxford, has specialised in Gothic fiction. He has contributed articles on aspects of nineteenth-century culture including that on John Cowper Powys and aestheticism for *The Powys Journal* II, 1992.

JANINA NORDIUS is engaged in doctoral research on John Cowper Powys and Solitude at the University of Gothenburg, Sweden.

DIANA PETRE lives in London. She is the author of several novels and *The Secret Orchard of Roger Ackerley*, the story of her childhood [1975] (Phoenix Paperbacks, 1993).

ROBIN WOOD lectures in English at the Memorial University of Newfoundland, Canada.

JOHN WILLIAMS, Reader in Literary Studies at the University of Greenwich, recently edited the Macmillan's New Casebook on Wordsworth. His biography, *Wordsworth, A Literary Life*, is to be published by Macmillan in January 1996. He has written several articles on T. F. Powys, and the 'Afterword' to The Powys Press edition of *Soliloquies of a Hermit* (1993).

ADVISORY BOARD

Michael Ballin	Wilfred Laurier University, Waterloo, Canada
Marius Buning	Free University, Amsterdam, Netherlands
Glen Cavaliero	St Catharine's College, Cambridge, UK
H. W. Fawkner	Gothenburg University, Sweden
Jeremy Hooker	Bath College of Higher Education, UK
Morine Krissdóttir	University of Guelph, Canada
Peter Mendes	University of Greenwich, London, UK
J. Lawrence Mitchell	Texas A & M University, USA
Elmar Schenkel	Leipzig University, Germany
John Williams	University of Greenwich, London, UK